In a world where we are bombarded by doubt and fear, we need to be equipped with God's truth to silence the lies of the enemy. *Daily Power* is an awesome tool that will help you connect with Jesus and his truth daily so that his power is activated in your life.

—CHRISTINE CAINE, founder, A21 and Propel Women

. . . . .

Daily Power shatters the stereotype of the broken New Year's resolution, providing the backbone needed to turn the idealistic dreams of a new year into reality. No matter how large or small the change you want to see, in Craig's words, "You're going to need God's power to do it." His daily bites of God's Word provide the encouragement, challenge, and steps needed to help you become all God created you to be.

—LISA BEVERE, *New York Times* bestselling author

. . . . .

Daily Power is exactly that. An explosion of grace and truth and mercy and insight that is accessible and helpful for you every day before you go off into your schools, jobs, or callings. Pastor Craig's words point you not only to truth the idea but Truth the person, Jesus.

—JEFFERSON BETHKE, author, *Jesus>Religion*

. . . . .

I've known Craig Groeschel for many years, and I never cease to be amazed at his ability to share God's Word in a way that just makes sense. In *Daily Power*, he offers a daily dose of wisdom and insight that's both simple and life-changing. If your goal is to get closer to God, this devotional can make a huge difference.

—DAVE RAMSEY, bestselling author and
nationally syndicated radio show host

. . . . .

When it comes to building healthy habits and cultivating discipline, there's no one I've learned more from than Craig Groeschel. I've seen him live out these principles and witnessed the results firsthand. If you're looking for a trustworthy guide to help you get the most out of each day, *Daily Power* is the resource you've been waiting for.

—STEVEN FURTICK, pastor, Elevation Church;
New York Times bestselling author

. . . . .

Pastor Craig Groeschel is a hero in my life. In *Daily Power* he gives us a concentrated daily dose of faith, page after page, like only he can. I'm grateful for his honest stories and applications, which remind us we are not alone on our journey. New Year's resolutions often crash and burn as quickly as they are constructed, but the daily encouragement Pastor Craig shares will empower you to start and finish your year with discipline, encouragement, and strength.

—PASTOR RICH WILKERSON, Vous Church

. . . . .

DAILY POWER

ALSO BY CRAIG GROESCHEL

DAILY
POWER

365 DAYS OF FUEL FOR YOUR SOUL

CRAIG GROESCHEL

ZONDERVAN®

ZONDERVAN

Daily Power
Copyright © 2017 by Craig Groeschel

Requests for information should be addressed to:
Zondervan, *3900 Sparks Dr. SE, Grand Rapids, Michigan 49546*

ISBN 978-0-310-34327-1 (international trade paper edition)

ISBN 978-0-310-34324-0 (ebook)

Library of Congress Cataloging-in-Publication Data

Names: Groeschel, Craig, author.
Title: Daily power : 365 days of fuel for your soul / Craig Groeschel.
Description: Grand Rapids, Michigan : Zondervan, [2017]
Identifiers: LCCN 2017024790 | ISBN 9780310343080 (hardcover)
Subjects: LCSH: Devotional calendars. | Devotional exercises. | Christian life.
Classification: LCC BV4811 .G67 2017 | DDC 242/.2--dc23 LC record available at https://lccn
    .loc.gov/2017024790

All Scripture quotations, unless otherwise indicated, are taken from the Holy Bible, New International Version®, NIV®. Copyright © 1973, 1978, 1984, 2011 by Biblica, Inc.® Used by permission of Zondervan. All rights reserved worldwide. www.Zondervan.com. The "NIV" and "New International Version" are trademarks registered in the United States Patent and Trademark Office by Biblica, Inc.®

Scripture quotations marked ESV are from the ESV® Bible (The Holy Bible, English Standard Version®). Copyright © 2001 by Crossway, a publishing ministry of Good News Publishers. Used by permission. All rights reserved.

Scripture quotations marked MSG are from *The Message*. Copyright © by Eugene H. Peterson 1993, 1994, 1995, 1996, 2000, 2001, 2002. Used by permission of NavPress. All rights reserved. Represented by Tyndale House Publishers, Inc.

Scripture quotations marked NASB are from New American Standard Bible®. Copyright © 1960, 1962, 1963, 1968, 1971, 1972, 1973, 1975, 1977, 1995 by The Lockman Foundation. Used by permission. (www.Lockman.org)

Scripture quotations marked NCV are from the New Century Version®. © 2005 by Thomas Nelson. Used by permission. All rights reserved.

Scripture quotations marked NKJV are from the New King James Version®. © 1982 by Thomas Nelson. Used by permission. All rights reserved.

Scripture quotations marked NLT are from the Holy Bible, New Living Translation. © 1996, 2004, 2007, 2013, 2015 by Tyndale House Foundation. Used by permission of Tyndale House Publishers, Inc., Carol Stream, Illinois 60188. All rights reserved.

Any Internet addresses (websites, blogs, etc.) and telephone numbers in this book are offered as a resource. They are not intended in any way to be or imply an endorsement by Zondervan, nor does Zondervan vouch for the content of these sites and numbers for the life of this book.

All rights reserved. No part of this publication may be reproduced, stored in a retrieval system, or transmitted in any form or by any means—electronic, mechanical, photocopy, recording, or any other—except for brief quotations in printed reviews, without the prior permission of the publisher.

Craig Groeschel is represented by Thomas J. Winters of Winters & King, Inc., Tulsa, Oklahoma.

Interior design: Denise Froehlich

First printing August 2017 / Printed in the United States of America

> "Do not despise these small beginnings, for the LORD
> rejoices to see the work begin." (Zech. 4:10 NLT)

A new year, another beginning, a fresh start.

More opportunities to grow closer to God. More chances to be the person he created you to be. More ways to serve those around you.

If you're like me, it's often hard to know where to begin making changes. Whether you have a lot you want to change this year or just a few things, you're going to need God's power to do it. And that's what this book is all about—providing you with bites of God's Word along with some encouragement and some challenges, always seasoned with his truth and the hope we have in Jesus Christ.

To get you started, consider this: What do you want your story to be a year from now? What major difference do you want to see in your life when you reflect after this new year is over? What's one tiny baby step you can take today to move in this direction?

Because you know how we grow? We practice daily.

Rarely does success come without time, discipline, and hard work. Successful people often joke that they spent years becoming an overnight success. What many don't realize is that it's the things no one sees that result in the things everyone wants. It's the faithfulness to do mundane things like flossing, walking around the block, eating better, and spending time with God before rushing out the door each morning.

The best way to think about changing your story is to focus on today, not tomorrow, next week, or next January.

It's time to take that first step.

Power Lift

Lord, give me wisdom to choose what to focus on during this next year. Help me to see my life, my story, the way you see it. Give me strength to take that first step today.

Since we live by the Spirit, let us keep in step with the Spirit. (Gal. 5:25)

One small decision today could have a big impact on tomorrow. Chances are you can think of something right now that you know God would love to include in your story. Just consider what might happen if you remember to floss tonight or work out tomorrow morning or attend church this Sunday or spend some special time with someone you love.

It doesn't always take a long time to see big differences in your life. What story do you believe God wants you to tell five or ten years from now? What does God want you to want? Jot down your thoughts about what you believe God wants for your future. Your ideas don't have to be perfect. You don't have to commit to what you write just yet. Just capture on paper the first thoughts that come to mind.

Based on what you believe God wants you to want, what discipline do you need to start doing to head toward where God wants you to go? Choose one thing. You'll be tempted to pick three, four, or even ten, but don't. Whatever you do, pick just one thing. Because if you pick more than one, you likely won't achieve any of them. But if you select just one, you absolutely can start writing the story God wants you to write.

. . . . **Power Lift** . . . .

Show me how you want me to grow this year, God. Give me your wisdom and discernment to know how to focus my habits, choices, and routines on one area of change.

> Therefore, if anyone is in Christ, the new creation has come:
> The old has gone, the new is here! (2 Cor. 5:17)

Vincent van Gogh said, "Great things are done by a series of small things brought together." He knew that a great life is built by small disciplines and wise decisions. For most of my adult life, I've followed his advice and started one new discipline every year. It might not sound like much, but the disciplines add up. Over the years, I've gotten in better physical shape, become a better student of God's Word, and grown to be a good financial steward. I started small and just kept at it.

Sure, I've slipped up and had to start over. But the disciplines that stick are the ones I practice hand-in-hand with God.

I'm convinced that two of the biggest mistakes you can make in life are not starting and not finishing. Maybe in the past you've had good intentions to start some new habits. Maybe you left many of them unfinished. Regret has set in. Sometimes you feel like a failure. You're too embarrassed even to try starting over.

But today that's going to change.

While you can't undo the past, you can start a new habit that could dramatically improve your future. If you're willing to take that first step, Jesus, the author and finisher of your faith, will help you complete what he's called you to begin.

Power Lift

I can only imagine how different my story will be, Lord, if I add one new discipline over this next year. With your help, I know I can make the change you're calling me to make!

But as for you, continue in what you have learned and have become convinced
of, because you know those from whom you learned it. (2 Tim. 3:14)

To the delight of dental hygienists everywhere, I'm an evangelist for
flossing. While I want us all to have healthy gums, I'm committed to
flossing because it represents the importance of personal habits and
routines in our lives.

Flossing matters to me because it's the easiest discipline for me to
quit. I've never liked it, and when I'm tired, I'd rather just brush my
teeth and fall into bed. But my choosing not to floss opens the door
for other challenges.

When I force myself to floss even though I don't want to, I feel
disciplined. Since I feel disciplined, I continue with my workout plan.
Since I work out, I eat better. I sleep better too. And when I sleep well,
I wake up early and do my Bible reading before work.

On the other hand, when I don't floss, I feel undisciplined and
more inclined to drop other habits as well. Since I didn't floss, I'm more
likely to skip a workout, which then helps me rationalize eating more
junk food. Those lazy, sloppy habits come back to haunt me when I
don't sleep as well at night.

Okay, I'm exaggerating—a little. But you have to agree: certain
disciplines lead to other positive actions. And the path to discipline
begins with the habits you cultivate. Yes, I encourage you to floss today,
but more important, I encourage you to commit to the habits that will
honor God, strengthen your faith, and improve the quality of your life.

• • • • • • • • • • • **Power Lift** • • • • • • • • • •

Dear God, today I will practice habits to cultivate discipline in my life. You are
the source of my strength, and I can do all things through you—even flossing.

> If any of you lacks wisdom, let him ask God, who gives generously
> to all without reproach, and it will be given him. (James 1:5 ESV)

Today you are one decision away from changing your life forever.

You might not even know exactly what that one decision will be. It's natural to assume that such a big, life-changing decision would be obvious. And sometimes it is, like deciding whether you should take a new job in another state or whether to return to school and finish your degree. Or whether you should marry the person you've been dating for the last few months. Huge decisions like these will send countless consequences rippling through your life.

But daily, smaller choices can also have a big impact. Our lives are constantly spilling into the lives of others, and theirs into ours. Like falling dominos, even our smallest decisions sometimes cascade into consequences—both positive and negative—we never could have seen coming.

Ultimately, the decisions you make today will determine the story you will tell about your life tomorrow. Each new day presents opportunities that could become the plot twists that carry you to a new page, a new chapter. Every day, all day, you make one small choice after another. Where to go, what to say, what to do.

And those choices just keep accumulating, each one twisting, folding into the next, until eventually they're all woven into the tapestry that is your life's story. Today ask God to guide you to the decisions you need to make to grow closer to him.

• • • • • • • • • • **Power Lift** • • • • • • • • • •

Father, give me your wisdom and discernment in all the choices I make today, both big and small. Remind me that each decision I make can draw me closer to you.

You need to persevere so that when you have done the will of
God, you will receive what he has promised. (Heb. 10:36)

I'm a sucker for those movies about great athletes and their teams—
you know, like *Rudy, Miracle, Hoosiers*, and *Remember the Titans*. I love
seeing underdogs refuse to give up as they overcome impossible odds to
achieve their dreams. In some cases, their friends and families believe in
them, and in others, they have to do it all on their own. Some of them
have a lot of natural talent, while others have to work twice as hard to
get to the top of their game. Most of them lose before they start winning.

True champions—not just winners—inspire us to persevere in our
faith. Like Christopher Morley says, "Big shots are only little shots who
keep shooting." Some days it's tough to keep going. We work hard only
to fail and get back up again, to keep trusting God to sustain us and
empower us to get back in the race. On those days, we must remember
God doesn't ask us to win every race. He asks us only to take the next
step, and the next, until we cross the finish line. That's what being a
champion is all about.

Power Lift

Lord, don't let me give up today. Help me to look to you as the source of my
power when I can't go on. Get me back on my feet and enable me to take the
next step.

My sacrifice, O God, is a broken spirit; a broken and contrite
heart you, God, will not despise. (Ps. 51:17)

As you reflect over the course of your years, chances are you have some chapters in your story that you'd rather not share with anyone. You might have secrets that you've never told another living person. You might have done things you wish you'd never done.

Maybe you've ended up somewhere you never wanted to be. You didn't mean to blow it, but you did. You made decisions that took you farther than you ever intended to go. You did some things that cost you more than you ever thought you'd have to pay. You hurt people. You compromised your values. You broke promises. You did things that you can't undo. There's no do-over like when you were a kid on the playground.

Sometimes you simply skip over those dark chapters of your life. Other times you edit the stories on the fly, making up a version that you like better than the truth, both to tell yourself and to tell others. You brush by the ugly parts and retell the happy ones.

No matter how you would describe your story right now, there's good news. Your story is not over. It's not too late to change the story you'll tell in the future. Regardless of what you've done (or haven't done) in the past, your future remains unwritten. There are more chapters to write, more victories to win, more friends to meet, more of a difference to make, more of God's goodness to experience.

Today, with God's help, you can start something new.

Power Lift

Forgive me, Lord, when I stumble and struggle to keep going. Give me the strength to get back on my feet and start again.

The heart of man plans his way, but the Lord
establishes his steps. (Prov. 16:9 ESV)

No matter how old we get, wisdom often hangs in the balance between a
good decision and one that becomes a slippery slope toward disaster. In
my case, this is often literally true. Or at least it was a while back when
I injured my foot during a savage game of indoor soccer. Immediately
after it happened, I could barely walk. When I went to my doctor, he
gave me a giant, heavy, ugly boot that I had to wear while it healed, a
sort of "man-UGG."

I tried to be a good patient, until the day that I remembered we
still had Christmas lights up on our house. And since I didn't want to
be that guy who leaves his Christmas lights up all year, I decided to take
them down—right then. Yes, I realize how crazy that sounds now, but
at the time it made perfect sense.

Just like many of our decisions seem to make sense in the moment,
it's not until later, when facing the consequences, that we realize how
impulsive or reckless or foolish we've been. Fortunately, after climb-
ing the ladder, I listened to the voice of reason—spoken through my
daughter—and came down. I had to step back, literally, and look at the
big picture and potential consequences in order to have clarity.

Today think about the choices you're making and their consequences. Are you allowing God to establish your steps? Or are you
trying to climb a ladder with a broken foot?

· · · · · · · · · · · **Power Lift** · · · · · · · · · · ·

Father, sometimes I rush ahead and make decisions that I later regret. Today I
want to slow down, step back, and allow you to show me my next move.

"I am the LORD, your God, who takes hold of your right hand
and says to you, Do not fear; I will help you." (Isa. 41:13)

When we were kids, our fears were often based on our imagination—monsters under the bed, scary clowns in the closet, and evil cats suffocating us in our sleep (okay, maybe that was just me). As adults, our fears often involve our health, our family, our job, and our finances. But sometimes, they still come back to those things jumping out at you in the dark.

Our family lives in a remote area, and several years ago I was putting out the trash cans at the end of our long, wooded driveway. It was dark, and once I had the cans in place, I thought I heard something. "Probably just a squirrel or raccoon," I thought and kept walking. Then I heard another rustle and something that sounded like a lion clearing his throat—that was no raccoon.

I'll admit it, I was scared.

Just then this huge golden beast lunged from behind a tree right at me! Well, maybe not right at me, but close enough.

It was a bobcat.

Ever since, I not only say a few prayers when I set the trash out, but I make sure I've got a flashlight and a baseball bat, just in case.

No matter what you fear—even bobcats—it's wise to petition God for safety and always put your trust in him.

Power Lift

Even though I still get scared sometimes, Lord, I know you are my shelter and will protect me. I have nothing to fear because you are with me today and every day.

Let the wise hear and increase in learning, and the one
who understands obtain guidance. (Prov. 1:5 ESV)

Remember when you were making the transition into adulthood? Becoming a grown-up meant learning to accept responsibility both for your choices and for their consequences. As you enjoyed more power to choose among more options, you also began to own the weight of your newfound freedom.

You learned that if you drove over the speed limit, you might get a ticket. If you dated the wrong person, you could end up heartbroken, struggling to trust again. And if you beer-bonged a six-pack of cheap beer in less than twenty minutes (not that I would know, of course), you likely found yourself hugging a toilet like you'd just asked it to marry you—and it said yes.

On the other hand, if you showed up at work on time every day and did your best work, you realized that your boss approved and might give you a raise. If you started exercising and you improved your diet, your pants size shrank and you felt better about yourself. And if you attended class, listened, took notes, and actually *studied* for exams, good grades were not out of your reach.

Every choice you make affects aspects of your life, both big and small. You either learn to take responsibility for your actions, or you learn to make excuses and find scapegoats. What's it going to be today?

You can make excuses or you can make progress.

But you can't make both.

Power Lift

I want to follow your ways, Lord, and not my own. Give me wisdom and patience so that I can know when to pause and wait on you instead of rushing ahead.

The way of a fool is right in his own eyes, but a wise
man listens to advice. (Prov. 12:15 ESV)

As a pastor, I have sat with so many people filled with regret, my heart aching for them as they asked tearfully, "Why did I do that? What was I thinking? I would give *anything* to be able to go back and make a different choice!"

One of the best decisions we can make when faced with an impulsive choice or high-stakes dilemma is simply to *stop*. Take a time-out. Hit Pause. Sleep on it. Think it over. Get some godly wisdom from others you trust.

During this interval, try to visualize what's likely to happen with each of your options. When faced with a decision, I try to picture the likely consequences of my various choices. I take stock of where I am, consider the distance between my present location and where I want to go, and then choose to move in the direction of my desired destination. Even if it seems like I'm taking baby steps, as long as I'm heading in the right direction, I know I'm getting closer to God's best for me.

Most of us have good intentions, or at least some kind of self-justification, for the things we do. And yet so many of us seem surprised when we find ourselves a long way from our desired destination. The big changes in our lives—both negative and positive—rarely happen without a series of decisions accumulating until their momentum creates significant impact.

Today make sure your steps are taking you in the right direction.

· · · · · · · · · · · **Power Lift** · · · · · · · · · ·

Jesus, today I will follow you instead of allowing my steps to stray. I trust you—not my feelings, circumstances, or other people—with the direction of my life.

"For I know the plans I have for you," declares the LORD, "plans to prosper you and not to harm you, plans to give you hope and a future." (Jer. 29:11)

Have you noticed how many New Year's sales are going on? Each January you see "new year, new you" marketing pitches everywhere you turn. Knowing we might not have received all we wanted for Christmas, stores encourage us to replace broken appliances, update our technology, and buy those products to help us keep our resolutions.

Retailers know it's often easier and more cost-efficient to discard something broken and purchase a new one rather than invest the time and money into repairing the old. Why bother fixing a broken coffee-maker when you can toss it and purchase a new one for the price of a few pounds of coffee?

As God's creation, however, we cannot be thrown away and discarded. While others may judge us, or we them, it's often our own self-condemnation, fueled by the Enemy's accusations, that blocks our fresh start. We end up feeling weak and defeated and unsure of how to begin again.

But with God, this is exactly what we get. He has promised never to abandon or forsake us. Our Father is committed to forgiving our sins, healing our wounds, and blessing us with an abundant life.

He is the source of the "new you."

· · · · · · · · · · · **Power Lift** · · · · · · · · · · ·

God, I'm so glad you don't discard me when I mess up. Thank you for your mercy and kindness, for the way you take my broken pieces and make me whole again.

Jesus told him, "Because you have seen me, you have believed; blessed
are those who have not seen and yet have believed." (John 20:29)

Do you remember when we had to buy stuff in stores—you know, things
like jeans, books, blankets, toys—even groceries? These days we can
order most anything online: clothes, food, appliances, computers—
even cars and houses. But usually, the more we're going to spend, the
more we want to see what we're getting for our money before we click
"complete order." While some people may be comfortable buying a car
online, sight unseen, most of us want to see it, touch it, and drive it
before we spend our hard-earned bucks to buy it.

It's hard to invest a lot of ourselves sight unseen.

Faith requires us to invest in our relationship with God in ways
that sometimes seem uncertain and unclear. We can't look and see
what's ahead or understand why God allowed certain events to happen
the way they did. And yet we're called to step out in faith, trusting that
our Father will guide us each step of the way, regardless of how clearly
we can see the path. But we don't have to see where we're going and
what will get us there—we just have to follow him.

Today don't worry about how clearly you can see what God's up
to—just take the next step.

Power Lift

Father, strengthen my faith in you as I face the unknowns ahead of me this day.
Remind me that you know where I'm going, even when I can't see ahead. You've
got this. Help me to trust you each step of the way.

*Let us also lay aside every encumbrance and the sin which
so easily entangles us, and let us run with endurance the
race that is set before us.* (Heb. 12:1 NASB)

Not so long ago, both Amy and my kids told me, "It seems like you're
always on your phone." At first, I made excuses and tried to justify it.
"But this thing I'm texting about is really important!" "I'm not on the
phone that often." "I've just got to post this one photo."

It's interesting how hard I fought against their sincere suggestions.
The more they prodded, the more I resisted. Eventually, in a moment of
humility, I recognized that they had a valid point. I *was* on my phone
all the time.

After finally admitting that I had a problem, I started to work on
detoxing from my phone addiction. Over time, I managed to stop bringing my phone to meals. I gradually learned to stop being a slave to my
phone. I want my story to be, "Dad was always engaged with us," not,
"Craig always replied to every text in five minutes or less."

Because which one matters most?

Is there something that those who are closest to you have been trying to tell you? Maybe you have an addiction, a hang-up, a weakness,
a blind spot. If more than one person who loves you has been trying to
help you see something that needs to change, maybe it's time to listen.

What one thing in your life needs to change?

· · · · · · · · · · · **Power Lift** · · · · · · · · · ·

Jesus, today I want to work on one issue in my life that I know needs to be
addressed. Give me the courage to face my own weakness and the strength to
experience your freedom.

For the Lord gives wisdom; from his mouth come
knowledge and understanding. (Prov. 2:6 ESV)

If you haven't already, someday you'll find yourself at a crossroads, a
place where you have to make a difficult decision about your life's direction. "Should I stay the course when it would be easier to walk away?
Or does God want me to stay put and wait on what he's doing here?"

Or maybe a better question you should ask is this:

"What does God want me to want?"

What is the one big thing you know God wants you to pursue?
Does he want you to spend more time with your family? To stop cutting corners at work? To evaluate an important relationship? It may be
that God wants you to stop pursuing your own dreams, to surrender
something to him that means a lot to you. Maybe he wants you to stop
living for things that don't matter. Even if the thing you're thinking of
isn't one of these, I'd be willing to bet you have some ideas of what it is
that God wants you to want.

In light of this, where does God want you to stay the course so that
ultimately you can tell the story he wants you to tell? Even though it
might be easier to walk away, is there some situation where you're realizing that God wants you to take a stand?

Power Lift

Father, I'm tempted to run away from my problems sometimes in order to avoid
conflict. Help me to face what I need to do, and show me where I need to stand
strong in my life today.

For still the vision awaits its appointed time; it hastens to the end—it will not lie.
If it seems slow, wait for it; it will surely come; it will not delay. (Hab. 2:3 ESV)

My senior year of high school, I played in the semifinals of the state tennis championships against a guy who was undefeated. My opponent was favored to win the tournament, so a college scout from a great university had come to watch him play. State semifinals were a big deal, so I really played my guts out, just giving everything I had. And lo and behold, I wiped the court with my (previously undefeated) opponent.

When I walked off the court, the recruiter walked right past him, straight to me, and offered me a full, four-year tennis scholarship to this awesome university! A little while after he left, I played my next match, in the finals, against a guy I had beaten just two weeks before. And he destroyed me. I played the worst match I've probably ever played.

Clearly, timing is everything. God had a plan, and it was no coincidence that the recruiter saw me play my best right before I played one of my worst matches ever. I never could have arranged events to synchronize that way if I'd tried. Sometimes we just have to show up and do our best and leave the outcome to God. Win or lose, he uses everything in our lives for good.

. . . . **Power Lift** . . . .

Dear God, forgive me for being impatient, because I know you are always right on time. I always want to do my best for you as you strengthen my ability to trust you with the outcome.

[Jesus] replied, "Blessed rather are those who hear
the word of God and obey it." (Luke 11:28)

I heard a story about a pastor who preached this incredibly powerful message to his congregation. The next week, he preached the exact same sermon. His congregation was confused but didn't want to embarrass him, so they didn't say anything. The third week, though, they were shocked and even angry when he delivered the exact same message, almost word for word. Finally, someone asked him why he kept giving the same sermon. The pastor replied, "When you start living it, I'll stop preaching it."

I wonder sometimes if this might be how God feels about the way we listen to him. It's one thing for us to study our Bibles, memorize verses, and hear teaching and preaching at church and in our small group. But it's another thing when we absorb the truth of God's Word into our hearts and act on this truth. He wants us to obey him by following the example set by his Son, Jesus.

If we love our Father and want to please him, then we will do more than just hear what he says. We will continually return to his Word and obey what he asks us to do for him.

Power Lift

Father, I'm so grateful for your Word. Allow me to be more than a hearer of your truth—I want to be a doer. Today I want to obey you in all that I do.

By his power God raised the Lord from the dead,
and he will raise us also. (1 Cor. 6:14)

I'm at the age where my kids are starting to leave home, to marry, and to start families of their own. Even though I feel too young to be called "Pops," the older I get, the more I think about what my legacy will be. Do you ever think about what you want to leave behind at the end of your life?

As we begin another year, it's natural to wonder how this year will be different from the last one, how we will grow, and what our legacies will be. What will we have accomplished this year that will endure after we've left this earth? Are we truly living out our God-given purpose, or are we settling for less?

It's tempting to let our circumstances dictate how we feel, which in turn influences how we act. If we get the raise or move to a nicer house or lose weight, then we'll feel like we're successful. But when we attach this kind of power to events beyond our control, we set ourselves up for dissatisfaction, disappointment, and discouragement.

This is not living the abundant life that Jesus came to bring. Yes, many circumstances remain beyond our control, and we will face disappointment sometimes. But when our hope is in Christ, then we can see beyond our momentary discomfort. We can trust God with this year and the next—knowing that with his help, we're creating an eternal legacy.

Power Lift

Dear Jesus, thank you for providing me with the power to face today. Help me to trust you fully, knowing that what I do is significant for your eternal kingdom.

> Seek the Kingdom of God above all else, and he will give
> you everything you need. (Luke 12:31 NLT)

I vividly remember the first real step of faith I took toward God. I was a sophomore in college, not a Christian yet, and part of a fraternity known for its outrageous behavior. When we met to brainstorm ways to improve our reputation, I had a radical idea. "Hey, let's start a Bible study! What could improve our image more than that?"

My fraternity brothers thought I was crazy, but I used my authority as vice president to insist. "Tuesday night at 7:00, starting this week, we're having our first Bible study!"

The next Tuesday, however, I panicked when it finally occurred to me that I didn't have a Bible. I was on my way to class when I noticed an older gentleman walking down the sidewalk toward me. He wore a suit and tie and had a broad, warm smile. As he approached, our eyes met, and with God as my witness, he said, "Would you like a free Bible?"

"Uh . . . sure. Yes, please . . . I need a Bible."

He handed me a tiny green paperback, small enough to fit in my pocket, and walked away, still smiling. (I would later learn that this man was with Gideons International, an organization that distributes free Bibles all over the world.)

Just like that, God provided me with the Bible I needed, even though I didn't know him yet. A few hours later, I strolled into my first-ever Bible study where seven of my party buddies were already waiting for me. If God could provide me with a Bible so easily, I knew he was about to do even more in our lives.

Power Lift

Lord, today I want to trust you with wherever I need to step out in faith and grow closer to you.

Submit yourselves, then, to God. Resist the devil,
and he will flee from you. (James 4:7)

Recently my wife, Amy, brought home a massive bag of M&M's. You know, the size of bag that looks like it belongs in the barn to feed grain to animals. The kind of bag you could use to do arm curls. I was intrigued because Amy almost never brings unhealthy food into our house. And I'm still not sure why she brought home this mega bag of chocolate delight that melts in your mouth but not in your hand, but I didn't question it.

I was secretly glad. Would it really be my fault if I were to eat one or two—pounds—of them? I didn't buy them in the industrial size. I just happened to open the kitchen cupboard one day, and there they were, emitting a multicolored aura and whispering my name.

And since the bag was already open, I decided I could just be a help to Amy and a role model for the kids and show them what moderation looks like. *I'll just have a few.*

Twenty minutes later, Amy came into kitchen to discover that I'd eaten a significant portion of the bag.

What's not so cool is that I knew what I was doing and had no one to blame but myself. If she hadn't stopped me, I could have eaten the whole bag. We all have our weaknesses, but the key to growing stronger is using our knowledge of them to protect ourselves. We are only as strong as we are honest. To resist those things that tempt us most, we must acknowledge where we are vulnerable and submit ourselves to God.

Power Lift

Lord, I surrender my heart and my will to you today. Give me strength to overcome the temptations I may face and to resist the Enemy's snares.

> I will instruct you and teach you in the way you should go; I
> will counsel you with my loving eye on you. (Ps. 32:8)

I love to play sports and was on the tennis team in college. When we "schooled" someone on the tennis court, it meant we taught them a lesson by beating them. What I've discovered as I've grown older, however, is the way God schools us every day.

He's not humiliating us—like I might've done with a few collegiate rivals—he's truly teaching us, giving us the counsel and instruction that's best for us. When we start thinking differently about how we relate to God, each day provides us with new learning opportunities.

We don't have to be in school or on the sports field or training for a new career in order to experience God's life lessons all around us. He delights in teaching us his truth. Through his Word, we have the opportunity to study his many lessons, each day discovering a new insight or a fresh angle to his truth that endures forever.

God also reveals his instructions to us through prayer and through our relationships with other people. While we may not always receive the answer we want when we want it, we can still know that he will guide us. Like a hiker lost in the woods who finds a compass, you don't have to rely on your knowledge alone.

Notice what God is trying to teach you today—about yourself, about your life, and about who he is.

Power Lift

Jesus, sometimes I still forget how much I have. Keep my spirit teachable and my heart humble. Open my eyes to see and my ears to hear the lessons of your truth before me today.

Say to those with fearful hearts, "Be strong, do not fear." (Isa. 35:4)

I work out with a buddy who pushes me beyond my physical limitations. He challenges me, taunts me, and encourages me. I'd never tell him this (after all, I'm a guy), but when he spots me, I can lift more because I'm not afraid of having the weights crash down on me. His presence in the weight room gives me confidence.

God's presence in our lives works the same way.

Most of our fears come from our perception that something is dangerous, uncertain, or unpredictable. Lightning may or may not strike our house, so we buy insurance. Illness and injury are more likely to occur if we don't exercise, eat right, and get adequate rest.

We do what we can to dispel and control our fears, but no matter how old we are or how mature in our faith, we still get scared sometimes.

Like a child walking through the woods on a moonless night, we're frightened by what we can't see. We worry about keeping our jobs or helping our kids or having enough money saved for retirement. We wonder how certain relationships will survive or if we'll remain healthy.

But we're not alone. When we're afraid, our Father spots us and makes sure we can lift the load we're carrying. He grips our hand and helps us push through whatever we face. Because God is with us, we have nothing to fear.

• • • • • • • • • • • **Power Lift** • • • • • • • • • • • •

Lord, today I appreciate the way you reassure me when I'm afraid. Thank you for going with me today, steadying my hand, and helping me push through whatever's ahead.

Sin shall no longer be your master. (Rom. 6:14)

So many Christian friends of mine struggle with something that started out as "no big deal" but, you guessed it, quickly became a big deal. That third cup of coffee became the need for a double-shot by 9:30 each morning. Buddies at the gym find that dipping snuff is something they need to do all day, not just when outdoors or playing sports. Others tell me they can't stop gambling—at first it was just fantasy football, but then it became online wagering. Soon they couldn't stop and were spending way more than they could afford to lose.

Even though we may struggle with sin for the rest of our lives, God's Word is clear that sin no longer has any power over us. Jesus died on the cross and paid for our sins once and for all. He rose from the dead and restored our relationship with his Father. We could never make ourselves presentable to our holy, perfect God, so he did it for us.

Too often, however, I see people living as though there's nothing they can do to overcome their addictions, both large and small. They live in denial, dismiss them as harmless, or resign themselves to managing their habits but not overcoming them. That's not how God wants us to live. If we're willing to trust him, God will give us more than enough power to defeat the "little sins" that trouble us the most.

Don't accept defeat today—focus on that one sinful habit you know you need to eliminate and ask God to help you overcome it.

Power Lift

Jesus, thank you for dying on the cross for my sins. I know that sin now has no more power over my life, so help me to live that way.

> Therefore, I urge you, brothers and sisters, in view of God's mercy, to offer your bodies as a living sacrifice, holy and pleasing to God—this is your true and proper worship. (Rom. 12:1)

Superman has his Kryptonite, and I have my Krispy Kremes.

Donuts are my weakness. But I know they're not good for me—and more important, I know if I eat just one, then I might have a second, and suddenly I'm cutting corners the rest of the day. And once I've blown what I ate on one day, it's that much easier to do it the next. So I've learned to stay away from my Kryptonite.

We all have our weaknesses. Day after day we make choices about what we will eat and drink, what to watch on Netflix, what to listen to in our car, or which blogs to read. We often think these little choices don't matter that much, at least not in the long run. But it's just the opposite: all of these decisions affect our body, our mind, and our spirit—what we think, how we feel, the way we act.

Our choices, even little ones, can bring us closer to God, but they can also pull us away. If we aren't careful and deliberate about all the daily choices that influence us, we open ourselves up for temptation and snares from our Enemy.

Your choices matter—every single one of them. Remember that change you began making a few weeks ago? Even if you've slipped a time or two, now is the time to get back on track. Today choose wisely, nourishing and protecting your body as a gift from God, caring for it as a good steward.

Power Lift

Dear God, I'm grateful for the body you've given me and want to make it a living sacrifice for your glory. Help me to take the best care possible in every choice I make today.

> Now when they saw the boldness of Peter and John, and perceived
> that they were uneducated, common men, they were astonished. And
> they recognized that they had been with Jesus. (Acts 4:13 ESV)

Have you ever noticed that what you believe determines how you behave? For example, if you believe that everybody is going to criticize you, you'll behave tentatively. If you believe that you're probably going to fail, you're going to venture out cautiously.

However, if you believe that the one true Lord God is calling you, empowering you, leading you, and equipping you, you will live very boldly. Why? Because boldness is behavior born out of belief.

The Greek word in Scripture that's translated as boldness is the word *parrhesia*, and this word means more than just speaking; it means outspokenness, it means assurance, it means courage, it means confidence, it means to act without fear.

To be honest, sometimes I get discouraged because the prayer I hear the most often is, "God, thank you for this day. Help us to get through this day. Amen." Now that's fine to include, especially if you're starting out, but you have to admit, it's not very bold. I've always wondered if God hears prayers like that and goes, "Okay, sure, but give me a tough one! I'm God of the universe—let me show you what I can do!"

In the Bible we see men and women who were just like us—scared, tired, unsure of themselves—who nonetheless were transformed into bold people. God delights in doing the same thing with us today— giving us the power to be bold. And it all starts with what we believe.

Power Lift

I want to be bold, Lord, and to step out in my faith. Today show me what risk to take that I may further your kingdom and draw others to you.

I urge you to live a life worthy of the calling you have received. (Eph. 4:1)

I suspect there's no greater satisfaction than the fulfillment that comes from doing what you know God made you to do. The last thing I want to do is sound like I'm bragging, but sometimes after I preach or speak, I feel "in the zone" and know I'm doing exactly what the Lord made me to do. There's no greater joy! I feel like the famous Olympic runner, Eric Liddell, who said, "God made me fast. When I run, I feel his pleasure."

I'm convinced it's this way for all of us. Once you've committed to a relationship with God by accepting Christ into your heart, then your calling becomes clear: to use your unique gifts and talents for your Father's kingdom.

Sometimes we become dissatisfied with life because we lose focus. We get pushed and pulled into other people's expectations and agendas, or we chase after goals we think will fulfill us. However, you're only going to be truly content when you're living within the purpose for which God created you. When you do what he created you to do, you feel his pleasure.

If you're still discovering this purpose, then ask him to reveal it more clearly to you. God has placed a call on you and your life and has equipped you for your unique purpose. Your life has meaning because it counts for eternity!

Power Lift

Jesus, I'm so grateful for the new life I have through you. You have given me a purpose and have equipped me to serve you so that others can know your love as well.

Consider the blameless, observe the upright; a future
awaits those who seek peace. (Ps. 37:37)

My second daughter, Mandy, recently got married. And I have to say, the planning that went into that event was amazing. Fortunately for me, almost all of it was done by my wife, my daughter, and the groom. As much as I love to plan, to organize details and follow a schedule to reach a goal, it would not have been pretty if I'd been in charge of the flowers, the cake, and the bridesmaids' dresses.

Planning for the future consumes a big part of each day. Sometimes we undertake events requiring many details—weddings, conferences, family reunions.

Others are simply future appointments, routine meetings, and events we want to attend. Sometimes, though, we invest so much time, energy, and money into our future endeavors that we overlook opportunities to impact our future right now.

I'm a firm believer that the actions you take today sow the seeds of your future. Your daily habits will create a cumulative impact on what you do tomorrow, next week, and next year. If you practice compassion, righteousness, and kindness, you know the future will yield peace, joy, and a closer relationship with your Father.

When you're planning for your future, don't forget that today's choices yield tomorrow's harvest.

Power Lift

Lord, I get so wrapped up in the future sometimes that I lose sight of the present. Today help me to focus on being more like Jesus, not on worrying about what tomorrow may hold.

> "Come to me, all you who are weary and burdened,
> and I will give you rest." (Matt. 11:28)

I have a hard time relaxing. I have such a tough time letting go of all the busyness in my life that a counselor once prescribed for me to spend five minutes each day doing absolutely *nothing*. Can you believe that? I paid someone to tell me not to do anything!

The sad thing is that I struggled to shut down even for five minutes. However, since that time, I've learned that to be my most productive, I must rest and recharge. Even God rested on the seventh day after creating everything, so it must be important.

How about you—when was the last time you felt truly rested? Do you struggle to slow down and get the rest you know you need?

As much as we want to catch up on all the busyness in our lives, we also long for soul-satisfying rest. Unfortunately, many people are just like me and don't find it easy to rest.

But what I discovered is that the secret to true rest isn't our activity—or lack of it—but our soul's anchor. When we choose to relax and let go of all our worries, our faith anchors us to the goodness and sovereignty of God. He's in charge, not us.

The secret to rest is anchoring yourself to a foundation that never moves. Our lives change constantly, but God's power, love, and sovereignty never change. He is the same now and forever.

So today you can rest easy.

. . . .   **Power Lift**   . . . .

God, like a child resting against their father's shoulder, let me lean on you, secure in the tender strength of your arms as I release all my worries.

Whoever dwells in the shelter of the Most High will rest
in the shadow of the Almighty. (Ps. 91:1)

As a pastor, I work most weekends. Consequently, I've often envied the relaxation and fun so many people seem to enjoy from Friday evening to Monday morning. But the more people I talk to about this, the more I realize their weekends are just as busy and hectic as mine. Even their Sundays can seem jam-packed with church services, family activities, and preparations for the upcoming week.

Maybe this is why God commands us to take a Sabbath, one day out of our weekly seven that's set aside to rest our bodies, renew our spirits, and recharge our minds.

Unfortunately, keeping the Sabbath as a time to recover from the week and to focus on our relationship with God is easier in theory than in practice.

But as God establishes in Genesis, when he created our world and everything in it, he took a day off. On the seventh day, he rested. Scripture doesn't say that he created only a couple of little things that day, or that he caught up on all those things he had been meaning to create. No, he *rested*.

Choose a day to honor as your Sabbath this week. And in the meantime, cancel an appointment, reschedule a meeting, or break your routine. Take a few minutes and simply rest your soul before God.

Power Lift

Lord, today I release my cares and worries to you. Help me to still my soul before you, to soak in your presence, and to practice keeping the Sabbath as my time to rest in you.

He makes me lie down in green pastures, he leads me beside
quiet waters, he refreshes my soul. (Ps. 23:2–3)

I recently overdid it at the gym and pulled a muscle in my back. It was nothing serious, but my doctor told me I had to rest for a few weeks. Once again, someone else had to tell me I needed to hit Pause if I wanted to get healthy. Once again, it was hard for me.

I know I'm not alone. Many of us never slow down until we're forced to. We get sick, have an accident, or sustain an injury.

Suddenly, we have no choice but to reduce our speed and alter our normally fast-paced routine. This process almost always yields positive results, even if we initially resist the required rest period or slower pace.

Similarly, I suspect sometimes our lives become so overwhelming that God intervenes and brings his supernatural peace into our minds. We can't explain it. Our to-do list remains just as long, the demands of our schedule just as overwhelming. But somehow we sense that it's all going to be okay. We know we're not alone.

It would be awesome to sit outside on a warm day, rest under a shade tree, and watch the sun set. Most of the time, especially in the midst of winter, we probably can't. Nonetheless, the same sense of tranquility can be ours when we allow God's peace to envelop us.

Power Lift

God, I feel so overwhelmed by life's demands most of the time. Remind me that your peace is always available to me, no matter how stressed I may feel today.

We are more than conquerors through him who loved us. (Rom. 8:37)

Cold weather gets me down.

It seems to last forever, and it's hard to believe there's anything living beneath the icy surface. But there is, of course, as the beauty of spring will eventually remind us. Ice and snow will melt, tender shoots will break the ground, and buds will blush with new color on vibrant branches.

But for now, we have to wait.

Our spiritual life is often the same way. Many times we can't see beyond the spiritual season of winter in which we sometimes find ourselves. We feel lifeless and flat, bored and uninterested in spending time in prayer or Bible study. We crave distractions—food, TV, social media, shopping, on and on—and try to fulfill our hunger for God with fast fixes that will never satisfy us. We face these days feeling weary and wondering how we will ever keep going.

This is when we must remember that spring will come.

We just need to keep the faith, remembering all that God has done for us, even if we don't feel as connected to him as we would like. During these times—especially during these winter seasons—we must remember that God's love is constant. It does not waver, increase, or decrease based on our feelings.

You will get through your present winter struggles as sure as spring will bring green shoots. God has already planted his new life within you.

Power Lift

God, thank you for loving me all the time, no matter how cold I might feel, and for providing all I need even when I can't see beyond my present season.

The goal of this command is love, which comes from a pure heart
and a good conscience and a sincere faith. (1 Tim. 1:5)

Back when I was in high school, I always dreaded February. The whole pressure of Valentine's Day felt like too much—especially too much money. I'm not proud of this, but I was the kind of guy who would break up with his girlfriend on February 12th and then miraculously reconsider and make up on February 15th. Sad, I know—and not very loving.

While February has become associated with love, mostly because of all the hearts and flowers, we know that God calls us to love others daily. Although Jesus remains our perfect model for loving, I'm grateful we have verses like today's to break it down. Clearly, in order to fulfill God's command to love, we need a pure heart, a good conscience, and a sincere faith.

Having a pure heart requires devotion to knowing God and obeying his commands. We don't have to be perfect; we just need to rely on God as the source of our daily power. A good conscience reminds us when we've sinned and are going astray. Knowing that our Father is quick to forgive us when we confess, we keep our conscience clear by asking for God's forgiveness when we sin.

Finally, having a sincere faith means we trust God with all our hearts—we give him our lives and hold nothing back. We don't play games, pursue self-righteousness, or pretend to have our lives together. We rely on God and follow Jesus as our example.

Following God's recipe, we discover the power to love every day of the year.

Power Lift

Dear God, you loved me first and are the source of all love. As I start this new month, help me rely on you as my power source for loving others around me.

Love must be sincere. (Rom. 12:9)

The word love gets thrown around a lot. We love our families. And the taste of chocolate and crazy cat videos on YouTube. We love our best friends, the latest *Star Wars* movie, and the beach.

But then there's the way God loves us and we love him. And one of the primary ways we show our love for him is by the way we love others—sincerely. We usually think of sincere as meaning genuine, earnest, unpretentious, and open about our feelings. But what does sincere really mean?

While we are uncertain about the root of the word sincere, some experts believe it comes from two Latin words, *sine* (meaning "without") and *cera* (meaning "wax"). In ancient Rome, sometimes slaves and builders would take shortcuts and use wax to gloss over gaps and imperfections when constructing homes. Saying someone was "without wax" meant they could be trusted as the real deal, not a phony.

We want our attitudes and actions around other people to be just as strong. In order to love sincerely, we must remain committed to God with a rock-solid faith. When we focus on Jesus and love the way he loved, then others will know our love is sincere.

Power Lift

Lord, I want to be sincere and authentic in my faith and in the way I love others. I'm sorry for those times when I glossed over opportunities to serve others. Show me how to love like Jesus and give others my best today.

> Jesus said, "Father, forgive them, for they do not
> know what they are doing." (Luke 23:34)

When I was growing up, I would perform magic tricks, and my sister, Lisa, three years younger, was usually my assistant. We often did the trick where I put her in a little box and made her disappear. Only sometimes I'd lock her in the box and just leave her locked in there, which I thought was hysterical—Lisa, not so much. (Okay, it might have been a lot of times.)

The amazing thing, though, is that my sister always forgave me—at least until I did it the next time. It didn't really make sense to me then, but looking back, I now realize I got a glimpse of Jesus' love in her forgiveness. Because Jesus forgave the very people who killed him—while they were doing it.

People spit on him, cursed him, mocked and laughed at him. "King of the Jews? Then why don't you save yourself!" they shouted. And instead of defending himself or explaining what was actually taking place, Jesus prayed for them: "Father, they don't know what they're doing—please forgive them."

I'm convinced that learning to love like Jesus means learning to forgive like him too. Ultimately, Jesus came to forgive all sinners—including you and me. But as we are forgiven, Jesus calls us to forgive each other. Forgiveness is the power of his love in action.

Power Lift

Jesus, give me the power to do what is not humanly possible—to forgive others when they hurt me. Just as you've forgiven me for my sins, today help me to forgive the people who have wounded me.

Bear with each other and forgive one another if any of you has a grievance
against someone. Forgive as the Lord forgave you. (Col. 3:13)

How do we love like Jesus? Especially when we consider deep hurts and
major wounds to our heart, it can be tough to forgive. Maybe someone
exploited you, abused you, betrayed you, lied to you, cheated you. Maybe
someone hurt the people you love the most, leaving them injured for life.

Most of us carry such wounds around inside us: the church that
excluded you, the boss who took credit for your work, the sibling who
turned against you, the parent who let you down. This person may even
be dead now, but still there's a dark, angry hunger gnawing inside you.
You may even wonder how God could forgive someone who could do
what they did to you.

But as we know, Jesus told us to pray for those people who hurt
us—and more specifically, to forgive them. As hard as it may be, we can
do it through the power of Christ. Why? Two reasons: first, Jesus knew
what he was asking of us because he himself suffered the worst, most
unfair, cruel abuse possible; and second, because even after suffering
through all of that, he chose to die to wash away our sins and forgive us.

Today consider the grudge you've been carrying around against
that certain person and begin the practice—and it will take daily practice for a while—of letting it go.

Power Lift

Lord, you know how hard it is for me to forgive certain people who have hurt
me. Help me to love them by choosing to forgive them as you have forgiven me.

> "You have heard that it was said, 'Love your neighbor and
> hate your enemy.' But I tell you, love your enemies and
> pray for those who persecute you." (Matt. 5:43–44)

There's this one guy in town who hates my guts. (Actually, I'm sure there's more than one, but I'm thinking about one in particular right now.) He takes every opportunity to trash my name, mock our church, and critique everything I say or do. To say he's hateful would be the understatement of the century. And when he hurls hate bombs my way, everything in me wants to fire back. There is just one problem.

Jesus told us not only to forgive those who have hurt us but also to love our enemies. He told his followers that when others wronged them, they were to turn the other cheek, go the extra mile, and forgive them. This was not what his listeners expected to hear. They had been taught an eye for an eye, a tooth for a tooth, and blood for blood. If someone wronged them, they were entitled to wrong that person back.

But Christ basically said, "Not so fast. It's easy to love people who are nice to you. And it's easy to hate people who act hatefully toward you. But if you really want to follow me, if you really want to love people, then you need to love your enemies."

· · · · · · · · · · · **Power Lift** · · · · · · · · · ·

Jesus, the only way I can love my enemies is with your help. Today give me the strength, love, and mercy I need to forgive those who are against me.

"The greatest among you will be your servant." (Matt. 23:11)

Imagine if you came to visit my home and I said, "Can I take your coat? Get you something to drink? Give you a pedicure?" After asking me to repeat myself to make sure you'd heard correctly, you would probably wonder about that last one. In our culture, it's good manners to welcome people into your home by offering to hang up their jacket and handing them a beverage. In Jesus' day, though, it was customary to ask guests if they would like their feet washed.

And if you think our feet are dirty today, just imagine what they must have been like back then. People wore sandals or went barefoot and walked almost everywhere—through dirt, mud, dust, and even much more disgusting things. So washing a visitor's feet was an act of humility, service, and honor—and a task most often left for slaves and servants to do.

However, Jesus did this self-sacrificing act for his disciples. After the final meal with his closest friends right before his betrayal, Jesus washed their feet. He knew about the power struggles taking place in each of their hearts and wanted to show them, in a very tangible and concrete way, how to be truly great: by serving others. Do the humbling, thankless, dirty job that no one likes to do. Love others by sacrificing yourself to meet their needs.

Today if you want to show others the love of God, find a way to "wash their feet." Notice someone's need and simply meet it. The same way Jesus would.

Power Lift

Lord, you demonstrated such loving service by washing your disciples' feet. Empower me to serve the needs of others with the same compassion and humility.

"My Father will honor the one who serves me." (John 12:26)

One time I was in a big home improvement store when I noticed a little old lady stretching to reach for the largest pair of hedge clippers I'd ever seen.

"Ma'am," I said, "can I help you with those?"

"Oh, thank you—yes, please," she said.

"Must be quite a job if you need clippers this big," I said and put them in her cart.

"Well, they haven't been trimmed in a long time," she said and went on to describe her yard and to explain why she hadn't been able to cut her hedges sooner. As we chatted, I asked who would be helping her, only to discover she planned to attempt this job by herself. Her family lived far away and she couldn't afford to pay someone.

It felt impulsive and a little crazy, but I offered to cut her hedges for her. After considering my offer for a moment, she asked, "Are you sure you're a lawn man?"

"Yes, ma'am," I said. "I am today. I got this."

I'm not sure why I happened to run into her that day, but I'd like to think it was because I had the chance to be a blessing to her—and to be blessed in the process. It's so easy to hear about someone in need or to find ourselves in a situation where we could help. And it's easy to smile, say something kind, and offer up a prayer. But if we truly want to love like Jesus, then we need to go one step farther. We need to serve.

Power Lift

Open my eyes, Lord, to the needs of those around me. Today I want to sacrifice my agenda to help someone experience your love.

We love because he first loved us. (1 John 4:19)

When I was dating in college, I tried to guard my heart by making sure I never needed any girl as much as I wanted her to need me. When I became a Christian, everything changed, especially my dating habits. So when I met my future wife, Amy, I quickly realized how much I needed her in my life. Fortunately, she felt the same way. We discovered how much we both needed each other, and it didn't matter who loved whom first.

With God, though, it's easy to see: we're able to love because he loved us first. It's not just that we need him and are created to be in relationship with him. It's simply a natural response when we experience his love for us. Even when it doesn't make sense to us, God loves us as his sons and daughters. He desires a relationship with us—so much so that he made the ultimate sacrifice, his only Son.

If you want to love others with the love of Jesus, then always make sure your heart is plugged into God's heart. He is your power source for loving even those people who at first may seem hard to love. We all need our Father's love, and he allows us the privilege of serving one another.

Power Lift

Dear God, help me to love others the way you love me. Allow me to demonstrate your patience, compassion, and mercy to everyone I see today.

"Give to the one who asks you, and do not turn away from
the one who wants to borrow from you." (Matt. 5:42)

Many years ago, my wife, Amy, bumped into a car that had just started to turn and then stopped. She and the driver both got out and looked, but they didn't see any real damage. The police came by and said neither was to blame and let them both go on their way since there was no damage.

However, a few days later, the man who had been driving the car called us and said there had been minor damage after all and that fixing it would cost several hundred dollars. We were stunned and didn't know what to do. On one hand, it seemed unlikely there was any damage done—the police didn't even file a report. On the other, though, we wanted to do our best to represent Christ for this man and his family. So we paid the money he requested, which was quite a lot for us at the time.

Fast forward seventeen years to a recent moment when Amy and I were coming out of the church. A young woman came up to us, introduced herself, and said, "When I was six years old, you accidentally hit our car. My dad asked for some money to fix our car, and you not only gave it to us but you acted so kindly and were so loving. Our family eventually started coming to your church, and it has been life-changing. So thank you!"

You never know how the way you act today could be used by God to change the lives of others tomorrow.

Power Lift

Lord, today let me plant seeds of kindness wherever I go. Let others see your love through my attitude and actions.

> Above all, love each other deeply, because love
> covers over a multitude of sins. (1 Peter 4:8)

When I was younger, before I had children, I used to wonder how my parents could love me when I did something disobedient and, well, stupid. I knew they loved me, yet I still seemed determined to test that love. At those times, I didn't feel like I deserved their love.

Even today sometimes, when we consider the way criminals murder, steal, and harm others, it's hard to understand how their families continue to love them. But even the most hardened criminal or heinous offender is someone's son or daughter, perhaps someone's spouse, sibling, or parent. The people who love them somehow see beyond the crimes committed to the individual they love underneath.

While most of us don't think of ourselves as criminals, we are just as sinful in our nature. Yet through the power of Christ's sacrificial death on the cross, God sees beyond our weaknesses and shortcomings and regards us as his beloved children. His love encompasses us in a way that is not conditional upon what we've done. Similarly, we can't earn his love with good behavior.

If we're honest, we know we've sinned and deserve to be punished. But our Father's love transcends even the worst things we've done. We are free to become new people, transformed by his Spirit.

Power Lift

Jesus, sometimes I judge others for what they do and condemn them in my heart. Help me to show the same mercy and love that you show to me to everyone I'm around today.

> Just as a body, though one, has many parts, but all its many
> parts form one body, so it is with Christ. (1 Cor. 12:12)

As a pastor, I often hear visitors tell me, "We've been to fourteen churches in this area and not one of them seems to meet our needs. However, we're really excited about this church and look forward to seeing if y'all can provide a spiritual home for us." During these moments, I have to exercise every bit of self-restraint I can muster not to reply, "Maybe you should keep looking! If you're a follower of Jesus, then you're a spiritual contributor, not a spiritual consumer!"

Of course, I try to welcome everyone who visits Life.Church. But I also try to make it clear that our church exists to do what Jesus did during his time on earth: serve the needs of others and spread the good news of the gospel. The church does not exist for us. We are the church and we exist for the world.

And when we give ourselves to serve as part of the body of Christ, we discover that thrill of knowing that God is using us. We feel our gifts, talents, and resources making an impact in other people's lives for eternity. We get the opportunity to make a difference in someone else's life every day. We get to reveal how much God loves them wherever they are and whatever they're going through.

When you serve others, God changes lives—and the first life he changes is yours.

• • • • • • • • • • • **Power Lift** • • • • • • • • • • •

Thank you, God, that I can make a difference today. I'm so grateful to be a part of the body of Christ and to show others your amazing love—through my attitude, my words, and my actions.

Love the LORD your God with all your heart and with all
your soul and with all your strength. (Deut. 6:5)

When Amy and I were first married, we quickly realized that the person we married was not perfect. One early battlefield, or should I say, "batter-field," for us was the breakfast table, because our weapon of choice was pancakes. You see, she made these little goopy circles of batter and called them "hotcakes," and I made these beautiful golden orbs of deliciousness called, understandably, pancakes. We even argued over whether to butter them and what kind of syrup to use!

It wasn't easy, but Amy and I knew that the commitment we had made to each other meant learning all there was to know—good and bad—and loving each other completely. I suspect it's this way for most of us. When we meet someone we love, someone who clearly loves us just for who we are, then we want them to know us completely. We want to be seen and understood fully.

The same is true with God. He wants us to love him with all areas of our being, not just when we go to church, say a prayer, or serve someone in need. Our relationship with him is the most important one we will ever have. So we must be committed to giving him everything we've got—our full attention, dedication, and devotion.

Consider how you can love God more fully by everything you think, say, and do today.

Power Lift

Lord, I love you so much and want to devote my heart, soul, and strength to showing others my love for you. Reveal to me any areas that I need to surrender in order to love you more fully.

They broke bread in their homes and ate together
with glad and sincere hearts. (Acts 2:46)

Amy and I have six children, and it's amazing to see how our eating habits have changed over the years. When we first got married, you would have thought the four food groups were McDonald's, Taco Bell, Wendy's, and Burger King! With little kids, we needed food to be fast and cheap, and if it came with a toy that didn't break before we got home, all the better.

These days if you were to open our refrigerator, you'd think you were in Whole Foods or at the farmer's market. There are some cage-free eggs next to the lactose-free almond milk beside the gluten-free noodles made from broccoli stalks. Now when I'm feeling really rebellious, I drink whole milk from cows that I'm assured were treated less than humanely. (Okay, maybe I'm exaggerating, but not by much.)

One of the ways Jesus showed his love to those around him was by breaking bread with them. From Zacchaeus, the wee little tax man, to Mary and her sister Martha and their brother Lazarus, Jesus frequently ate with other people in their homes. He created quite a stir with the Jewish religious leaders who considered him scandalous for eating with sinners.

We can love people by finding common ground, especially if it involves sharing a meal together. When we dine together over the same food, we can experience a true and meaningful fellowship that honors our Savior and draws us closer to each other.

Today invite someone to share a meal with you.

· · · · · · · · · · · **Power Lift** · · · · · · · · · · ·

God, help me to love others by finding ways to break bread with them. Today guide me to the person I can share lunch or coffee with, or at least invite to join me on another day.

"How precious is Your lovingkindness, O God!" (Ps 36:7 NKJV)

"I'm really proud of you."

Just five little words. That's all it took to #MeltDadsHeart. My oldest daughter, Catie, had texted me at 8:22 p.m. one Sunday night not long ago (I know because I saved it). It was one of those special moments where she surprised me with the simple gift of those five little words. It means more to me now that Catie's an adult and married, because it was totally unexpected. The fact that she was thinking of me, and was *proud* of me, meant more to me than she could ever know.

One quick text is all it took to make me feel #SoHappy #LoveThatGirl #LifeIsGreat.

Sometimes the smallest acts of kindness can produce enormous rewards. When someone holds the door for us, surprises us with a cup of coffee, or thanks us for our help, we feel respected, appreciated, and valued. Often these little gifts of courtesy and compassion have a larger impact than anything else that person could have given.

When we give these same kinds of gifts to others, we may have no idea how we're impacting their day. But those little kindnesses add up and remind each of us—both giving and receiving—of God's abundant blessings in our lives. Today let your attitude of kindness toward others reflect your Father's kindness toward you.

Power Lift

Lord, I'm amazed at the way you continue to shower me with blessings and reveal your unfailing kindness to me. Allow me to bless others with the same spirit of loving generosity.

And let us consider how we may spur one another on
toward love and good deeds. (Heb. 10:24)

It's not unusual to get together with friends and hear, "Hey, let's go see the new movie that just came out!" or, "When's our next potluck dinner?" or, "Let's get tickets to the big game next weekend." We don't have trouble coming up with ideas for how to have fun and enjoy being with our friends.

But when it comes to serving others as the body of Christ, we seem to struggle with fresh ways to serve and meet the needs of those around us. I mean, when was the last time you heard someone say, "Let's host a themed meal for the homeless," or, "Come over to my place this Saturday—my elderly neighbor needs a new roof"?

I understand how hard it can be just to get together, let alone organize a time when you can all serve together. But the Bible tells us it's important for us to meet together and to practice "good deeds" for those in need around us. There's something about serving together that unites our hearts in a unique way, a way that reflects the heart of God to those we're serving.

It's what we are called to do—come together to demonstrate God's love.

· · · · · · · · · · · · **Power Lift** · · · · · · · · · · · ·

Dear Father, I know it's good to fellowship with other believers. But please keep our hearts focused on serving those around us more than just having short-term fun. I know we can experience longer-lasting joy when we unite in a common goal empowered by your love.

> "Greater love has no one than this: to lay down
> one's life for one's friends." (John 15:13)

Not so long ago, if one person said another person was their "friend," you knew exactly what they meant. A friend was someone who shared common interests or bonds, who you enjoyed being around, someone you did life with. But in our social-media-savvy world, it's not that simple anymore, is it?

A "friend" can be someone you've never met #IRL (in real life). Now it might be some person who follows what you post on Pinterest or Instagram. And if they follow you, but you don't follow them back, that's one kind of friend. And if you follow them, but they don't follow you, then that's another kind of friend. And if you both follow each other, even that's a different kind of friend.

Sadly enough, however, the average American now says they have only two friends they would consider "close." Sadder still, about 25 percent of Americans say they have zero friends—no one! With technology and social media, we have an infinite number of connections, but few friends whom we really know and love.

Jesus chose only twelve men to work with closely during the three years of his public ministry. He didn't count the thousands who came to hear him speak as confidants. He concentrated his attention and invested in only a dozen.

Who are you investing in as your friend? How can you love your real friends, not just your virtual ones, more like Jesus today?

Power Lift

Lord, I want to be a true friend and invest in the people you've brought into my life. Give me wisdom about who to love and trust and about how best to love them the way you do.

"Here I am! I stand at the door and knock. If anyone hears my voice and opens the door, I will come in and eat with that person, and they with me." (Rev. 3:20)

Some friends of mine have what we call "refrigerator privileges." When we visit each other, we have the right to get up, wander to the kitchen, open the fridge, and grab something to drink or even a snack. We treat each other like family and enjoy that familiar sense of being "at home" with one another.

Jesus wants to have this same kind of intimate fellowship with us, much like two old friends sitting around the kitchen and enjoying an impromptu meal. He certainly seemed to enjoy breaking bread with a diverse company of people. From feeding the five thousand to the Last Supper, Jesus knew that eating together creates a shared experience and reminds us of what we have in common. Even after his resurrection, he prepared breakfast on the beach for his disciples who had been out fishing all night.

When we invite Christ into our lives, we open the door to an intimate relationship with our Savior. He's not some aloof, distant, detached emperor who rules from afar. No, he enters into our lives with the comfortable, intimate familiarity of sharing a meal with a friend. Our relationship with Jesus is the basis for every friendship we have.

• • • • • • • • • • • • **Power Lift** • • • • • • • • • •

Dear Jesus, thank you for entering my heart and giving me new life. I love you, Lord, and want to follow you in all areas of my life. Help me to love my friends the way you love me.

"The LORD is slow to anger, abounding in love and
forgiving sin and rebellion." (Num. 14:18)

I remember one time when our church staff was having lunch together. As we came out of the restaurant, a truck pulled up and the driver said some very graphic and disrespectful words to one of the women in our group. I was instantly enraged and began chasing the truck as it sped away—and I'd probably still be chasing it if my buddies hadn't held onto me and calmed me down.

You may handle anger differently. Some people fight back immediately when something sets them off, like I did that day, and they make anger part of their default defensive setting. Others don't seem to get angry much at all and may go weeks or even months before they reach their boiling points. Some people express their anger through words, while others take action—or avoid taking action—to communicate their feelings.

The Bible tells us that God is slow to anger. Even when we disappoint him through our disobedience, if we confess our sin, he loves us so much that he instantly forgives us. He doesn't blow up like a hothead with a short fuse. Even when God is angry, his love and compassion remain. He will not become so furious with us that he cannot forgive us. His nature is love, and through the gift of his Son, Jesus, he's chosen to always forgive us so that we can be with him forever.

· · · · · · · · · · ·   **Power Lift**   · · · · · · · · · · ·

Lord, I'm grateful that you are slow to anger, that you don't express your anger the way I do sometimes. Help me to control my anger and to show forgiveness and mercy to others, even when they provoke me.

Love each other with genuine affection, and take delight
in honoring each other. (Rom. 12:10 NLT)

Imagine that someone you care about is hurting because they just received bad news. Maybe it was unexpected test results from the doctor or news that their position has been eliminated at the office. Maybe they just found out their child has a serious medical condition or their spouse has betrayed them. How would you show them you love them?

Sure, you could send them a text: "Hey, just thinking about you" or "Praying for you! Let me know if I can help." But surely, as a follower of Jesus, you can do better than this. What if you used that device you text with to *call* your friend and have a real-live conversation? Or maybe you decide to get really crazy and take it to the next level—you go *see* them face to face.

You could ask them a few questions, and then just listen to them. If it seems appropriate, maybe put your hand on their shoulder. Maybe even hold hands across the table and pray with them. And if they happen to start crying, it's okay. Just wrap your arm around their shoulders. Or, if you're a guy, punch them in the arm to help cheer them up. Just let them know that you're right there in it with them.

Presence is powerful.

It reminds us that God is with us. And it reminds others that God is with them. Today remind someone of how much you, as well as God, love them—especially in light of whatever challenge they're facing.

. . . . **Power Lift** . . . .

Jesus, as I try to love others as you did, empower me to be present in the midst of someone else's pain. Allow me to comfort them with your undeniable love and peace.

"I will give them an undivided heart and put a new spirit in them; I will remove from them their heart of stone and give them a heart of flesh." (Ezek. 11:19)

If I've learned one thing from working out, it's what happens when I stop for a while. Usually because of injury, and sometimes when my schedule gets too busy, I'm forced to skip the gym. But I can always tell the difference when I return.

Without exercise, our muscles atrophy. They become weaker and get stiffer at the same time. Without the benefit of regular exercise, our muscles deteriorate until they can no longer support us or perform the regular functions they once maintained. To be healthy, we must keep moving, stimulating our muscles in order for them to grow stronger.

Our heart muscles work the same way, both literally and figuratively. When we're not praying, giving, serving, and loving on a daily basis, it becomes harder and harder to feel connected to God, to relate to other people, and to feel the joy that comes from serving them.

Stone hearts don't harden overnight. They gradually atrophy until we find ourselves with a heart as cold as granite. Regular exercise allows us to love more deeply and serve more humbly. It keeps our heart tender and compassionate, alive and grateful.

· · · · · · · · · · · **Power Lift** · · · · · · · · · · ·

Dear Lord, I want my heart to be alive and tender, not hard and cold. Even when it's painful, help me to be sensitive to the needs of others.

> Most important of all, continue to show deep love
> for each other. (1 Peter 4:8 NLT)

My teenage daughters will invite friends over, and they'll all be so excited as they're pouring into the house, chattering and laughing together. They head straight for some comfy room where they can all lounge around in big chairs or on the couch. They'll all sit down by each other—some of them even leaning against each other—and they'll each stare intently at their own tiny screens. They're alone together! A teenage girl doesn't think anything of sending a text to her friend who's sitting right next to her!

We adults are no better. We've either seen, or if we're honest, been, that family in a restaurant with each member glued to their phone or tablet—texting, gaming, emailing, surfing, whatever. We're losing the ability to relate to one another in natural ways.

Being physically present is important. But if you're doing it just so you can check some box and say, "Well, I tried. I met with them, but it felt awkward. I guess I'm not really a people person," then I can guarantee you it's not going to make a difference in their life—or yours. Yes, you should be physically present with people. But you should be emotionally engaged too. Don't just be "present"; be *all there.*

Engage deeply spiritually. Go all in. Make sure that the person you're in the room with is the most important person in the world when you're together. Show them the same kind of love and attention God lavishes on you.

* * * * * * * * * **Power Lift** * * * * * * * * *

Father, allow me to focus on the hearts of the people around me. Help me to be fully present, showing them how much you love them by my concern and attentive spirit.

Therefore if you have any encouragement from being united with Christ, if any comfort from his love, if any common sharing in the Spirit, if any tenderness and compassion, then make my joy complete by being like-minded, having the same love, being one in spirit and of one mind. (Phil. 2:1–2)

The state of Oklahoma, where I live, has seen plenty of tragedy lately. From shootings to tornados, when a crisis disrupts one life, it unsettles all of us. And I know it's not only our state, or even our country—we see unexpected unpleasant events unfold around the world. The only silver lining, or so it seems, is the way people come together to mourn, grieve, and regroup. Sometimes they band together to take action to prevent the calamity from happening again. Other times they simply unite to serve, restore, and rebuild.

This unity borne of tragedy helps us survive and recover, but we don't have to wait until there's a loss to unite as a community. We can show the love of Christ to one another without any reason other than fulfilling the purpose God has called us to and to express our joy in doing it.

As we become one in spirit and unified in our shared beliefs, we become stronger than any one individual. God dwells among us and promises to bless us with his presence, both in good times and in bad. We can meet one another's needs and experience the transformation that comes from both giving and receiving his love every day.

Power Lift

Jesus, today I want to connect with other people and serve them with your love. Help me to unite with others who love you or want to know you.

"For whoever wants to save their life will lose it, but whoever loses their life for me will find it." (Matt. 16:25)

When I was a kid, we didn't have selfies. Even that word is relatively new, simply referring to any picture you take of yourself, usually with a mobile or smartphone. Most people post selfies online to show off something: the fun they're having, the cool people they're meeting, the new clothes they're wearing, or just their latest purchase or personal accomplishment.

While selfies have been around for a few years, coinciding mostly with the combination of smartphones and social networks, they seem to keep building momentum. I just discovered more than 300 *million* posts using the hashtag #Selfie—and I'm sure there are more since I checked!

It's no exaggeration to say we've become a selfie-obsessed culture.

If your latest selfie needs to be touched up a little, you can just apply a filter to it. You can change the color saturation, brighten it, soften it, or make it black and white. You can even get rid of red-eye and erase that second chin! You can change the color of your eyes and raise your cheekbones. Basically, you can filter your life and show people, "This is the photoshopped me that I want you to see."

Selfies aren't bad—I just worry that they cause us to focus even more time and attention on ourselves than on other people. If we want to love others like Jesus, then we have to become selfie-less.

Power Lift

Jesus, today I pray you would allow me to take my eyes off of myself and focus instead on those people around me. Let them see less of me and more of you.

Now the Lord is the Spirit, and where the Spirit of the
Lord is, there is freedom. (2 Cor. 3:17)

For as long as I can remember, my toes have been my worst physical fea-
ture. Even my wife agrees: "Craig, I love everything about you. You're
perfect in every way. I love you from the top of your head to the bottom of your . . . ankles."

Amy knows my feet are the ugliest and often says, "Be sure to put
on socks before you come in the bedroom." She's not being mean; she's
just being honest.

So for years, I've been self-conscious about my toes.

Finally, this past year, I had a breakthrough. For the first time ever,
I thought, *I'm middle-aged. I'm happily married. My wife loves me. Why
should I care what anybody else thinks?*

So I bought a pair of sandals and wore them without shame—to
restaurants, the park, even to church. So what if little kids screamed
and cried when they saw my toes? Where the Spirit of the Lord is, there
is freedom, baby! And I have been set free.

I'm exaggerating—but honestly, only a little. It may seem silly, but
this struggle has lasted for decades. Over the years, I've learned we all
have something we've become ashamed of, some part of ourselves or
our lives that we feel we must hide.

But not with God. While our culture may condition us to hide
our flaws or filter our selfies, God loves every part of us—ugly feet
and all. What image are you trying to portray in your life that doesn't
reflect the real you?

Power Lift

Dear God, help me to embrace the freedom that comes from experiencing your
unconditional love and to extend it to others—including myself.

God . . . reconciled us to himself through Christ and gave
us the ministry of reconciliation. (2 Cor. 5:18)

Both as a pastor and as a dad, I've learned that much of what I'm called
to do is resolve conflict and help people love each other better. If you're a
follower of Jesus, you have the same calling. You don't have to be a politi-
cian or Nobel Peace Prize winner to be in the business of reconciliation.

Unfortunately, in our world today, there are plenty of individuals, groups, tribes, and nations at odds with each other. We don't have
to look far to find certain people who take a combative stance against
almost everyone they encounter. Maybe you even feel this way sometimes yourself—I sure do.

But God is in the business of forgiving, reconciling, and healing. Having been at odds with us because of our sinfulness, our Father
knew that the only way to reconcile with us permanently was to pay
our debt once and for all. And that's what Christ did for us—he is the
ultimate mediator, bridging heaven and earth, fulfilling a penalty we
could never pay.

As people who bear the image of Christ, we must seek to reconcile those around us. Whether in the boardroom or the classroom, at
home or at church, we bring God's peace wherever we go. And God's
peace reigns supreme.

Power Lift

Father, I long to reconcile people in conflict the same way you do. Provide me
with the strength, courage, and wisdom to bring peace to everyone I encounter
today.

> Love is patient, love is kind. It does not envy, it does not boast, it is not proud. It does not dishonor others, it is not self-seeking. (1 Cor. 13:4–5)

Social media encourages us—it absolutely *trains* us—to become more narcissistic and full of ourselves. One recent study indicated that 80 percent of what a person posts on social media is directly related to that user. Makes sense. After all, think about what you often check first when you're online. What people are saying about you. Are people "liking" my posts? Are people commenting on the things I've posted? What can I do to attract more of the kind of positive affirmation I enjoy?

Why do we do this? It's emotional, sure, but it's also scientific. Every time we see something about ourselves—especially if it's positive—our brains release a tiny dose of a chemical called dopamine. That rush gives us a little (completely legal) buzz, a little "A-ha! I like this!" moment.

So when we participate in social media, both posting and casual surfing, it's conditioning us—like little laboratory rats tapping a food bar—to become more and more self-centered over time. Social media causes us to care less about other people by transforming our bodies to become more self-centered (#ThatsMessedUp).

However, God reminds us that real love is not self-centered. His kind of love doesn't need the buzz of self-adoration, whether online or in person. The essence of love is what Jesus did for us on the cross. This kind of love can motivate everything you do—if you keep your eyes on Christ and not on your home page.

Power Lift

Jesus, so much of my day revolves around me and my needs and wants. Today let me look beyond my online image and focus on others with your selfless love.

Whoever is kind to the needy honors God. (Prov. 14:31)

Depending on our present circumstances, we usually don't consider ourselves as being needy—you know, like those people in really tough situations with nowhere to turn. Like homeless people or those in crisis, the ones caught up in domestic dysfunction or addictions who so obviously need help.

But here's the truth: we are all needy. No matter how hard we work to disguise our needs and appear self-sufficient, we need the support, encouragement, and assistance of other people. As a guy, I especially don't want to appear as if I need anybody's help. Instead I want to be seen like Jason Bourne or Jack Reacher—tough guys who can handle anything, and anyone, all by themselves. Guys who don't need help from other people—ever.

However, those guys exist only in the movies.

God designed us not to be robotic action heroes but to be men and women with strong character and tender hearts. He made us as relational and social beings, to need each other so we can help each other. Whether it's money for groceries or encouragement to ask for a promotion, our sense of interdependency reflects the way God made us. He doesn't expect us to have everything together and take care of ourselves alone. He created us to be in relationships as part of a larger community.

Sometimes you need to let your guard down and allow others to see how much you really need them.

• • • • • • • • • • • **Power Lift** • • • • • • • • • •

Lord, I know that I always need you, even when circumstances seem to be going well. Help me to serve others but also to receive what I need as you provide it through them.

Jesus had compassion on them and touched their eyes. Immediately
they received their sight and followed him. (Matt. 20:34)

I'm terribly sad to confess this, but I'm not always as sensitive to the
suffering of others as I used to be. Years ago, if I was channel-surfing
and came across a commercial or program showing some sweet, mal-
nourished child with flies buzzing around her face, my heart stopped. I
would feel so guilty sitting in my comfortable home, watching on a big,
color flat-screen TV, that I often had to change the channel.

But after a while, I had seen so many of these images that they
simply didn't bother me like they once did. I became immune to them.
They were invisible, just more background noise. You see, repeating a
stimulus causes it to register less and less each time you're exposed to
it. That poor hungry child doesn't burden me now as much as before
because I've become desensitized to such a sight. It's familiar and not
nearly as disturbing unless I intentionally pause and remember this is a
human being—a real flesh-and-blood child suffering needlessly.

Why is this such a problem? Because the more indifferent we become
to the suffering of others, the more we become unwilling to love them,
help them, serve them. Because if we have chosen to follow Christ, then
we need to understand that God has called us to so much more than
changing the channel or closing the pop-up window.

Compassion counts.

He calls us to serve.

He calls us to love.

● ● ● ● ● ● ● ● ● ● ● ● **Power Lift** ● ● ● ● ● ● ● ● ● ●

Lord, prevent me from becoming desensitized so that I may have eyes to see
and a tender heart to feel the suffering of others.

For we live by faith, not by sight. (2 Cor. 5:7)

March is one of those months that often comes in like a lion and goes out like a lamb, as the saying goes. As a kid, I remember the winter weather would start to turn, rushed along by windy days that signaled kite-flying and baseball games just weeks away. In Oklahoma, some days were so windy that I had a hard time standing at the bus stop or on the playground.

The winds of life often leave us feeling the same way. Peer pressure, cultural trends, and social media leave us feeling strained to keep our faith and stand up for what we believe. In order to grow in our faith, we have to ask ourselves: How do we stand out, in the right ways, at the right time, for the right reasons? I'm convinced that when we stand out and stand up—in the right ways, at the right time, for the right reasons—it can change the direction of our lives.

The flip side is true as well. When we compromise on the wrong things, in the wrong ways, at the wrong times, it can cost us way more than we can even imagine in that moment of weakness. It's always so important to make the presence of God a priority in your life, where you seek him, where you depend on him, where you're living and dwelling in his Word no matter what the winds of change might bring. This is how we learn to walk by faith, not by sight.

• • • • • • • • • • • **Power Lift** • • • • • • • • • • •

Dear God, today help me to stand strong in my faith and to trust you with what matters most. Give me your peace when storm winds blow. You are my solid rock.

We know that we have come to know him if we
keep his commands. (1 John 2:3)

When I was growing up, my family was what I'd call "cultural Christians." We'd go to church on Christmas and Easter. We'd help a neighbor in need. We'd donate canned goods to food drives. We'd pray over our meal at Thanksgiving. But that was basically the extent of it.

Even though I believed in God, all I knew was *about* him—and very little of that. I didn't *know* him. And because I didn't know him the way best friends or spouses know each other, I lived according to my own rules.

Once I gave my life to Christ, I began a relationship with God that continues to this day. As part of this relationship, I submitted to his rules, including his command to love others as I love myself.

God cares about how you live. And your relationship with him will naturally flow into your daily attitudes and actions. If you're struggling in your faith, ask yourself if you need to return to your source. Are you trying to obey him because you know him and love him? Or because you think you have to?

Power Lift

Dear God, I want to know you and grow more in love with you. Show me your heart as I give you more and more of mine.

Those who live according to the flesh have their minds set on what the flesh desires; but those who live in accordance with the Spirit have their minds set on what the Spirit desires. The mind governed by the flesh is death, but the mind governed by the Spirit is life and peace. (Rom. 8:5–6)

Are you looking for full-time benefits from a part-time investment? Can you work out just once a year and still be physically in shape? What if you told your spouse you loved them only on your anniversary? Would they believe you? Sometimes we become similarly lax in our pursuit of Christ. But it's impossible to be sort of a Christian and expect to grow in our faith. We can't be a cultural Christian—like I was growing up—and have spiritual success.

How do you know if you're a cultural Christian? "Well, I go to church—always at Easter and Christmas. And I try to be a good person—you know, not over the top like those weirdo types who take religion too seriously. Yeah, I'm a Christian. I believe in God and all that stuff."

Believing in God doesn't mean you know God. Scripture teaches that even the demons believe in God. If you're always blending in, going with the flow, not wanting to stand out because of your faith, then it's time to re-evaluate your faith.

Today make sure you have a full-time faith, not just part-time. Don't be a cultural Christian—be a whole-hearted, all-in follower of the living God.

Power Lift

Lord, I want to be so much more than a cultural Christian. Help me give my whole heart to you and to trust you in every area of my life.

But if from there you seek the Lord your God, you will find him if you
seek him with all your heart and with all your soul. (Deut. 4:29)

I'm afraid a lot of people who say they're Christians are really Christian
atheists. They claim to believe in God, but they live as if he doesn't really
exist. What they say they believe about God doesn't line up with their
behavior and lifestyle. They say one thing and do another.

How do you make sure you're not a Christian atheist?

You get to know God and give your life to him.

You let him change you from the inside out.

If you don't know God well, you can. If you used to be close, you
can be close again. Getting to know God is not difficult, and it's not
about a bunch of rules. Yes, God wants your obedience, but he wants
your heart even more. In addition to today's verse, he says over and over
again in the Bible that if you seek him, you will find him (see Jer. 29:13;
Matt. 7:7–8; Acts 17:27).

God has been there all along. You can find him by reading your
Bible. You can pray. You can spend time with him and learn more about
who he really is and what he's really like. And as you begin to draw
closer to him, you will quickly see that he's already running toward
you, his beloved child.

Get to know him and allow his presence to impact every area of
your life, every day.

. . . . **Power Lift** . . . .

Lord, I invite you into all areas of my life today so that I can know who you really
are.

"Everyone who calls on the name of the Lord will be saved." (Rom. 10:13)

What people call me clearly reveals how well they know me—or if they know me at all. When I answer my phone and hear, "Hello, Mr. Gress-shull, I'm seeking donations for our community kids' fund," I know right away that this person doesn't know me because they don't even know how to pronounce my name!

Or if my wife and I are in a restaurant, I give the hostess our name and then wait for a table. After a few minutes, the hostess calls out, "Grow-SHELL? Party of two? Your table's ready." The hostess knows my name and how to pronounce it, but she still doesn't know me.

If you call me "Pastor Craig," then that means you know a little bit about me. Maybe you've been to our church and you've heard me preach. If you call me "Craig," like many friends do, then you probably have shaken my hand and talked with me about something important.

But if you call me "Groesch," then it means we've been friends for a long time. We've got shared stories to tell. We go way back and know each other really well. There's familiarity and depth of relationship.

What you call God reflects what you believe about him. If to you, he's the "big man" or the "guy upstairs," you probably don't know him well. But as you draw close to him, he may become "Father," "Shepherd," "Provider," or "Friend." He becomes your refuge, your shelter, your redeemer, your savior, your righteousness, your rock, and so much more.

What name do you use for God? What name do you *want* to use?

- - - - - - - - - - **Power Lift** - - - - - - - - - -

Thank you, God, that I can have a personal relationship with you through your Son, Jesus Christ. Today I want to spend extra time getting to know you better.

Because of the LORD's great love we are not consumed, for
his compassions never fail. They are new every morning;
great is your faithfulness. (Lam. 3:22–23)

Once you begin to know God better, you will change. A vibrant and intimate relationship with God will empower you to heal from the hurts from your past, forgive what seems unforgivable, and change what seems unchangeable about yourself. Walking with God will break the power of materialism in your life and lead you to a radically generous life.

Instead of living for yourself and for the moment, you'll live for Christ and for eternity. Your heart will begin to break for the same things that cause God's heart to break. You'll serve him faithfully as part of the body of Christ, the church. The old temptations will lose most of their appeal, and you will be compelled to obey God because of how much you love him, because you know how much he's done for you.

Instead of living in anxiety and fear, you'll experience peace, grace, and trust. The more you get to know God, the more you will become excited about sharing your faith with others, and the less concerned you'll become about fitting in with those around you. Knowing God will make you ache to tell others what he's doing in your life.

Draw closer to God today. Your life will never be the same.

Power Lift

I'm a work in progress, Lord, and I'm so grateful for the way you are transforming my life. Thank you for changing me and giving me the power to live for you.

As far as the east is from the west, so far has he removed
our transgressions from us. (Ps. 103:12)

When I became a pastor, I quickly discovered that many people struggle
to grow in their faith because they feel paralyzed by shame. Some are
ashamed of their poor financial condition, plagued with guilt about
their irresponsible spending and debt. Others carry shame about sexual sin from their past. Many drag shame with them into their future
relationships. Countless others remain crippled by their shame over
secret addictions.

Many years ago, our church built the website www.mysecret.tv,
where people could anonymously confess to anything and invite others to
pray for them. The response blew me away. Many of the gut-wrenchingly
honest confessions broke my heart as thousands of people poured out
their anguish, pain, and shame. So many lives had clearly been shattered and shackled by the power of shame.

But Jesus came to crush shame. No matter what you've done or
the secrets you're keeping, God can set you free. When we confess our
sins to him, we are forgiven. We don't have to carry the burden of our
past mistakes any longer.

Christ has set you free. Once you make him the Lord of your life,
there is no condemnation anymore. Today you can stand strong in God's
grace, knowing that shame has no power over you.

. . . . **Power Lift** . . . .

It's so hard sometimes, Lord, to understand how you can forgive me for all the
things I've done. Today protect me from the accusations of the Enemy and remind me of the security of my salvation in Christ Jesus.

For everyone who has been born of God overcomes the world. And this is the victory that has overcome the world—our faith. (1 John 5:4 ESV)

Rebecca was a faithful volunteer at our church, a wife, and the mother of two children. She seemed happy enough but eventually shared her dark secret: for years she had eaten whatever she wanted only to regurgitate that food a few minutes later. Ashamed of her struggles, she had managed to keep her sickness hidden from everyone around her. Then one day Rebecca's three-year-old daughter began sticking her little finger down her throat, mimicking what she had seen her mommy do. At that moment, Rebecca knew it was time to come clean about her struggle.

She confessed to everyone—her husband, her family, and our team at church. She sought help from a Christian counselor and slowly pushed through her darkness into the light of Christ's healing. Best of all, God has transformed her past struggles into a ministry. Rebecca regularly meets with other women struggling with the same private battle she endured for years.

No matter what your struggle is, God can do a similar miracle for you. Once a broken bone heals, it is often strongest at the point of the fracture. In the same way, God can take the shame of past failures and amazingly redirect their outcome toward our future success. He loves to transform our weaknesses with his strength so that others can see his power at work in our lives.

Power Lift

I give my struggles to you, Father, and thank you for the way you change my mistakes into your masterpieces.

"I have loved you with an everlasting love; I have drawn
you with unfailing kindness." (Jer. 31:3)

I once heard about a teenage girl who gave her boyfriend a framed picture of herself. On the front she wrote, "Todd, I love you more than life itself! Yours forever, Ashley." However, later after they broke up, Todd discovered Ashley had left him another note written on the back of her picture: "If we ever break up, I want this picture back—and my mom wants the frame!"

Life often conditions many of us to view love as temporary and conditional. As a result, we are tempted to apply the same mindset to the way God loves us. If we have a good day at work, we think he must really love us. If the car breaks down or the kids get sick, then we wonder why God doesn't love us anymore. But that's not the way God's love operates.

Our Father's love is permanent and unchanging. While others may love you today and abandon you tomorrow, God's love never changes. And because of his love, you will always be a valuable, worthwhile individual. His very nature is love and he sacrificed all he could to show you just how much he loves you. He gave his only Son to die on the cross.

Today stop doubting God's love for you and bask in being his beloved child.

· · · · · · · · · · · **Power Lift** · · · · · · · · ·

Lord, your love is beyond anything I can experience from the people in my life. Thank you that your unconditional love never changes.

"Therefore I tell you, whatever you ask for in prayer, believe that
you have received it, and it will be yours." (Mark 11:24)

A pastor once asked his church to pray that God would shut down a
strip club in their neighborhood. The whole church gathered for an
evening prayer meeting, pleading with God to rid their community of
the evils of this place. The next week, lightning struck the club and it
burned to the ground.

Hearing about the church's prayer crusade, the club owner promptly
sued the church. When the court date arrived, the owner argued that it
was the church members' prayers that caused him to lose his valuable
business. The pastor dismissed these accusations by admitting that no
one actually believed their prayers would do any good.

"Let me get this straight," the judge said. "I've got a strip club
owner who believes in the power of prayer and a pastor who doesn't."

Sometimes we struggle to grow in our faith, not because we're not
praying but because we're not believing. Prayer should be like talking
to a close friend with whom you can share your heart. Even when God
doesn't seem to be answering your prayers the way you want, it doesn't
mean he isn't listening.

God's responsibility is the outcome. Our responsibility is faithful
obedience. Trust him today to answer your prayers.

· · · · · · · · · · · **Power Lift** · · · · · · · · · · ·

Thank you for hearing my prayers, Lord, and providing for all my needs. Give me
patience when I have to wait on your perfect timing.

Not that I have already obtained all this, or have already arrived at my goal, but I press on to take hold of that for which Christ Jesus took hold of me. (Phil. 3:12)

It was one of those rare occasions when I was grocery shopping with my wife. I was stunned to see so many varieties of, well, everything! From kinds of mustard (mild, spicy, hot, zesty, sweet) to breakfast cereals (with berries, without berries, vanilla, chocolate, apple), dozens of possibilities smiled back from every aisle.

And it's not just the grocery store. Today we have more options, choices, and opportunities than ever before in human history. From what we want on our burgers to the color of our homes, from where we stay on vacation to where we go to church, we're encouraged to choose the "best"—usually what is popular or appears to be the "perfect" choice.

As a result, we often put pressure on ourselves to have our lives together before we start over with God. But he doesn't expect us to be perfect. God doesn't call us to live a perfect life and didn't create us for a problem-free existence.

Each day will hold enough trouble of its own. And God will provide all the power we need to overcome these challenges. We don't have to face our problems alone. We don't have to get our lives in order before we ask God for help.

He loves you just the way you are.

And he loves you too much to let you stay that way.

. . . . **Power Lift** . . . .

I'm so glad that you don't expect more from me than I'm capable of giving, God. Thank you that I don't have to be perfect. Help me to believe that you love me just as I am. And give me the eyes to see the ways that you are transforming me.

A thousand years in your sight are like a day that has just
gone by, or like a watch in the night. (Ps. 90:4)

I'm not a very patient person. Some days I feel like I don't even understand the concept of time. Some weeks are over before you know it, and
other ones seem to contain three Mondays. Sometimes I can't believe
a couple of my kids are grown and other days I wonder why it took so
long for them to grow up. God continues to teach me patience, often
reminding me that standing strong in my faith means traveling not at
my preferred speed but at his perfect speed.

God sees all of time at once. I believe he knows every moment
as "right now." There is no such thing as being late in God's timeline.
Everything is happening exactly when it should, at the perfect time. He
sees the "big picture"—past, present, and future all at once.

While we may never understand this (and may not even like it),
God gives us opportunities to trust him every day, to believe that he
has everything under control and that nothing happens by accident.
He uses everything in our lives, even time, to let us know that he has a
plan for us. He gives us everything in its time.

Today when others are late to your meeting or when you get stuck
in traffic or have to wait at the doctor's office, trust God enough to
relax and say, "All in good time."

. . . . **Power Lift** . . . .

God, I know everything that happens in my life is for a reason. Help me to trust
your perfect timing. Give me patience—with myself, with others, and with you—
as I go through my day.

> What does the LORD require of you? To act justly and to love
> mercy and to walk humbly with your God. (Mic. 6:8)

Early in my days as a pastor, a group of men told me I wasn't cut out for ministry. I was leveled and questioned whether God had really called me to lead and pastor a church. Fortunately, my pastor reminded me that God's job requirements aren't the same as man's.

Many bosses and employers want us to meet certain specific requirements, like a particular educational degree or years of experience in the field. They may want us to have training with certain software or knowledge of industry systems. It often can be frustrating when you are just starting out, because everyone wants you to have work experience, but no one wants to give you the opportunity.

But God accepts us and has special plans for us even when others—or even when we ourselves—can't see it. We don't have to apply for a position with God. We're family. He adopts us as his sons and daughters when we accept Christ into our hearts and commit to following him. This doesn't mean that God doesn't require anything from us, but it does reassure us that he takes us just as we are. We don't have to fulfill certain prerequisites before we can be saved by his grace.

Today remember that with God, you've already got the job: to act justly, to love mercy, and to walk humbly with your Father.

Power Lift

Father God, thank you for creating me for your purposes and empowering me to do the job. Help me to keep my eyes on you as I go through my day, allowing me to walk humbly wherever you lead me.

"When you stand praying, if you hold anything against anyone, forgive them, so that your Father in heaven may forgive you your sins." (Mark 11:25)

When life doesn't work out the way we want, it's tempting to blame other people. Maybe it's our parents, kids, spouse, siblings, or other family members, but we often hold them responsible for holding us back. Sometimes we pin blame on our teachers, boss, coworkers, or employees. It's especially easy to play the blame game when one of these people offends us, hurts us, or says something critical that wounds our pride. That's how they then end up in the bull's-eye of our blame circle.

But Jesus reminds us over and over again that there's a direct correlation between how we handle the offenses of others and how we handle God's grace. If we're not willing to forgive others—let alone quit blaming them for our decisions and actions—then we're not able to embrace the grace of God.

It's not that he withholds it from us based on our unwillingness to forgive; it wouldn't be grace if that were the case. It's simply that when we experience the fullness of God's forgiveness in our lives, we're prepared to forgive others. True grace is always contagious.

With God's help, stop blaming others and start forgiving them just as God has forgiven you.

Power Lift

Dear God, I'm overwhelmed by the way you love me and forgive my sins. Remind me of your mercy as I encounter those who sin against me today.

The mind governed by the Spirit is life and peace. (Rom. 8:6)

I've been accused of being a bit of a control freak. But I don't usually think of myself that way—I just like to stay on top of things. My mind tends to race ahead and think about all the steps and details that need to be done to reach my goals. Sometimes, though, I get so caught up in my own thoughts and plans that I don't leave room for God. I obsess about what I want and lose focus on what he wants.

How about you—what's on your mind today? Or maybe the better question is *who's* controlling your mind today? I'm not talking about aliens or brain implants or government conspiracies, those kinds of stories that show up in science fiction or in big-screen spy thrillers. What I mean is the biblical truth that God has given us the ability to decide what we allow into our minds. What we think about determines who we become. Our lives tend to move in the direction of our strongest thoughts.

When we focus on our fears, responsibilities, obligations, and problems, we allow our minds to be stressed with anxiety and worry. But when we anchor our thoughts with God's Spirit, then we experience life and peace. Today consider how your thoughts shape your expectations, color your perspective, and influence your actions. Remember, you can relax because God is the source of your power and peace. You're not in control. He is.

Power Lift

Lord, you are always in control—not me. Keep your truth as the anchor in my thoughts today and keep me steady when I'm tempted to try to take control.

"You will call on me and come to me and pray to me, and I will listen to you. You will seek me and find me when you seek me with all your heart." (Jer. 29:12–13)

My wife once lost her wedding ring, and we thought we would never find it. We looked in every nook and cranny, every toy box and cupboard, every bedroom and bookshelf. Still no ring. After it had been missing for close to a year, I bought a new ring and surprised Amy with it on a weekend getaway. But the surprise was on me a few weeks later when we found her old ring in one of the seams of a chair in our living room!

It's so frustrating and inconvenient when we misplace something that's important to us. We have to retrace our steps, searching for the missing item in obvious places, and then it always seems to be in some place we never expected. But you can never find it if you never start looking. Sometimes we may feel like we've lost our faith or that somehow God is no longer close to us. We feel powerless, untethered from our anchor. We get scared that we'll never be close to God again.

But all you have to do is call out to your Father. God is never far away. He's right here with you right now. When you seek him with all your heart, you discover that he was there all along.

. . . . **Power Lift** . . . .

Father, I'm so grateful that you are always with me. I want to seek you with my whole heart today in all that I do. Help me to find you and to know you are always with me.

> If our hearts do not condemn us, we have confidence before God
> and receive from him anything we ask. (1 John 3:21–22)

I hold myself and others to a high standard. While I like pursuing excellence, I also know the way our Enemy can play mind games and use it against me.

I believe this is the case for most of us—we are our own worst critics.

While others may criticize us, they're only reinforcing what we're already telling ourselves. Especially when we begin comparing ourselves to others, we start holding ourselves to an impossible standard that traps us in a cycle of trying harder, failing, then feeling ashamed, only to try harder again. Throw in a few of life's curveballs, and it's no wonder we often struggle in our faith.

But this fight has already been won for us.

When we accept God's free gift of salvation and embrace his forgiveness through Christ, we no longer face condemnation from anyone—including ourselves.

When it feels that God has forgiven us more easily than we can forgive ourselves, we must learn to quiet our inner critic.

As we grow in our faith, we become more aware of our true identity. We are God's children, created in his image for good works.

God says you are worthy. He forgives you when you fail. Your confidence comes from relying on him as your power source. Don't believe what anyone else—including yourself—may try to tell you when it's contrary to his truth.

Power Lift

Dear Jesus, thank you for dying on the cross for my sins. I know that there is now nothing that separates me from God's love. Remind me today to hold onto this truth whenever I feel like I'm not good enough.

And my God will supply all your needs according to His
riches in glory in Christ Jesus. (Phil. 4:19 NASB)

Several years ago, my wife, Amy, after spending time with victims of
human trafficking, believed she should open a transitional home for
women breaking free from abuse and other hardships. But all the advice
she received said she shouldn't. She didn't know much about this type
of home. There are bureaucratic obstacles. And the list of reasons not
to go forward grew longer each day.

But Amy believed she should go ahead and take a step of faith. So
with no money, no staff, and no house, she gathered people who might
be interested and shared her vision for helping marginalized women.
A few days later someone suggested we visit a house that was for rent.
When we walked into the home, we saw a lady named Janet that we
knew from the church. Janet had just remodeled an older home as a
rental property, not realizing she was turning it into the perfect home
for Amy's ministry.

When she heard Amy's vision to serve women, Janet started crying.
After some time in prayer, she explained she wanted to donate the house
as a gift to the ministry. I will never forget the moment she told us. She
cried. We cried. Even the repair guy who came in to fix something cried!

When Amy took a step of faith, God met a need in a way that we
never could have predicted or dreamed. You may be in a similar place.
Take that next step of faith—and trust him with the details.

· · · · · · · · · · **Power Lift** · · · · · · · · · ·

God, I want to step out in faith and take risks for your kingdom. Give me wisdom,
guidance, and provision to fulfill the goals you set before me.

> Walk with the wise and become wise, for a companion
> of fools suffers harm. (Prov. 13:20)

My mom used to share with me tons of motherly wisdom. When our team lost a ballgame and I was feeling disappointed, she might say, "It doesn't matter if you win or lose; it's how you play the game." Or if I got frustrated because I couldn't follow the directions for assembling a model plane: "You can do anything you set your mind to."

But the clincher, the one she told me most often, dealt directly with my friends: "You are who you run with." Sometimes I wasn't sure if she was approving of my buddies or encouraging me to find better replacements. She probably wasn't sure either. What became clear, though, was the truth in her wisdom.

It's almost impossible to live the right life when you have the wrong friends.

Whether you're a kid, a tween, a teenager, a young adult, or middle-aged, you *will* become like your closest friends. Count on it. When we connect with another person, we become a conduit for their values, beliefs, and decisions. This isn't just from my mom—the Bible states this truth repeatedly. If you stick close to people who are wise, you'll become wiser. If you hang out with people who are godly, you're likely going to grow closer to God. If you become close friends with people who make good decisions, chances are you'll make better decisions too.

Today run with people who love God as much or more than you do.

· · · · · · · · · · · **Power Lift** · · · · · · · · · ·

Jesus, give me wisdom about who I choose to spend my time with and how and when to trust them. Bring me friends who make me more like you and empower me to be a blessing to them.

If anyone obeys his word, love for God is truly made complete in them. (1 John 2:5)

When I had just gotten my driver's license, I once sat at a stoplight at 2:00 a.m. waiting for it to change. There was no traffic at that time, and I didn't see any other cars. Still, I didn't want to risk a ticket from some officer hidden in a patrol car nearby. So I sat there. One minute, two, three—finally, after five minutes, I ran the red light and held my breath to see if a dozen cops were about to descend upon me for the violation. But none did.

What would you have done? And how much would your choice be influenced if you knew you wouldn't be caught? In day-to-day life, we often obey rules and regulations based on our ability or willingness to understand their purpose. When we understand the reason for a rule—such as the obvious necessity for a stoplight to regulate a busy traffic intersection—it's easy to comply. But if no one else is around, why stop?

Because it's the law. Because God doesn't give us options to consider but gives commands to obey. If we cut corners in one area, it's that much easier to cut corners somewhere else. We don't just obey God because we fear him; we obey him because we love him.

- - - - - - - - - - - - **Power Lift** - - - - - - - - - - - -

Thank you, Lord, that I can trust you with every area of my life. Give me the strength to obey you in all I do today.

"If the Son sets you free, you will be free indeed." (John 8:36)

Sometimes we feel stuck and begin to wonder if we will ever change. We let others label us and we start to believe them. We feel haunted by past mistakes and don't know how to move forward.

No matter what you've done or haven't done, God's power is big enough to change you. There is no sin too great for God's grace. There is no habit too big for his healing. There is no label too strong for his love. Let me put it another way, because I want you to believe this: *God's power is bigger than your past.*

And his power is rooted in his love for you. He knows who you really are no matter what others may label you—or what you label yourself. What's true about you now doesn't have to be true about you later. The goal is not to "reinvent" yourself by striving to be some perfect person but to allow God to give you an extreme makeover by uncovering your true self in his image, redeemed through Christ. What once was no longer has to be. God can and will break the labels that have held you hostage.

You have freedom in Christ to become who you were meant to be.

. . . . **Power Lift** . . . .

Dear Father, I'm so grateful that you know everything I've done and still love me. Give me strength to overcome my past mistakes and to move into the fullness of who you created me to be.

For we are God's masterpiece. He has created us anew in Christ Jesus, so we can do the good things he planned for us long ago. (Eph. 2:10 NLT)

The *Mona Lisa*. Michelangelo's *David*. *The Last Supper*. If you imagine the greatest works of art in human history, even these have flaws. A human artist strives to create work that captures the essence of her subject as close as possible to perfection. Regardless of the art form or medium, the artist attempting to reflect certain facets of his image or theme as precisely as possible will never reach perfection.

However, when we consider that we are God's work of art in progress, we discover that we are already his perfect workmanship in Christ Jesus—we don't have to try harder to earn it. It doesn't matter how hard you try, how religious you act. You can't earn your way to salvation. You can't save yourself. There's a crucial distinction here about who we are and how we are to live. We are not saved *by* good works. We are saved *for* good works.

Specifically, we're not saved *by* the good things that we have done, but we are saved *to do* good things on behalf of the one who saved us. And the good that we do is not for us to brag about. He saves us so we can make a difference in this world and bring glory to him.

Now that's a true work of art.

Power Lift

Dear God, you are the potter who shapes the clay of my life into your perfect masterpiece. Today I thank you for using even my mistakes to transform me for your purposes.

I rise before dawn and cry for help; I have put
my hope in your word. (Ps. 119:147)

Sometimes I wake up in the middle of the night and can't go back to sleep. My mind spins with thoughts of appointments, responsibilities, and obligations for the following day. I worry about my kids, my friends, and members of our church. When everyone seems to be doing okay, I worry that I can't think of anything to worry about! The best thing I do, though, is simply pray about all that's weighing on me.

Sometimes people say, "All we can do now is pray." It's tempting to treat prayer like it's a last line of defense. In actuality, though, prayer is our first line of offense.

We all have so many people depending on us that it can be hard to feel strong enough to do all that needs doing. We want to keep standing firm in our faith, but we become weary and feel so exhausted. That's when we have to cry out for help, just like the psalmist says in today's verse. We have to put our hope in the promises of God's Word.

When you wake early because your mind and heart are troubled, you can rest in remembering what your Father has promised. He is with you and will never abandon you. He is in control and devoted to your growth for his good purposes. You don't have to do everything that's spinning around in your mind.

Today you can rest easy knowing that your hope is in God and not in your own efforts.

Power Lift

Today I cast my burdens before you, Lord, and trust that you can handle all that weighs on me and more. My hope is in you and I trust your timing to meet my needs as you show me my next step.

> And God is faithful; he will not let you be tempted beyond what
> you can bear. But when you are tempted, he will also provide
> a way out so that you can endure it. (1 Cor. 10:13)

So often we think we're the exception to the rule, the person who can handle what others can't. When I went away to college, I was stupid enough to believe that I could drink and party without being affected the way others were. Even though I knew my family had problems with alcoholism throughout several generations, I still thought it couldn't happen to me.

Until it did.

Even my fraternity brothers and teammates started to worry. Even those who were also partiers said, "Uh, Craig, you might have a problem." I figured, no big deal, I can handle this. But then I started drinking one night and tried to stop after one beer, and there was no way I could stop. Not that night. Not the next day. Or the day after that. Fortunately, not long after this realization, I became a Christian and with God's help overcame an addiction that had plagued my family for several generations.

What is temptation anyway? Temptation is anything that promises satisfaction at the cost of obedience to God. But today's verse reminds us that God always gives us a way out. And why resist temptation in the future when you have the power to eliminate it today?

God is the only one who can satisfy our souls.

And he is the only one who can help us overcome the temptations we face each day.

Power Lift

God, I'm so grateful for the way you meet the needs of my heart and satisfy my thirsty soul. Thank you for the power to overcome any temptation that comes my way today.

Be made new in the attitude of your minds. (Eph. 4:23)

I love being around positive people. You know, the ones who genuinely seem to care and show an interest in me and my day. They have this optimistic quality, this calm attitude, that draws me to them and makes me want to be the same way.

You can't deny the power that someone else's genuinely positive attitude can have on you. It can be a coworker, family member, friend from church, or even a stranger, but if they exude joy and confidence, it's contagious.

On the other hand, it can be really frustrating when we're struggling through a hard day. If only we had a switch to flip that would change our attitude instantly. While it's not usually that quick and simple, we can still train our minds to filter our thoughts through God's truth. When we focus on God's character and the power of his Word, we directly influence our attitude and subsequently our feelings.

Scientists tell us it takes twenty minutes for our brains to receive the message from our stomachs that we're full. Similarly, it may take a little while between the digestion of truth in our hearts and a sense of satisfaction reflected in our daily attitude. But it will come if we keep up a steady diet of prayer, Bible study, and ministry to others.

. . . . **Power Lift** . . . .

Today God, draw my attention to the power of your timeless truth. Allow me to develop an attitude of grace and hope based on the promises of your Word.

The Lord is my shepherd; I shall not want. (Ps. 23:1 ESV)

Whether it's hours in the day or money in the bank, sometimes you feel like you will never have enough, that you can never get caught up, let alone get ahead. Especially when we look online or check social media and see what others have, we often feel like we're missing out.

We see other people eating incredible meals, taking amazing vacations, and having fun with family and friends. They look beautiful and wear amazing clothes, live in houses straight out of HGTV, and drive new cars.

And then we wonder why we feel so disappointed with our own lives.

Here's what you need to remember. When your contentment is based on comparing yourself with everyone else—especially on social media—then you will never be satisfied. Even when you know everyone else is simply posing and photoshopping their lives, as long as you compare, you'll come up short.

However, when your desires for your life align with God's, you'll never feel envious or jealous. Instead, you'll feel just the opposite—content, joyful, fulfilled.

Our primary need each day is to know him, grow closer to him, and know his peace.

When we focus on this truth and follow our Good Shepherd, we become content in a way that Instagram can never convey.

· · · · · · · · · · · **Power Lift** · · · · · · · · · · · ·

Dear Jesus, you alone are the Lord of my life and my power source. Remind me that I have more than enough of what my heart truly desires through my relationship with you.

"Call to me and I will answer you and tell you great and
unsearchable things you do not know." (Jer. 33:3)

Have you ever been around someone you respect so much that you
stumble over your words? Because you look up to them, you want to
make a good impression. But in the pressure to perform, you end up
saying the wrong things. Instead of winning them with your wisdom,
you walk away feeling stupid and embarrassed.

I remember the first time I met my pastor. He had impacted my
life in such a significant way, I wanted to make the best impression
possible. After making awkward small talk during our first conversation, my pastor asked me what I wanted to do with my life. Knowing
that I wanted to be a pastor, I accidentally said, "I want your job." He
laughed and said, "Well, maybe I should quit then so you can have it,"
and then he laughed out loud. Even though he was being playful, I was
so embarrassed I could barely utter another word.

I'm so glad that we don't have to feel pressure when we approach
God. We don't have to worry about getting the words right or being
afraid that we might say the wrong things.

Like a child approaching a loving dad, we can approach our heavenly Father knowing that he loves us and is ready to hear the cries of
our hearts. When we call on him, he will always answer.

. . . . **Power Lift** . . . .

Father, thank you for hearing my prayers and for answering them. I'm grateful
that you speak to me through your Word and through your Spirit. Help me to hear
your voice today.

> Do everything without grumbling or arguing, so that you
> may become blameless and pure. (Phil. 2:14–15)

When I was in college, I worked each summer to make money for the next school year. What I remember most about those thankless jobs is how much they taught me about the importance of attitude. I discovered that washing dishes or working the front desk could be fun if your coworkers had positive attitudes and gave themselves to the task at hand.

Similarly, even easy jobs seemed tedious and frustrating when the people around me grumbled and criticized everything.

Sure, it's tempting to complain when faced with doing something we don't like to do. We've all worked jobs that had to be done while making sure the people around us knew how we felt about it.

Whether a menial chore at home or drudge work at the office, we do it, but we also want everyone else to notice us, acknowledge us, or admire us. Maybe we talk the whole time we're doing it, calling attention to ourselves and the great sacrifice we're making.

As we mature, however, we realize that these attitudes do not glorify God or reflect his generous, loving character. When we grumble, complain, whine, and bicker, we're allowing opportunities for strife, competition, comparison, and bitterness to creep in.

We're focusing more on our comfort and selfish desires than on serving others with a Christlike spirit.

Today try doing everything as if you were doing it for the Lord. Perform your job the way Jesus would, humbly yet confidently.

∙ ∙ ∙ ∙ ∙ ∙ ∙ ∙ ∙ ∙ ∙ ∙ **Power Lift** ∙ ∙ ∙ ∙ ∙ ∙ ∙ ∙ ∙ ∙ ∙

God, I offer you my heart, hands, and resources today. Anything I do, I want it to be a sacrificial gift of service, not an opportunity to boost my ego or show off my abilities.

Set an example for the believers in speech, in conduct
in love, in faith, and in purity. (1 Tim. 4:12)

I'm always blessed and humbled when people follow me on different
social media platforms. But knowing that so many people from around
the world can view whatever I tweet or post always gives me pause. I
want to do my best to reflect Jesus in everything I say and do, whether
online or face to face.

You may not even be aware of how many people watch you on a
daily basis, but I would guess it's more than you might think. Now more
than ever, others scroll, click, or follow what you do and say online.
Others post pics, snapshots, or pin common interests too. A careless
comment, mean-spirited tweet, or prideful page status could send the
wrong signal to people who look to you as an example.

With so many people expressing their opinions, especially online,
it's tempting to think that no one will even notice your positive attitude—or lack of it. But they will.

Many people who don't know God base their understanding of
the gospel on what they see in your life.

Don't let this responsibility pressure you. After all, it's a privilege
to reflect the love of God and the truth of Christ to those around you.

You don't have to be perfect; just do your best to allow others to
see your faith in action.

. . . . **Power Lift** . . . .

Dear Jesus, thank you for being my perfect role model and holy example. Remind me that others will see you in the things I do and say, whether online or in
person. Help me reflect you today.

When I called, you answered me; you greatly emboldened me. (Ps. 138:3)

Do you remember how large cell phones were when they first came out? I can remember thinking, "Why would anybody want to have one of those?" Even as they became more popular and portable, I was still reluctant to adopt them. I couldn't imagine having to live with a device that allowed people to call me anytime, day or night.

Nowadays, it's rare that we can't reach someone with whom we want to connect. We text them, and if they don't respond, we do it the old-fashioned way and call them. If they don't answer, we look for them on Facebook or other social media, or we shoot them an email. We've become so conditioned to reaching the other people in our lives that when we can't connect with someone, we're easily frustrated.

Sometimes we may feel like God isn't responding to our attempts to reach him either. But even if we don't hear from him the way we want, when we want, we can know that he's still there, listening and caring. He does answer us and he does embolden us with his power, strength, and grace.

We have to remember that God never ignores our calls or fails to answer our requests. He is always available to us, no technology needed.

· · · · · · · · · · · **Power Lift** · · · · · · · · · · ·

I'm so grateful, Lord, for your presence and the way you are always there for me. Stay by my side today and reassure me with the security of your loving presence.

"The LORD does not look at the things people look at. People look at the outward appearance, but the LORD looks at the heart." (1 Sam.16:7)

People tend to show only their best side on social media. They curate and try to control what gets posted, who sees it, and how others respond to it. Most of the time, they're hoping everyone will think they're the coolest, smartest, most attractive, successful version of themselves.

But rarely does our profile picture show who we truly are. Those comments and captions don't often express what's really inside. Wouldn't it be interesting if there were an app allowing others to know what you're really thinking, not just what you post online?

If the people around you could look inside your heart right now, what would they see? Would they be surprised by what's there? Would *you* be surprised by what's there?

Most of us hide our problems and disguise our disappointments, trying to appear pleasant and professional. When someone asks how we're doing at work, we say, "Just fine, thanks. And you?" Rarely are we authentic with most of the people we encounter throughout the day.

But we can't fool God. No matter what our online profile looks like, he knows what's really inside us, both the good and the bad. But the best news is that through the power of Christ, we don't have to try to fool anyone. We're free to be authentic, to drop our masks, and to share the truth of our Father's love with everyone around us.

Power Lift

Dear Lord, today let others see Jesus in me. Help me to live with integrity and display an authentic attitude of love, kindness, and gentleness—the real deal.

> But grow in the grace and knowledge of our Lord and Savior Jesus Christ.
> To Him be the glory, both now and to the day of eternity. (2 Peter 3:18 ESV)

I love those little signs that spring is right around the corner. Those tiny green shoots that eventually become daffodils. The buds on trees. Chocolate bunnies in the stores. Okay, maybe that last one is just a personal temptation. Seriously, though, the natural world is changing and will soon explode with color and new life.

Do you sense the same kind of dynamic change inside your heart? What does it mean to follow Christ and be his new creation? How is he changing you?

Jesus is the Son of God, who came to earth and showed us God's love. He hung out with those the religious people rejected: the sinners, the tax collectors, the prostitutes. He loved them where they were. He forgave their sins. He changed them and they became born again, new creations.

When we call on Jesus, he makes us new in that same way. Not just a better version of the old us. But new. Every sin forgiven. We're filled with his Spirit. We're transformed. If you're standing firm in your faith, then you can trust God to change you and make you like his Son.

Because when you follow him, your life will look different from before. You will be holy—set apart—from the world around you. Never forget that the old you has passed away; you're a new person in Christ.

Power Lift

Sometimes it's hard to feel like I'm really growing in my faith, Lord. But I know I can trust your promise to forgive my sins and make me a new creation. Thank you that I'm becoming more like Jesus every day.

In the morning, LORD, you hear my voice; in the morning I lay
my requests before you and wait expectantly. (Ps. 5:3)

For much of my life, I've felt guilty for not praying enough. At times, I wondered if my requests were too small. I'd think, "God is all-powerful and all-knowing. Why would he be concerned about this little thing that's bothering me? I'd better focus on praying for people I know who are dealing with much bigger problems."

And if I'm honest, sometimes I get bored or distracted while I'm praying. Some mornings I'm thirty seconds into it, feeling some prayer momentum, and then the next thing I know, I'm thinking, "Lord, please be with—oh, my goodness, I need to change the oil in my car. And Amy said we need butter if I stop at the store today . . . uh, sorry, Lord, where were we?"

I know I'm not alone in this struggle. While I don't always feel like a mighty prayer warrior, because I'm a pastor, people sometimes ask me, "Am I praying the right way? Am I praying too little? Too loud? Am I doing it right? What exactly *is* prayer anyway?"

That's when I tell them—and remind myself—that prayer is simply communicating with God. That's it. When you talk, God listens. This month, I want to encourage you to focus on your prayer life. With so many questions and issues surrounding prayer, it's no wonder we struggle occasionally. But Scripture makes it clear there's no "right way" to pray. It's not the words that matter to God so much as our hearts. God simply wants to talk with us.

We only have to open our hearts to begin the conversation.

• • • • • • • • • • • **Power Lift** • • • • • • • • • • •

Dear God, I'm so grateful I can talk to you anytime, anywhere. Today I want to talk to you more than usual, and I want to listen for your voice.

Look to the LORD and his strength; seek his face always. (1 Chron. 16:11)

I've got six kids, and I've always related differently to each of them, especially when they were little. One daughter always wanted to read with me before she opened up to talk about what was on her heart. Another daughter seemed to be quiet as a mouse all day, but then around bedtime, she was like, boom!—a DJ on talk radio! One of my sons would say, "Daddy, can we go on a walk?" and take my hand. There was something special about holding hands with my little boy as he reflected on his day. My other son needed an hour or so of wrestling and giggling before he was exhausted enough to want to talk.

I think we all connect to God in different ways too. Prayer is not just kneeling by your bed with hands clasped. You might love to sing and enjoy making up little melodies as you pray to God. Maybe you like to take your time and write out your thoughts to him. Maybe you talk to him out loud, and especially after a hard day, you just unload your heart to your Father, talking and crying and even yelling.

Or if you're having a great day, you may be like, "God, wow, I love that sunset! You're just showing off. You are so awesome, God." You might even have heard something funny, so you tell God a joke. Sure, he's heard it before, but you know, like a loving Daddy with his child in his arms, he laughs and shares your joy just the same.

Whatever you do, and however you do it, seek God daily.

Power Lift

Daddy God, thank you that I can be myself with you today, praying any way I want. Thank you for listening to me. I'm glad that you love spending time with me.

> At dusk, dawn, and noon I sigh deep sighs—he
> hears, he rescues. (Ps. 55:17 MSG)

When was the last time you let out a deep sigh of contentment?

When Amy sits next to me, sometimes she sighs out of frustration—you know, like, "There he goes again, just being a guy." Other times, she snuggles in close and lets out a sigh of contentment, of closeness and security, of connection and intimacy. Obviously, I prefer the second kind of sigh from her, and I know that sometimes I experience a similar feeling in God's presence.

When I pray and open my heart to him, I don't have to be strong and have all the answers. He already knows my weaknesses and limitations better than I do, so I don't have to pretend to have things figured out or to be in control. I can just relax and let my soul breathe, resting in the fullness of his presence, secure in my knowledge of who he is and how much he loves me.

You can enjoy this same sense of security and contentment as you talk to your Father. When you rest in just being his child and acknowledge that he loves you enough to die for you, then you don't have to rely on circumstances, achievements, or addictive substances for satisfaction. You can simply relax, knowing you are loved by the one who created you.

Power Lift

Lord, thank you that I have all I need in you. Today I'm grateful for our time together and for your showing me just how much you love me.

"But when you pray, go into your room, close the door and
pray to your Father, who is unseen." (Matt. 6:6)

"Dude, what's kickin'?" my friend asked. "Good to see you, Craig."

"Man, it's good to see you too," I said. We were meeting for lunch
to catch up but also to discuss how my buddy and his family might
plug in to our church. We chatted and then when our food came, I
realized something.

"Oh, heavenly Father, gracious creator and sustainer of all goodness," my friend began to pray. His voice suddenly sounded like he had
a cold, and at first I looked around to see who he was talking to. Then
I realized that this was his "praying voice." I don't want to be judgmen-
tal, but it seemed more like he was performing than praying.

Sometimes we forget that we can talk to God just like we talk to
everyone else. Just imagine if one of my kids came up to me, stopped
several feet away, and said, "Grand, omnipotent father of our house-
hold, we beseech thy blessing in the form of lunch money for school
this very day." I'd rush them to the doctor, right?

When my kids were young, they would just come running up and
crawl in my lap. They'd say, "Daddy, I love you. Want to go to the playground?" Their loving innocence and sincerity moved my heart every
time I heard their voices.

God, as our heavenly Father, wants us to talk to him with the same
authenticity. You don't need to sound like Shakespeare or King James.
In Scripture we see people talking to God in the midst of almost every
emotional situation, including anger, fear, and desperation.

While you should always be reverent, you can pray honestly to God.

Power Lift

Father, today I want to talk to you without trying to get the words right, knowing
you will hear my heart.

And my God will meet all your needs according to the
riches of his glory in Christ Jesus. (Phil. 4:19)

Some days it feels like we never have enough—enough time, energy, money, patience—enough of anything. Sometimes our families, our coworkers, and even our friends drain us and leave us feeling empty. We aren't giving our family the time and attention we want, nor are we contributing our best to our work. Paychecks just seem to evaporate, one after another, even as the clock keeps ticking and the calendar pages keep turning.

Just. Not. Enough.

On those days, it's especially important to remember that God promises to meet all our needs—as this verse says—"according to the riches of his glory in Christ." It's easy to assume this refers to physical needs, but it also includes other needs—those emotional, spiritual, psychological deficits we carry. God meets these needs even as he provides food, shelter, and transportation for us.

Sometimes we're so focused on meeting everyone else's needs that we overlook our own. We forget that we have to keep our tanks filled so we can lead and serve those around us. Tackling so many goals, chores, and responsibilities, we forget our "invisible" needs—for rest, for reflection, for peace.

But God doesn't forget. When he says he'll meet all our needs, he means *all*, including the ones we may overlook.

• • • • • • • • • • • **Power Lift** • • • • • • • • • • •

Remind me, Lord, to stay connected to you throughout my day. Bathe me in your peace and help me to pass it on to those around me.

> "Are not two sparrows sold for a penny? Yet not one of them will
> fall to the ground outside your Father's care. . . . So don't be afraid;
> you are worth more than many sparrows." (Matt. 10:29–31)

Whatever is important to you, talk to God about it.

Recently I had some news to tell my kids that I knew would upset them. So I called a little family meeting and said, "Kids, here's the deal," and then shared the hard stuff. I feared my daughters would take the news especially hard. "I know it's tough, so let's talk about this."

"Oh, we're fine, Dad," they said. "Thanks for telling us."

After more assurances from them, I went to work but couldn't stop worrying about them. When I came home, I found Amy comforting one of our daughters, who had obviously been crying all day.

"Why didn't you talk to your dad about this?" Amy asked her.

My little girl, almost a grown woman, said, "Dad's got so much going on with work and church and stuff. I just didn't want to bother him with this. It's just a little thing."

When I heard this, my heart broke. I went to her and said, "Sweetheart, you need to understand that if there's something that matters to you, it matters to me. Even if it seems small, if it matters to you at all, I promise you, it matters to me."

Today you must remember this. If it's important to you, because you are God's child, it's important to him. Don't hold back—tell him.

. . . . **Power Lift** . . . .

Lord, thank you for letting me share my heart, knowing that no problem is too small, no concern of mine too trivial. I'm so glad you care about the details of my day.

The name of the LORD is a strong tower; the righteous
run to it and are safe. (Prov. 18:10 NKJV)

When my kids are hurting, I want them to know they can come to me, that they have a safe place to share their pain and disappointment. I want them to know our home is a place where we care about and respect one another, a shelter from the scary stuff that often happens in the world around us.

We all need such a place. And with news cycles now trumpeting tragic stories and doomsday headlines 24/7, it's easy to feel overwhelmed and afraid. Life happens at a crazy pace. Some relationships come and go, and new opportunities flash before you while other doors close. Even when we're connected with dozens of family and friends on social media, we can still end up feeling alone.

This is another reason we run to God in prayer. We can't survive without his rock-solid foundation of love, protection, and provision. God remains the same regardless of what the stock market does, who's elected to be our leaders, or if you lose your job. No matter what today might bring, you can rest in the knowledge that your relationship with your Father does not change.

· · · · · · · · · · · **Power Lift** · · · · · · · · · · ·

I'm so grateful that you're always the same, Lord. The uncertainty of all that can change in my life sometimes scares me. But then I remember that you're in control.

"Give us today our daily bread." (Matt. 6:11)

Years ago when my kids were small, they begged me to get a dog. Now, I've always loved dogs, but at the time we simply had too many pets—hamsters, birds, fish, cats (and I don't even like cats). But my kids wouldn't let it go, so I said, "I'll tell you what, kids. You pray, and if God provides the right dog, I'll consider it."

My kids had the most passionate prayer meeting you've ever seen—it made Pentecost look small! They gathered, they got on their knees, they took turns praying, and they stayed with it. I could've been fighting for my life in the hospital, and I don't think they would've prayed as long as they prayed for that dog.

The next day when I came home from work, all six of them were out at the end of our driveway to greet me. They were jumping up and down, high-fiving each other, laughing, and squealing with joy. I got out and asked my son Sam, who was about seven then, "What's going on, little buddy?" His eyes got so big as he said, "Daddy! It worked! God heard our prayer and sent us a dog!"

I couldn't believe it. We lived out in the middle of nowhere, and apparently someone had abandoned a puppy and an angel of the Lord had guided him to our house—or something along those lines. And that's how we ended up with Sadie, the perfect dog for our family. I'm still in awe—God answered the prayer of my children, because it mattered to them.

What matters to you today? Pray about it.

· · · · · · · · · · · · **Power Lift** · · · · · · · · · ·

Thank you, Lord, for caring about what matters to me today. I trust you to answer my prayers in your time.

Praise be to the Lord, to God our Savior, who
daily bears our burdens. (Ps. 68:19)

Back when my children were toddlers, they loved for me to carry them—to and from the car, in the mall, at church, whenever they felt tired or wanted to be close to dear old dad. And I loved it too. At least, for the first few minutes—and the first few kids! With six growing kids, it was more of a workout than going to the gym.

Maybe you've carried a child in your arms for a long time, or a heavy backpack, or several grocery bags. Remember how good it feels when you can finally set down whatever you're carrying? Your arms tingle, your back straightens, and you can breathe again. Perhaps you've carried a heavy load and had someone come along to lighten it, to lend a hand or share your work.

When we ask him to, God will provide that same relief every day. From the list of worries we continually seem to carry to the new items we'll add today, our Father can lift them all. There's no need to strain, strive, and struggle alone. With his power, sovereignty, and wisdom, God knows exactly how to relieve us of those things, big and small, that weigh on us.

Today you can rest in the knowledge that God bears your burdens.

Power Lift

Lord, sometimes I feel so weighed down by my life. Thanks for the ways you will bear my burdens and lighten my load today.

Rejoice always, pray continually, give thanks in all circumstances;
for this is God's will for you in Christ Jesus. (1 Thess. 5:16–18)

The most positive change in my prayer life resulted from learning to pray continually. Maybe you're thinking, "Well, that's nice for you, Craig—you're a pastor. I've got a family, a job, commitments to fulfill—you know, a life. I don't have time to pray continually." But I promise you, I have spiritual ADD and can't pray in long spurts.

My wife, on the other hand, amazes me with the duration of her prayer time. She gets up early, before everyone else, and spends an hour on her knees praying—every day. If I tried to do that, I'd fall back asleep!

In addition to the early hour, though, I'm just not good at praying for a long time all at once. But what I've learned to do instead is pray quickly and frequently during my day. I've conditioned myself to be mindful of God's presence and to pray throughout the day. When I wake up, I open with, "Lord, thank you again for this new day. Please use me today for your glory." Then I just keep praying in short prayer bursts like that all day long.

Smith Wigglesworth, a British evangelist from years ago, said he never prayed for more than twenty minutes at a time and never went twenty minutes without praying. I love that! His model of "continual prayer" works for me. I don't pray for long periods of time, but I never go long periods of time without praying.

Talk to God in the midst of everything you do today—it could change your life.

· · · · · · · · · · **Power Lift** · · · · · · · · · · ·

Dear God, help me to find the best way to stay in touch with you throughout my day. I'll talk to you again soon.

LORD, be gracious to us; we long for you. Be our strength every morning, our salvation in time of distress. (Isa. 33:2)

As with anything in our lives, whether physical, emotional, or spiritual, the things that we feed grow, and the things that we starve shrink. It takes practice and consistency to build a strong prayer life. The kind of faithful, fervent prayer life we long for won't happen in a week. Just like working out in the weight room builds muscle, time spent in the prayer closet builds consistency. We can't become a super prayer warrior without putting in our time and attention on a regular basis.

And this is easier said than done. Sometimes we don't feel like praying and have to push through painful disappointments and grieve private losses, expressing our emotions but not allowing them to control us. After all, God can handle all our feelings, no matter how angry, volatile, or hurt we may feel.

As the source of our strength, God loves for us to spend time with him and to tell him everything that's on our minds and in our hearts. He wants to renew our spiritual strength so we can get through the day with peace, purpose, and passion for all he's doing in our lives.

When we're committed to loving and seeking him, then building our prayer life is a natural (and supernatural) way to strengthen the muscles of our heart.

Power Lift

God, you are my source of strength, and I have full confidence that you are empowering me to get through this day.

> After the earthquake came a fire, but the LORD was not in the fire.
> And after the fire came a gentle whisper. (1 Kings 19:12)

God not only wants to hear us, but he wants us to hear him. What does he sound like? How does that happen? From my experience, it occurs in many different ways. A lot of people tell me, "Well, I waited to hear the voice of God boom across the heavens, but it was pretty quiet."

Not that he can't boom when he wants, but I suspect he more often speaks to us the way he spoke to Elijah, as indicated in today's verse.

Scripture says very clearly that there was a wind that tore through the mountains and shattered the rocks, but God was not in the wind. Then there was a huge earthquake, where most people would probably expect to find God, but God was not in the earthquake. Then there was a blazing fire, but God was not in the fire. Finally, there came a "gentle whisper"—and that's how God spoke to Elijah.

God may speak to you in the same way: a gentle whisper. It may happen when you're in prayer, or as you open up his Word and soak in the truth you find there. God may speak to you through other people or even through circumstances. When you have eyes to see what he's doing and ears to hear what he's saying, God may speak to you directly.

Today pay attention and listen closely for the voice of God. What is he saying to you?

Power Lift

I'm grateful for how you listen to my prayers, Lord, but I also want to listen and hear your voice. Speak to me, God, and give me ears to hear.

Let us hold unswervingly to the hope we profess, for
he who promised is faithful. (Heb. 10:23)

I've worked hard in my marriage and in my relationships with my kids never to break a promise. If I question my ability to keep my word, I try not to promise. I want my promise to mean something true and definite, something the people who love me can depend on.

I also suspect that promises today have lost their value because there's often so little to back them up. Political candidates make promises, knowing full well they may change their minds tomorrow or after they're elected. Big companies promise us whatever it takes to convince us to buy their products, but they may not always deliver with superior customer service. Married couples commit to vows of unbreakable love for one another, yet still our divorce rate hovers around 50 percent.

Sometimes even our friends don't keep their promises. We get jaded and skeptical, unable to rely on those who give us their word. They promise to help us but then forget to show up. They commit to stand by us through thick and thin but drift away once they move out of town.

Promises mean something to God—they mean everything. He is immovable, unshakable, eternal. He's our rock and never breaks his promises to us. The more we get to know him in prayer, the more we realize he's always faithful.

We are not changed by the promises we make to God.

We are changed by the promises God makes to us.

· · · · · · · · · · **Power Lift** · · · · · · · · · ·

I'll admit, Lord, it can be hard for me to trust you sometimes, mainly because a lot of people have let me down. Today remind me that I can always count on you.

"My sheep listen to my voice; I know them, and
they follow me." (John 10:27 NLT)

Whose voice do you love to hear when you answer the phone? Your
spouse? Your kids? A best friend you've had since school days? We all
have caller ID these days and can usually know before we answer who's
on the other end of the call. But I can remember that back before cell
phones (yes, there were these ancient telephonic devices called "rotary
phones"—you can google it), I wouldn't know who was going to be on
the phone when I answered it. It could be a telemarketer, or it could be
my sister Lisa, or it could be Amy.

Obviously, I would recognize my sister's voice or Amy's, and they
could tell it was me from my deep, he-man voice growling back, "Hello?"
Sometimes it's not so easy, though, even with caller ID. If there's a lot
of ambient noise, like in a busy restaurant or at a big event, it can be
hard to tell who you're talking to.

I worry that sometimes people today have so much background
noise in their lives that they don't recognize God's voice when they
hear it. With all the sound bites, songs, rants and raves, comments,
and commentaries, it can be tough to find a few minutes to sit quietly
with God. But becoming comfortable with stillness is essential if we're
to recognize his gentle whisper.

Try to reduce the unnecessary noise around you today and listen
for your Shepherd's voice.

Power Lift

Help me, God, as I become more intimate with you in prayer, to be someone who
recognizes your voice. I want you to know me, and I want to follow you.

> We have not stopped praying for you. We continually ask God
> to fill you with the knowledge of his will through all the wisdom
> and understanding that the Spirit gives. (Col. 1:9)

When Amy and I were dating, we were both committed to keeping our relationship with each other sexually pure because of our relationship with God. While this wasn't easy, we also learned that there are other ways that we could grow closer to one another and share intimacy. One of the healthiest intimacy-building things we did—and still do—was to pray together.

As uncomfortable as it can be, praying with another person can also be a very intimate experience—and maybe that's why it's scary and sometimes feels awkward. When you pray with another person, you're not just sharing words and information with them. You're revealing everything about yourself—your struggles, needs, hopes, and dreams. Shared prayer has a way of bonding people together toward common goals for God's kingdom.

When we commit to pray for someone else, we're sharing their burdens and offering to make their needs known before our Father. God already knows their needs, of course, but our participation through prayer benefits us as much as it benefits them. Aligning our hearts in prayer with another person changes us. Prayer not only gives us access to the most powerful force in existence but also connects us with other people.

. . . . **Power Lift** . . . .

Lord, I'm so grateful that you allow me to share my needs as well as those of others. Today I lift up the needs of the special people in my life. Please also give me the courage to invite them to join me.

"Therefore I tell you, whatever you ask for in prayer, believe that you have received it, and it will be yours." (Mark 11:24)

In college, I was on the tennis team, the only American among a rowdy group of Australians. After I became a Christian, I was always looking for ways to be a positive influence on my teammates and get them to take God seriously.

Once we were at a tournament and noticed a high-jump bar set up near the tennis courts. They started trying to jump and could barely clear more than three or four feet. So I set the bar at *six* feet and said, "If I pray and ask God to help me clear this and I make it, will you guys come to church with me and give your lives to Christ?"

They laughed, thinking there was no way I could clear such a height, and agreed. I prayed, they sort of mock-prayed, and I began counting off my steps. These guys didn't know that in high school I had been a high jumper! A six-foot jump was almost automatic for me.

Only this time I didn't clear it. I almost made it, but at the last second, my trailing foot slightly clipped the bar.

I didn't understand—why didn't God answer my prayer? I was pretty sure I could make the jump, even without God's help. Since then, many other prayers, including much more important ones, have also gone unanswered. But I've learned to trust God's plan even when I can't see what he's up to. So I pray for him to act, but I surrender to his will, not mine.

Prayer reminds us we are not in control, while keeping us close to the one who is.

Power Lift

Lord, today I yield to your will. You know my needs and concerns, and I trust you to meet them in your perfect way at the perfect time.

"And when you stand praying, if you hold anything against anyone, forgive them, so that your Father in heaven may forgive you your sins." (Mark 11:25)

If you haven't forgiven someone who has wronged you, it may limit the power of your prayers. Not because God doesn't hear you or requires you to jump through hoops but because of the condition of your heart. You can't say you love God while you hate your brother.

When my kids were small, they loved playing with Webkinz, these little stuffed toys they could play with on the computer. My kids were addicted to them, so we came up with rules about when they could play—usually after they had first completed their normal chores, as well as some additional "Webkinz reward" chores. One day I was working from home and saw my kids being mean to each other. They had turned sibling rivalry into a spiritual gift!

After they had been acting out all day, they said, "We did our chores and earned our rewards, Daddy. Can we play Webkinz now?"

I said, "No, you can't. Because you were fighting, your lack of relationship and love trumps your obedience on the chores. You're not getting your coupons today because you haven't been showing love to each other."

"But that's not fair!" they argued.

As a father, the way they treat each other matters to me.

With your heavenly Father, the way you treat one another matters to God. How can we receive forgiveness from God over and over and over, yet be unwilling to forgive those who have wronged us?

Who do you need to forgive today?

• • • • • • • • • • • **Power Lift** • • • • • • • • •

Father, you know who I need to forgive in order to make things right—with them and with you. Give me the strength to show them the same grace and mercy you show me.

"My thoughts are not your thoughts, neither are your ways my ways," declares the LORD. (Isa. 55:8)

When I joined the tennis team in college, I had to get used to my Aussie teammates' manner of speaking. I realized pretty quickly that the English they spoke was not the same English I spoke!

Sometimes even people who speak the same language still can't communicate. We hear each other, but we struggle to listen and hear the message being conveyed. I knew nothing about footie, "Waltzing Matilda," or wallabies, and they weren't always willing to stop and explain every little reference or meaning.

Sometimes I wonder whether our prayers seem just as curious and strange to God. Of course, he understands us and knows our hearts. But it must be hard to hear us pray one thing and then say and do another. Because we're so limited by what we can see with our eyes, we tend to rely on the physical world as the basis for our understanding. We're still sinful despite having been saved by Christ. As a result, our prayer language may seem very limited.

Nonetheless, God hears us and knows what we are not even able to put into words. With his Spirit dwelling in us, we can communicate fully with our Father—despite our sinful mistakes or those times when we can't understand what God's doing.

Prayer isn't just asking; it's also trusting.

Power Lift

Lord, I can't always understand why you do what you're doing, but I don't need to. Today I'm reminded that I can trust you regardless of my limited perspective.

"Which of you, if your son asks for bread, will give him a stone? Or if he asks for a fish, will give him a snake? If you, then, though you are evil, know how to give good gifts to your children, how much more will your Father in heaven give good gifts to those who ask him!" (Matt. 7:9–11)

Sometimes we find ourselves praying over and over again with the same request. We know that God hears us and has a plan based on his wisdom, knowledge, and sovereignty, but we're still waiting for an answer to our prayers. When God doesn't seem to answer our prayers right away, we naturally assume that the timing must not be right for him to reveal his answer.

Our Father knows our needs. Our concerns, big and small, matter to him, and he hears our prayers and responds in his perfect timing. Jesus reminds us that even a sinful earthly father would never give his child a snake when he asks for a fish, or a stone when his kid asks for bread.

As a father, I love giving my six kids what they ask for. But sometimes I know better than they do what they can handle or whether they're even ready to receive it. If our human parental instincts are loving and generous, then our heavenly Father's must be beyond our imagination. God always wants what's best for his children. We may not get what we ask for, but we always get what's in our best interests.

Your Father loves you and will give you what you need.

Power Lift

Father God, I know that you hear my prayers, even when I'm forced to wait patiently for your answer. Today I will trust in you, knowing that you always want what's truly best for me.

When you ask, you do not receive, because you ask with wrong motives,
that you may spend what you get on your pleasures. (James 4:3)

The motives you carry into your prayers matter to God. Over and over
again in the New Testament, we see Pharisees, the Jewish religious leaders of Jesus' day, praying with wrong motives. They usually wanted to
show off their self-righteous pride. "Hey, did you hear what a beautiful
prayer I prayed? Wasn't it amazing? And I'm so humble about it too."

God's not fooled; he knows our hearts and what's behind our prayer
requests. And if we're honest, we've all prayed with selfish motives
before. "Oh, Lord, let me win the lottery! If I win, I promise to give
you half!" But God might be thinking, "Hmm, you're not giving me
a tenth now! You're not really thinking about giving. You're really just
thinking about yourself."

Sometimes we pray for other people just to make our own lives
easier. "God, please give my boss that big promotion! And if I end up
getting her job, well, that's okay too." Rather than disguising our request
as kindness toward others, we should just be honest with God. When we
tell our Father the truth, we can often talk ourselves out of the request
we were originally going to make! Our motives truly matter to God.

If God answered every prayer you prayed last week, what would
be better in the world today?

· · · · · · · · · · · **Power Lift** · · · · · · · · · · · ·

Dear God, I want to come before you with a pure heart. Keep my motives focused on glorifying you and expanding your kingdom. Help me to put you first,
not myself.

"Truly I tell you, unless you change and become like little children,
you will never enter the kingdom of heaven." (Matt. 18:3)

Have you ever listened to children pray? Their prayers are great—so honest, so sincere and innocent. I love hearing the things kids are thankful for: puppies, hamburgers, stuffed animals, their Disney karaoke machines, and their invisible friends. Children's prayers remind adults to keep it real when we come before God.

Kids revel in reflecting their view of the world around them and sharing it with God in their prayers, and we should do the same. And like a parent basking in the joy of their child's latest finger-painted masterpiece, God loves us with the same intensity and compassionate kindness. We're his creation, made in his image, his sons and daughters as heirs through Christ.

Sometimes we lose our perspective on prayer because we pray the same way about the same things over and over again. If you sense your prayer life getting in a rut, then find some way to be creative and child-like again. Singing, writing poetry, journaling, walking in nature, drawing—there are all kinds of unique ways to enhance your alone time with God.

Today pray like a kid again, knowing that God loves you as his precious child.

· · · · · · · · · · **Power Lift** · · · · · · · · · ·

Thank you, Father, for the way you love me as your child. I want to keep my heart open to you, sharing honestly and sincerely. Thank you for reminding me of your unconditional love.

The prayer of a righteous person is powerful and effective. (James 5:16)

Sometimes people wonder why their prayers seem ineffective. They pray faithfully believing that God will hear their prayers and move on their behalf. But nothing seems to happen. One thing some of us fail to consider is that the way we live matters. How we act and the motives behind our behavior matter to God, and they matter when we pray.

While we all have the same access to God, we may not see the same results from our prayers. The Bible indicates that the way you live impacts the power of your prayers. Notice in today's verse, it doesn't say "the prayer of an unrighteous person" or "an okay person." It doesn't say "the prayer of a casual churchgoer" or "the prayer of someone who likes Jesus."

Need more evidence? Consider Proverbs 15:29: "The LORD is far from the wicked, but he hears the prayer of the righteous." Now, we're never going to be perfect. The good news is that our righteousness comes from accepting Jesus as our Savior. But in these verses, the emphasis is on living righteously, which means following God, obeying his commands, and relying on his Word.

If you're struggling in your prayer life, I encourage you to think back over your past week. How are you living? Do others see Jesus through your attitude and actions? Or do they only see you?

• • • • • • • • • • • **Power Lift** • • • • • • • • • • • •

Today I want to live for you, God, and I want my actions to reflect this desire. Help me to live in a way that others will see Christ through all that I say and do.

When he had gone indoors, the blind men came to him, and he asked them, "Do you believe that I am able to do this?" "Yes, Lord," they replied. Then he touched their eyes and said, "According to your faith let it be done to you"; and their sight was restored. (Matt. 9:28–30)

When my oldest daughter Catie was maybe two or three, she got a terrible case of poison ivy. The doctor gave us some ointment but said Catie would just have to endure the painful itching for at least a week.

Once we were home, Catie was crying and scratching, and I said, "Baby, I know it's hard but don't scratch and it'll get better in a few days, okay?"

"No, Daddy," she said, "Jesus is going to heal me."

It was such a sweet moment, so innocent and pure. But I wanted Catie to understand that Jesus doesn't always heal us the way we want when we want it, so I tried to explain it to her.

"No, Daddy," she insisted. "Jesus is going to make my poison ivy go away. I prayed and he's going to heal me."

I decided not to argue with her but dreaded seeing her crushed the next day when she was still itchy. The next morning, Amy and I were still in bed when Catie ran in wearing nothing but her Barney panties and beamed, "Mommy and Daddy, look! Ta-da!"

"Put some clothes on, young lady!" Amy said. "Where are your pajamas?"

"No, Mommy—look! It's gone."

There wasn't a sign of poison ivy anywhere on Catie's little body. God had honored the faith of a little child. He will honor your faith too.

Power Lift

My faith is in you, Lord, even for things that seem impossible. Today I'm all in, trusting you fully each step of the way.

"Praise be to the name of God forever and ever;
wisdom and power are his." (Dan. 2:20)

At our house, spring cleaning often resulted in more chaos and clutter than when we started. Once the weather turned warmer, Amy and I usually picked a Saturday when all of us—six kids and two parents—could be there, which was no small feat. Each child was responsible for collecting his or her broken toys along with the ones they had outgrown. Amy and I tried to go room by room and get rid of as much clutter as possible before moving on to our garage.

The only problem was that what one kid wanted to get rid of, her brother or sister would start playing with. And what Amy wanted to throw out, I usually knew we better save. You never know when you might need a weight bench with ripped padding or that old tire that would make a perfect tree swing someday. You get the picture.

Our spiritual lives can benefit from a good spring cleaning too. When we confess our sins to God, he forgives us and grants us a clean slate. When we face our secrets, addictions, and ongoing struggles, God gives us his power to find help and win our battles. Sometimes he prunes our lives and shows us what to focus on cleaning up. Other times, he just wants us to experience the joy and peace of knowing we're forgiven.

Clear out the clutter of sin and let God cleanse your heart.

Power Lift

Jesus, today I want to clean out my heart and let go of all the worries, guilt, and sinfulness that has accumulated there. Thank you for bearing my sins so that I can be white as snow.

> "Father, if you are willing, take this cup from me; yet
> not my will, but yours be done." (Luke 22:42)

Years ago my wife's brother, David, was very sick. He was in the hospital, so we had everyone we knew praying for him—for his health, for healing, for a full recovery. For weeks and weeks, we prayed and prayed. But after several months, God healed David in a way we hadn't planned. My brother-in-law, who was only thirty-four, left this earth and joined God in heaven.

My wife lost her only brother. My in-laws lost their only son. We were devastated and it was hard not to wonder, "Where was God in that? Why did we have to lose David?"

I helped do the funeral, and I invited people to know the Jesus who had changed David's life and set him free from the bondage of a dark past. That day so many people said yes and invited Christ into their hearts, including Uncle Blue, a great guy and one of our family's favorite people.

Recently Amy and I were reflecting on the positive ripple effect we could see in so many lives—all because God did not answer our prayer the way we wanted. "Would you trade everything that's happened to get your brother back?" I asked. Without hesitating, she said, "No way. What God has done through our loss is greater than anything I could imagine."

God's will matters in the midst of our prayers. You don't always get what you want when you want it. But you can always walk by faith and trust in God's will.

Power Lift

Dear God, there's so much I don't understand about your ways. Today help me walk by faith and not by sight, trusting in your perfect and holy plan for my life.

"We know that God does not listen to sinners. He listens to
the godly person who does his will." (John 9:31)

I recently visited one of our church's locations in another city. Standing there with the leadership team, with a huge grin on his face, was the former assistant coach from my college tennis team, one of those wild Australian guys who once loved to party so much. He had become a Christian years before and now served alongside me on our church team. How awesome is that?

It made me think back to when I was a new believer, devastated because God didn't help me clear a six-foot-high bar so my Aussie buddies would come to Christ. But in hindsight, I know that if I'd made that jump, not much would've changed with them. They would've said, "Oh, you must've been a high jumper!" and then they'd have laughed, drank more beer, and gone back to telling me how weird I was.

But because I missed the bar that day, I continued praying for all of them for years and years. And now I was seeing God answer my prayers. Not only with this guy at my church but with other former teammates who had emailed me from Australia telling me about watching our church's podcasts. I still pray for them and know God is at work in their hearts.

It's tempting to get discouraged when our prayers seem to go unanswered. But God is faithful and always comes through. We can count on him—today and always.

Your prayer for others may or may not change them. But it always changes you.

· · · · · · · · · · · **Power Lift** · · · · · · · · · · ·

Lord, give me patience to persevere and continue praying for those people in my life who need you.

Set your hope on the grace to be brought to you when Jesus
Christ is revealed at his coming. (1 Peter 1:13)

Around this time of year in my part of the world, spring is usually in full bloom and summer is right around the corner. If you're like me, you start making plans for vacations, family visits, conferences, and other events that will fill up your calendar for the rest of the year. Before you know it, school will be out and your family will be putting away the coats and hats and getting out the shorts and T-shirts.

However, before the rest of this year starts to take off like a speeding train, take some time to honor your commitment to spend time with God—both alone and with others, in prayer and in silence. Just like any strong relationship, the amount of time together and the frequency of honest communication affects your bond. And as your schedule begins to get away from you, you will need time to quiet your heart and listen to God's voice.

Instead of squeezing your prayer time around all the other events and commitments you have, what if you scheduled them around your prayer time? Today look at your calendar for the next few months and plan days when you will dedicate yourself to prayer and time alone with your Father.

Think you don't have time to pray each day? The truth is you don't have time *not* to pray.

· · · · · · · · · · · **Power Lift** · · · · · · · · · ·

Dear God, I'm grateful for the change of seasons and for the season ahead. During the busyness, though, help me to make our relationship my number-one priority.

When I think of all this, I fall to my knees and pray to the Father. (Eph. 3:14 NLT)

Growing up, I had a picture by my bed of a child kneeling in prayer, hands clasped together lifted toward heaven. There was something about this image that seemed to draw me toward God.

Years later, I've learned that when it comes to prayer, posture matters. While it may or may not matter to God, it matters to me. There is something profoundly powerful about kneeling before a holy God.

Kneeling represents humility, dependence, and submission. Without a doubt, God will hear our prayers whether we are standing, kneeling, or sitting. But when things are especially tough, challenging, or desperate, I love to honor God by kneeling.

When I'm on my knees crying out to God, I'm not just praying with my heart and words, but I'm praying with my whole body. My position says to God, "I worship you. I depend on you. I honor you. I need you. I submit to you."

If you feel like your prayer life is a little flat or stale, why don't you consider changing your posture? Give yourself a little more time than usual. Find a quiet spot in your home or outside. Remind yourself who God is to you as you kneel before him in need.

You might just find that kneeling to pray gives you the strength to stand.

· · · · · · · · · · · **Power Lift** · · · · · · · · · · ·

Lord, I bow before you and acknowledge that you are my King. On my knees before you, I thank you for the many ways you strengthen me to stand firm in my faith.

> "This, then, is how you should pray: 'Our Father in heaven,
> hallowed be your name, your kingdom come, your will be
> done, on earth as it is in heaven.'" (Matt. 6:9–10)

Every morning I've learned to pray a similar version of the same prayer. Just as Jesus prayed the Lord's Prayer, depending on God for provision, for forgiveness, and for his will, I pray a prayer of surrender.

Many people talk about our country's Declaration of Independence. Well, my prayer is what I call my daily declaration of *dependence*. Each day I remind myself that I need God's help, and I devote my whole being to his service.

Before leaving the house, I pray.

"God, I give you my mind. Renew it with your truth.

"I give you my eyes. May I only see the things that matter to you. Keep my eyes pure and focused on only what matters most.

"Take my ears. May I only hear your truth. Silence the lies of the Evil One. Fill me with your Word.

"I offer you my mouth. May all my words be pleasing to you.

"Take my heart. I know it is deceitful above all things. Make it new.

"Use my hands. May they be instruments to serve and strengthen others.

"And take my feet, Lord. Lead me on righteous paths. I need you in every area of my life. May my steps take me only toward your perfect will."

As you start your day, consider a declaration of dependence. You need God. Ask him to take all of you and use you for his glory today.

Power Lift

Dear God, I need you and depend on you for all that I am and all that I have. Today I trust you to lead, guide, and direct me for your purposes.

> Let us not become weary in doing good, for at the proper time
> we will reap a harvest if we do not give up. (Gal. 6:9)

When our kids were little, I loved how excited they got about spring-time. They'd bring home these little sprouts in paper cups, and we'd line them up on our kitchen windowsill. It was a race to see whose tiny green shoot would grow the fastest.

As our kids got older, I made sure that they knew real gardening was a lot more work.

Even a flowerbed or herb garden requires so much attention—watering, fertilizing, weeding, guarding from raccoons and bobcats. The harvest comes only after the investment of dedicated hard work begun long before the first rose bush blooms or you smell the first lavender.

Our faith requires the same kind of commitment and consistent effort. This month is about growing and cultivating different facets of our faith: patience, compassion, kindness, joy, and peace. To reap a har-vest of any of these qualities, we must be diligent on a daily basis. As we saw last month, prayer is essential, but Bible study, worship, com-munity, and fellowship are vital too.

Today assess your relationship with God—what areas need more time and attention? What can you do to produce the kind of fruit you know that God wants to see in your life?

• • • • • • • • • • • • **Power Lift** • • • • • • • • • • • •

I want to grow in my faith, Lord. This month I want to work on growing in those qualities that will strengthen my faith and enhance my relationship with you.

> Better a patient person than a warrior, one with self-
> control than one who takes a city. (Prov. 16:32)

How often do you get impatient during a typical day? If you're like me, it's more often than you'd like. It's not only wishing rush-hour traffic would move faster, but it's wanting people and situations to happen at our speed and not some slower, unknown pace. You think, why won't she do the right thing? Why won't he apologize? Why can't the kids obey me this one time? Why doesn't my boss recognize my talent? Why do I put up with this?

The sad thing is that many of us show our impatience most frequently with the people we love. We snap and bite our spouse's head off with our response. We raise our voices at our kids or follow through with the consequences we've been threatening. "Don't make me pull this car over! Okay, that's it!" (Sound familiar, or is it just me?)

It's only natural that we get impatient and want to control the people and events around us. We want our lives paced to our preferred speed and not determined by factors that are out of our hands. But the reality is that no matter how much we think we can control our lives, ultimately, we have to trust God and his timing.

His eternal perspective reminds us that most of what feels urgent to us today isn't all that important. So cultivate patience for those moments—especially with other people—when you're forced to wait.

. . . . **Power Lift** . . . .

Lord, you know how much I struggle with being patient. Today I want to slow down, relax, and follow your perfect sense of timing.

But if we hope for what we do not yet have, we wait for it patiently. (Rom. 8:25)

By God's grace, I've been a pastor for over half my life now. When I became a Christian, I was still in college, working toward a business degree. Soon I knew God wanted me to be a pastor, and my home church hired me to minister to single adults. The learning curve was huge, but I couldn't learn fast enough. Within a few months, the singles group, which had about a hundred people to begin with, was down to a half dozen—and Amy and I were two of those!

The church board met with me and told me I might not be cut out for the job. I was devastated and confused. I was discouraged and tempted to quit, but my wife reminded me of the ways we had seen God confirm our calling. She encouraged me to talk things over with our pastor, Nick Harris.

While he encouraged me to take the board's critique to heart, he also said something I've never forgotten: "The more God wants to use you, the more likely you'll be tempted to quit. But I see real potential in you. You came here for my advice. So here it is: *don't you dare quit.* Stay the course. Wait on God."

In what area of your life do you need to wait on God instead of listening to what other people are saying? Today exercise patience by staying the course when it would be easier to quit.

Power Lift

Thank you, God, for giving me a calling and a purpose for my life. I know I'll face obstacles, but give me patience to persevere when I'm tempted to run away.

Let us not grow weary of doing good, for in due season
we will reap, if we do not give up. (Gal. 6:9 ESV)

Sometimes the greatest act of faith is faithfulness, staying where you're planted, remaining patient when you're itching to force a change. Staying in your marriage when it only gets harder instead of easier to love your spouse. Keeping your job even though you keep getting passed by for a promotion. Supporting a friend who always seems to need help, although they seldom offer thanks for what you do. Taking care of family members with chronic illnesses.

If you haven't already, you will someday find yourself at a crossroads, a place where you have to make a difficult decision about your life's direction. "Should I stay the course when it would be easier to walk away? Or does God want me to stay put and wait on what he's doing here? If he wants me to wait, I'll need a lot of patience."

Patience is best exercised when you'd rather take a shortcut, make something happen, or force others to do things your way. But waiting on God shows just how much you trust him. Today keep on keeping on, knowing that God will move you forward according to his perfect schedule.

· · · · · · · · · · · **Power Lift** · · · · · · · · · ·

It's hard to stick things out, Lord, especially when I keep waiting and waiting and nothing seems to change. Despite how frustrated I may get, help me to stay put, knowing that you have me exactly where I should be today.

And this world is fading away, along with everything that people crave. But anyone who does what pleases God will live forever. (1 John 2:17 NLT)

You see it every day. A grown man throwing a tirade because his fast-food burger took three minutes to make. A mom coming unglued because her iPhone is taking too long to download the app she wants. A young couple complaining because they were denied the loan to buy their dream home (that was way over their budget), so now they have to do something they've never done before—wait.

Our society has trained us that if it's worth having, it's worth having now. If you are going to do it, you should never be forced to wait. In order to feel important, our culture tells us we should get what we want when we want it. Commercials and ads tell us, "You deserve the best." "Have it your way." "Live for today."

But God tells us to take the long view, an eternal perspective that sees beyond our daily frustrations and momentary inconvenience. When we wait on God, we acknowledge that we're not in control and that we're no more important than any other human being. Yes, we want what we want right now—but God knows what's best for us.

Today practice patience by being kind to the people around you, especially those who are serving you in some way.

Lord, I get so caught up in what's going on around me that I grow impatient if I have to wait longer than expected. Give me your perspective today so that I can invest my time, energy, and resources into an eternal legacy that furthers your kingdom.

Whoever is patient has great understanding, but one who
is quick-tempered displays folly. (Prov. 14:29)

My grandma always said, "If you play now, you'll pay later." If you know anyone who grew up during the Great Depression, perhaps a parent or grandparent, then you know that their worldview differs radically from that of the generations following them. Because they grew up lacking what we take for granted, they conserved, they saved, and they planned. They exercised patience on a daily basis.

However, those generations coming after the most resourceful generation in recent history have allowed the pendulum to swing to the other side. Most of my parents' peers (the boomers), borrowed, charged, and leveraged their way to a "better" lifestyle. Now approaching their seventies, that generation is waking up and their material dream is turning into a financial nightmare. After decades of living for the moment, most are not financially prepared for the later years in their lives.

Delayed gratification keeps our patience in practice. Which helps us be better stewards of all God's gifts and allows us to be more generous to those in need.

Today consider your finances. Are you exercising patience with your purchases? Or do you get caught up in getting all you want now? What does God want you to do? What change can you make today toward a more patient, responsible financial attitude?

Power Lift

Dear God, give me divine wisdom to go with your patience so that I can be a saver who gives generously instead of a spender who has nothing left to give.

> Better to be patient than powerful; better to have self-
> control than to conquer a city. (Prov. 16:32 NLT)

So how do we move away from impatience? How do we overcome the cultural pull toward immediate gratification? How do we practice patience in ways that strengthen our faith?

We pursue God with all our hearts until his desires become our desires. Rather than craving what our peers crave, we learn about the things that matter to God's heart, and we begin leading our hearts toward his. The Bible says, "Delight yourself in the LORD, and he will give you the desires of your heart" (Ps. 37:4 ESV).

As we seek God, his desires become ours. The Hebrew word translated as "delight" is the word *anag*. It carries with it the idea of being made soft or pliable. You could say that as we enjoy or delight in God, he shapes our hearts and desires to look like his. Then instead of desiring the immediate cravings of our fleshly nature, we learn to crave the kingdom desires of our God.

All of us want to make a difference in this world. And when we don't have the immediate impact we desire, we often feel frustrated or discouraged, as if we've failed at being a Christian. But the truth is that God works in us even when we can't see it—perhaps especially when we can't see it!

· · · · · · · · · · · **Power Lift** · · · · · · · · · · ·

Jesus, I want my desires to be your desires. Keep my heart soft and pliable so that I can be patient, compassionate, and loving as I serve those around me.

"Who has known the mind of the Lord so as to instruct
him?" But we have the mind of Christ. (1 Cor. 2:16)

Scripture tells us that Jesus faced the same temptations that we face and
yet did not sin. He obeyed his parents, loved his friends, and got angry
at his enemies. He ate food and drank water, slept and wept, walked
and talked. His hair got longer, his fingernails grew, and he bled whenever he got cut, which, when he was beaten by the Roman guards right
before he was crucified, was a lot.

Just as all mortal bodies eventually expire, Jesus' did too. His family and loved ones mourned his loss and buried him. Because Jesus was
also God, though, the story doesn't end there.

Christ did what no one else could ever do—defeat the power of sin
and death once and for all. When he left earth, he promised to send his
followers a gift, the Holy Spirit, who would dwell in them and guide
them. With God's Spirit living in us, we start to become more like
Christ in the ways we see the world and other people. We begin thinking differently and acting differently. We have new minds that enable
us to overcome the power sin has on our bodies.

We have the power to love others more than we love ourselves. We
can see the needs of others and be moved with compassion, just like
Jesus was. Compassion fuels our ability to serve those around us and
show them Christ's love in action.

· · · · · · · · · · · · **Power Lift** · · · · · · · · · · · ·

Today I want to cultivate more compassion in the way I see and serve others. I
want them to see Jesus in me, Lord, so that they may know your love and mercy
the same way I do.

Give me a sign of your goodness, that my enemies may see it and be put to shame, for you, LORD, have helped me and comforted me. (PS. 86:17)

Whenever I used to talk to people, I was easily distracted. As I talked to someone, I'd be looking around, over their shoulder, out the window, even stealing glances at my phone screen. Finally, some loving friends confronted me about it and Amy confirmed that what they were saying was true. Since then, I've worked hard to engage and be present with anyone I'm talking to. I try to imagine how Jesus would focus on them.

But it requires practice.

Most days we go through our routines and barely notice anyone else. It's not hard to start running on autopilot, cruising through our day with scripted responses to the people around us while our mind spins in a hundred different directions. We can call it multitasking if we want, but the truth is that it's not very loving.

We might take others for granted as we remain fixated on ourselves and our little world. We miss opportunities to be a blessing to others. And serving others blesses us.

It's not hard to show others the compassion of Christ. Simply listen to what they're telling you instead of thinking about what you're having for lunch today. Send a friend an encouraging text to let her know you're praying for her. Leave a note for your spouse in the car. Pick up your kid from school and grab a milkshake.

Compassion is in the caring.

Power Lift

Lord, I want to love others the same way you love me. Today give me your eyes and ears and help me really see and hear the people around me. Let them see you by the way I care for them.

And let us consider how we may spur one another on
toward love and good deeds. (Heb. 10:24)

Some people blame our lack of genuine community on the invention of the air conditioner. Before AC, people would sit on their front porches in the evenings and try to catch a breeze to cool off. They would wave at neighbors and visit with the ones who stopped to chat over a glass of lemonade. With air conditioning installed, people can stay inside and don't have to interact with their neighbors.

Attaching garages to our houses didn't help either. Instead of walking from our driveways or detached garages and exchanging greetings with neighbors along the way, we pull in, shut the door, and we're inside our house. Fences, gated communities, answering machines, and caller ID reinforced this notion that we want to be left alone. We don't have to interact with anyone, so we don't. Now people interact online and through social media and really never have to *interact*. You can even shop online.

But Jesus always had time for other people. He talked to them, fed them, healed them, and forgave them. He often met physical needs in order to address spiritual needs. If we're too busy even to interact with the people around us, let alone engage with their struggles, then we're not following Christ's example. And we're also missing out on the blessing of loving and serving one another.

Today take the time to stop, listen, and talk with someone you see every day but rarely slow down to get to know.

Power Lift

Lord, it's easy to make excuses about why I don't engage with more people in my daily life. But you remind me to show your love to everyone I meet. Give me wisdom to know when to interrupt my schedule in order to bless those around me.

One of them, when he saw he was healed, came back, praising God in a loud
voice. He threw himself at Jesus' feet and thanked him. (Luke 17:15–16)

Have you ever gone to a lot of trouble to do something special for someone, but they barely acknowledged your effort? You planned. You saved.
You prepared. You thought of every detail. You made everything just
right. You worked like crazy to surprise someone, bless someone, honor
someone. And they didn't even say thank you.

Of course you didn't do it to be rewarded, but an acknowledgment
would have been nice. Imagine how God feels when he gives us life, his
love, his presence, his blessings, his Son. And we ignore him, continuing to do our own thing. Or perhaps we're a bit more gracious and give
a polite, token "Thanks, God."

We show up for church once or twice a month, if we're not too tired
or have a chance to take a weekend trip. We might halfheartedly sing
a few songs, listen to the sermon, and nod to acknowledge God before
rushing to our favorite restaurants to enjoy our normal lives.

If you want to cultivate compassion and grow in your faith, then you
must embrace gratitude. It's like plant food for the quality of compassion.
Gratitude kills pride. Gratitude slays self-sufficiency. Gratitude crushes
the spirit of entitlement. Gratitude turns what we have into enough.

Today remember: you are blessed so you can be a blessing.

Power Lift

Jesus, I have so much to be thankful for—my family and friends, my home, my
job, my church. Let me appreciate how many blessings I have so that I can serve
and bless others.

Every good and perfect gift is from above. (James 1:17)

Years ago we were raising money for a new playground for the kids at our church. You know, the cool kind of playground with slides and tubes to crawl through, monkey bars, swings—the works.

Knowing our church parents would be excited to get behind this project, I recorded a short video to show an example of the playground we'd get for our kids. When the video was almost over, I looked into the lens and said, "Let's give big because our kids deserve the best."

At the time, I didn't think anything of the video. It looked good, sounded good, felt good. Until a buddy approached me after watching the video during one of the weekend services at church. Steve had just returned from a mission trip to a very poor part of the world. The people in the village he served didn't have running water, plumbing, or electricity. They fought daily to get enough food to survive. Most people died young, either from starvation or some treatable sickness. Steve told me all about the trip and showed me pictures of the kids that had nothing. Then he said, "Next time you make a video to raise money for a luxury like a very expensive playground, maybe you shouldn't say that our kids 'deserve' it. They really don't."

Steve was right. Without even knowing it, I've been sucked into an entitled, demanding, and ungrateful culture. He helped me remember the importance of focusing our compassion on those with the greatest needs.

• • • • • • • • • • • **Power Lift** • • • • • • • • • •

Lord, please give me wisdom and discernment so that I can channel my compassion toward the people who need the most help.

Therefore, as we have opportunity, let us do good to all people, especially to those who belong to the family of believers. (Gal. 6:10)

Jesus said people would know that we're his followers by the love we show to others. I'm convinced this is especially true for how we as believers treat one another. Most people might not expect us to show love and kindness to our enemies. But they would likely be surprised or even disappointed if we didn't treat our brothers and sisters in Christ with respect and compassion. While we're called to be like Christ to all people, if we fail to do it with those who share our faith, then we've truly failed indeed.

Through our compassion toward one another, we can change the way nonbelievers understand what it means to follow Jesus. Too often the world sees people who claim to be Christians arguing, fighting, judging, condemning, and tearing down people within their own church, denomination, or religion. God must be especially grieved when our behavior creates an offensive and inaccurate impression of what it means to know him.

Today you have a chance to influence how others understand and define the Christian faith. So many people are tired of hearing about the love of Jesus. They don't want to hear about it. They want to see it. Your actions speak louder than you may realize. Let the people around you see the love of Jesus in all that you do.

Power Lift

Dear God, forgive me for those times when I have criticized or torn down other people, especially my brothers and sisters within your family. I want to show everyone your love, grace, and kindness in all that I do.

"Do not seek revenge or bear a grudge against anyone among your people, but love your neighbor as yourself." (Lev. 19:18)

Because my family lives out in the boonies, our nearest neighbor is a long walk away. With such distance between our house and our neighbors' homes, I'm tempted to feel like we're off the hook. It's not that hard to be nice when you only pass each other on the street every now and then.

Jesus redefined neighbor to include basically everyone, not just those in physical proximity. Neighbors are all around us, whether we know their names or notice them at all.

The lady serving our coffee in the diner, the older man sitting across from us on the bus, the awkward kid in our youth group at church. That coworker who annoys us with her strangely flavored lattes and constant cat videos. The extended family member who just went into the nursing home. The single mom and her two little girls across the hall.

Jesus told us that anyone we come in contact with is our neighbor. We're told to treat them—actually, to *love* them—the same way we love ourselves, especially if they're in need and we can help them.

Today notice every neighbor you encounter, not just those who live across the street. Try to show them the love of Christ through your attitude and actions.

Power Lift

Dear God, help me to love my neighbors as myself, to put them and their needs above my own.

> Do nothing out of selfish ambition or vain conceit. Rather, in humility
> value others above yourselves, not looking to your own interests
> but each of you to the interests of the others. (Phil. 2:3–4)

When was the last time you snapped a selfie? Last night? When you woke up today? Last weekend?

On the other hand, if I asked you, "Are you vain and self-absorbed?" you would probably say, "Of course not, Craig!" and then you'd think what a rude person I must be for asking. But the truth is that in our social-media-saturated world, we face more temptations than ever before to value ourselves too highly. From what we post as our status to our ubiquitous selfies, we become the star in our very own reality series called life.

As followers of Jesus, however, we're called to put others before ourselves. God tells us not to be so focused on our appearance and what we're going to wear and eat and do next. Instead we should look for ways we can serve those in need. Our culture encourages us to chase after our fifteen minutes of fame, but God tells us to focus on investing ourselves in things with eternal value. While it's not always easy, with Christ as our role model, putting others first is always possible.

Today step out of your spotlight and let someone else be the star of the show as you serve them.

Power Lift

Lord, it's not always easy to quit thinking about myself, but I want to put others first. Remind me that in order to find my life I must lose it.

Since we have such a hope, we are very bold. (2 Cor. 3:12 ESV)

When was the last time someone was amazed by your boldness? When was the last time you stopped someone in their tracks with your bold speech and actions?

Now, I'm not talking about the wacky, cheesy, thirty-three-bumper-stickers-on-your-SUV kind of Christian drive-by witness. I'm not talking about being bold in a bad-Christian-television way to make people dislike you or ridicule you.

I'm talking about being bold with integrity, with grace and compassion. The kind of boldness where you're serving people faithfully in Jesus' name, where you're encouraging them, where you're living in a way that reflects Christ's compassion and selflessness, where others look at you and say, "There's something different about this person." Where you're so generous with your money and your heart and your time, where you've served your way into people's lives, and therefore you've earned the right to say, "I really do love you—may I tell you about my God?"

Spiritual boldness is not our goal; knowing Christ is our goal. Boldness is merely a byproduct of following Jesus and living as he lived, showing others the love of the Father. Spiritual boldness comes from knowing Christ.

Power Lift

It can be scary for me to talk to other people about you, Lord. But I want them to know you and experience your love the way I have. Give me the courage I need to be bold in the best way today so that others see you through me.

The members of the council were amazed when they saw the boldness
of Peter and John, for they could see that they were ordinary men
with no special training in the Scriptures. They also recognized
them as men who had been with Jesus. (Acts 4:13 NLT)

You don't have to be an expert or a scholar, have a seminary degree or
experience as a missionary to serve Christ with amazing power. God
gives ordinary people extraordinary boldness. I'm living proof of that—
and so were Jesus' disciples!

Don't believe me? Consider this: the Greek word translated as
"ordinary" in today's verse is the word *idiotas*. This word can mean
"unlearned" or "unschooled" or "ordinary," but the most literal translation
for the word *idiotas* is, you guessed it, the word idiot! Don't you love it?

Sometimes I think the Bible translators are just too polite. Yes, the
most literal translation renders this verse as, "These guys were amazed
and couldn't believe the boldness of these idiots." There's no mean-
spirited name calling here; it's just a fact, these guys had no special
training or religious education that qualified them to heal a lame man.

Here's the deal: if you're like the best of the best, the brightest of
the brightest, God will still use you for his kingdom. It's just that he
specializes in using idiots—normal, everyday people like you and me!
God loves, absolutely loves, using ordinary people to step out boldly so
that others can see his power shining through them.

· · · · · · · · · · · **Power Lift** · · · · · · · · · · · ·

Lord, I'm grateful that I don't have to be some perfect, superstar Christian for you
to use me. As much as I want to boldly serve others, I still stumble and even miss
opportunities right in front of me. Today let me be an ordinary, everyday conduit
for your grace and power.

So we can confidently say, "The Lord is my helper; I will not fear; what can man do to me?" (Heb. 13:6 ESV)

After I became a Christian in college, I remained on the tennis team and promised God that I would use the sport to represent him in any and every way possible. The following season, I went undefeated—which was hard to believe after struggling my first year to stay on the team. I was a decent player, but God (and some hard work) made me a better one.

At the end of that year, the college had this big sports awards ceremony. I had just met Amy so I invited her to go, and my parents had been invited so I knew I must be getting some award. But what I didn't expect was to be named Athlete of the Year, the school's most prestigious athletic honor.

When I walked to the podium to accept the award, the presenter asked if I wanted to say a few words. Immediately I remembered my promise to God, grabbed the microphone, and preached my first sermon. It had something like 73 points as I rambled for a good ten minutes. But it didn't matter because my heart was open and God shone through.

Closing my little impromptu sermon, I became mortified at what I'd just done. So imagine how shocked I was when everyone in the banquet room gave me a standing ovation! When I returned to my seat, I passed another athlete who extended his hand to shake. "That's the boldest thing that I've ever seen in my entire life!" I thanked him, well aware that it was all God.

His same power is available to you. Right now, today.

Power Lift

Dear God, take me out of my comfort zone and give me your boldness and power. Help me grow in faith so others can know you.

> On the day I called, you answered me; my strength
> of soul you increased. (Ps. 138:3 ESV)

Remember the guy I told you about at the awards ceremony? He wasn't a Christian, but he shook my hand and said that it was the boldest thing he'd ever seen. Well, I hadn't seen that guy for years until recently when I bumped into him. "Hey, you're the guy from back in school! How's it going?"

He said, "Yeah, it's great to see you! I'm doing well. And I'm really enjoying that sermon series you're doing right now."

"Say what?! I didn't know you were in our church. That's awesome!"

The guy smiled, nodded, and said, "Man, Groeschel, I remember back in school when you gave that bold speech at the awards dinner. I wanted to believe you were different because I knew how you were, but honestly I thought it would wear off. Then a couple years ago somebody invited me to Life.Church. When I walked in and saw you up there, I freaked. All these years later, there you were—with the same passionate message. Your faith hadn't worn off. Jesus had truly changed you. And because he changed you, I wanted him to change me."

Jesus loves you and me enough to change us and use us to show others what he can do. He'll grow your faith, and give you boldness, and you'll see results that will blow your mind. Refuse to be a half-hearted, lukewarm Christian. Fall so in love with God that everywhere you go, you overflow with a spiritual boldness of love and compassion that draws people to Christ.

Power Lift

Jesus, help me to be consistently bold in what I say and what I do so that others can see your power at work transforming my heart and life.

In whom we have boldness and access with confidence
through our faith in him. (Eph. 3:12 ESV)

My mom is an amazing lady who isn't afraid to speak her mind. She was in the hospital a number of years ago and was about to go into surgery. I had come to be with her and could tell she was nervous. Shortly before it was time for her operation, a hospital chaplain stopped by and asked if she would like him to pray with her.

"I'm so glad you're here! Yes, please pray with me!" Mom said.

"What's your religious preference?" asked the chaplain.

"Christian," she said.

"And denomination?" the chaplain continued.

"Well, I'm not hung up on denomination—I'm just a Christian."

The chaplain smiled and said, "Ma'am, in order to pray with you, I need to know your specific denomination—what kind of church did you grow up in?"

Mom and I were both confused. She said, "I grew up in the Methodist Church."

"Great! Give me one second." And he whipped out his little prayer book, turned to the table of contents, apparently found the appropriate Methodist prayer, and started reading. "Dear God, I pray for—"

"Wait, wait, wait!" Mom interrupted. "Get this guy out of here and get me someone who knows how to pray their own prayers!"

I might've been embarrassed if I hadn't been so busy laughing!

Mom knew that we can pray boldly just by being ourselves. We don't have to have it written out or read it from a prayer book. Bold prayers come from the heart.

• • • • • • • • • • **Power Lift** • • • • • • • • • •

Today, Lord, I want others to see how much I love you. Give me the courage and strength to step out on my own, knowing that you provide the words I'll need. I don't have to rely on anyone else's.

"If you abide in me, and my words abide in you, ask whatever
you wish, and it will be done for you." (John 15:7 ESV)

There's no better mirror for someone's theology than the content of their prayers. What you pray for reflects what you believe about God—who he is, what his character is like, and his disposition toward us, his children. It's as if the words we use in our prayers are like mirrored pieces of glass, each one reflecting back our beliefs about the one we're addressing.

For example, if you pray very small prayers all the time, then you probably don't really believe in a God who answers big prayers. If almost all of your prayers are for yourself and your comfort and convenience, then this reflects your belief that God is just there to serve you. Or maybe you've noticed the way someone facing a tough situation will say, "Well, we've exhausted all possible solutions—all we can do now is pray." If prayer for you is a last resort, this reflects what you believe about God.

Today pray boldly and rely on God as your first choice—not your last option by default. Trust him enough to pray for his will and not just what you think you need right now. Being bold means letting him lead you—even when you can't see where he's taking you.

Power Lift

Lord, it's hard for me to let go and trust you completely. But that's what I want to do today. I want to get out of the way and rely on you to guide my steps and reveal your path for me.

Anyone who belongs to Christ has become a new person. The old life is gone; a new life has begun! (2 Cor. 5:17 NLT)

It's no secret that I've always been financially conservative—at least that's the way I've described myself. Others haven't been as kind. "Cheapskate Craig" and "Craig the tightwad" were the labels I heard well into adulthood, when I became a Christian and God challenged me to see the way I saved money was a way to try to control life. Don't get me wrong— saving money and being a good steward is important. But knowing that what I had was God's and not my own freed me up to become extravagantly generous.

The closer I became to God, the more I believed God was calling me to a life of radical generosity. Over time, God changed me from being a tightwad to being someone who lived to give. Though it started slowly, I grew into God's calling. Without question, I now know that one of my greatest purposes is to live well beneath my means and to sacrificially give to make a difference around the world.

If you will take the risk to step out in faith, God will take one of your greatest weaknesses and turn it into one of your greatest strengths. It has been said that our weakness is our genius: our greatest struggle often yields the greatest opportunity for our growth. That's exactly what God did through me. By the grace of God, he transformed my heart and gave me a new name that carried a new purpose.

• • • • • • • • • • • **Power Lift** • • • • • • • • •

With your help, Lord, today I will live in the new identity I have in Christ and will take risks for your kingdom that the old me could never have taken.

"Be strong and courageous, and do the work. Do not be afraid or discouraged, for the LORD God, my God, is with you." (1 Chron 28:20)

Most people seem to think I'm confident. Many people tell me I'm a natural leader, strong and even-keeled. But the truth is that I doubt myself every day. I've been haunted my whole life with feelings that I'm not good enough, worrying that I might not measure up.

I had hoped that when I became a Christian my insecurities would disappear. But that wasn't necessarily the case. It wasn't long after I committed my life to Christ that I had opportunities to speak publicly and to teach the Bible. At first, I declined every invitation, never feeling good enough to teach the Word of God.

Finally, my pastor convinced me to give it a try. I was so nervous that I threw up in a garbage can right before taking the pulpit—a habit that continued for some time. For years, every time I spoke publicly my face would get blotchy, my neck would flush red, and I'd feel like I couldn't breathe.

But I know God has called me to pastor, to preach and teach. So I've had to trust that he will give me the confidence and power needed to do what he wants me to do. I do my part to prepare and do my best, and this includes wrestling my fears.

You don't have to be perfect. You just have to be willing.

Power Lift

Dear God, pull me out of my comfort zone as I grow into being the person you created me to be. Today let me put my fears aside knowing my confidence is in you.

> For the love of Christ controls us, because we have concluded this:
> that one has died for all, therefore all have died. (2 Cor. 5:14 ESV)

After I'd been preaching a while, my physical symptoms of anxiety began to fade. However, I continued to second-guess myself. After speaking or preaching, convinced I'd done a horrible job, I'd avoid interacting with anyone.

However, one Sunday I thought, "That message wasn't so bad—I did okay and I'm getting better." So I went to the door, finally courageous enough to talk to people on their way out of church.

The very first woman to approach me was a sweet, tiny lady in her late seventies. She walked up and patted me on the shoulder, and I prepared to receive her generous words. Knowing what a kind, devoted, lifelong Christian she was, I expected to hear, "That was a fine sermon!"

Instead, she said, "Nice try. You know, if you keep practicing, you might just be a real preacher one day!"

I did my best to keep smiling, even though her words punctured my already deflated ego, carving my old insecurities deeper than ever before.

Can you relate? Sometimes no matter how hard you try, you feel like your best just isn't good enough. You try to please everyone in your life and yet no one seems satisfied. You feel inadequate, inferior, and afraid of being found out.

But God says you are enough.

The love of Christ is what controls you now.

No matter what others may say or forget to say, don't let their feedback slow you down. Keep taking risks to do what God has called you to do.

Power Lift

Dear Lord, I get discouraged when others criticize me or tear me down. Help me to rise above those moments and concentrate only on pleasing you.

Who shall separate us from the love of Christ? Shall trouble or hardship or persecution or famine or nakedness or danger or sword? . . . No, in all these things we are more than conquerors through him who loved us. (Rom. 8:35, 37)

Today, some two thousand years after Paul wrote this Q&A in Romans, these potential obstacles remain just as relevant. Troubles and hardships certainly transcend time. You might be facing some kind of trouble or hardship right now—marriage struggles, physical injury, trouble with your kids.

Thanks to social media, persecution can take the form of cyber-bullying. Maybe people make fun of you for reading your Bible or for remaining a virgin until marriage. Maybe others ridicule you for walking away from shady business deals.

Even if you're not naked or in famine, like millions of people in our world, what about financial challenges? Does it ever feel like there's more month left than money?

In my country, fortunately, our lives are not endangered by our public worship like in some nations around the globe. But you might still be in danger—from a chronic illness, an abusive relationship, or PTSD from old wounds.

Paul answered his own question. He knew in all these various obstacles and challenges, we are more than conquerors. It's important that we acknowledge that this promise is not fulfilled under our own power—but through the power of the risen Christ, who loves us.

If you follow Christ, you are more than a conqueror—you are an overcomer.

· · · · · · · · · · · **Power Lift** · · · · · · · · · · ·

Jesus, thank you that nothing and no one can come between us. I'm so grateful for the power of your love and the way it fuels me on my journey. Today, with your help, I will overcome every obstacle that comes my way.

"They triumphed over him by the blood of the Lamb and
by the word of their testimony." (Rev. 12:11)

In the Old Testament, to receive forgiveness for sins, people offered animals (often a lamb) to God as a sacrifice. The shedding of this precious blood—the source of life—was what would cleanse them of their sin.

Then Jesus presented himself as the ultimate Lamb of God, a final sacrifice for the forgiveness of our sins. His blood alone had the power to forgive us once and for all. Because he chose to shed his blood for us, we have overcome the sin that held us hostage.

The other factor contributing to our ability to triumph according to this verse is our testimony. This refers to our stories, but specifically how we've encountered Jesus firsthand, personally. If you witness something happening, and you're called in to court as a witness to testify—or to give your testimony about what happened—then you're an eyewitness to events establishing the truth for all the people who weren't there. The judge has you swear that you'll tell the whole truth about everything you saw. And your testimony isn't about you either. It's about events that you happened to be present for, to see, to experience, to observe.

So your testimony is your story with Christ. Who were you before you gave your life to him? Who are you now because of Christ? The transformation of your life by his power is your story, the words of your testimony. When was the last time you shared your testimony with someone?

Power Lift

Lord, give me courage and wisdom today so I can step out in faith and share the difference you've made in my life.

> We are therefore Christ's ambassadors, as though God
> were making his appeal through us. We implore you on
> Christ's behalf: Be reconciled to God. (2 Cor. 5:20)

Years ago, I was looking out my office window one afternoon when I saw at least thirty cars screech into the parking lot. Within moments, dozens of high school students gathered in a big circle around two muscular jocks who were obviously about to fight.

Instinctively, I got really excited and ran through our office yelling, "Fight! Fight! Fight!" A friend and fellow pastor joined me, and the two of us couldn't wait to get outside to watch these two kids beat the crud out of each other. Fueled by adrenaline and more testosterone than two middle-aged pastors should feel, we yelled, "Hit him, *yeah*! Harder!"

However, a few seconds into the fight, we looked at each other. What were we thinking? We were grown-ups, we were Christians, and we were pastors! We weren't supposed to be acting like spectators at a World Cagefighting title bout. We were supposed to be stopping the fight and restoring order! Finally, we both ran closer and shouted, "Break it up! Come on, guys, it's over!"

Now, before you judge me for watching too much ultimate fighting on late-night cable, I think this little incident clearly illustrates a problem that many of us seem to battle: spiritual amnesia. We forget that we no longer have to act like we used to act.

We are new creatures as well as Christ's ambassadors.

We are peacemakers and reconcile others to God.

Where is there relational tension surrounding you? What can you do today to help bring peace?

Sometimes I forget, Lord, that I'm no longer the person I used to be. Help me to act like your ambassador so that others may come to know you.

He has committed to us the message of reconciliation. (2 Cor. 5:19)

At big banquets, dinners, and holidays, when it's time to eat, someone will inevitably say, "Pastor Craig, would you bless the meal?" Now, I'm certainly happy to pray, but in these situations, I love to turn the tables. "I'd be glad to, but why don't *you* pray a blessing on our meal?"

Almost every time I say this, the other person protests, "Oh no, no, no! You're the pastor and I'm just a regular Christian!" I love seeing people squirm! Maybe it's because I squirmed for so long whenever God dragged me out of my comfort zone. And so I tell them that I may have more practice praying out loud but that my prayers are no better than theirs.

All Christians are called to be Christ's representatives here on earth. The message of reconciliation that God has committed to us means we can help other people get right with him. Each one of us is called to help others know who Christ is so they can be whole and made right with God.

If you're a follower of Jesus, then God has committed you to the message of reconciliation so that others may know him. It's not easy stepping out in faith and talking about God with other people, but it's part of who we are as we grow closer to him. Similar to praying in public, don't worry about the "right words"—just speak from your heart.

Power Lift

Father, I get nervous telling others about you. Give me courage and boldness so that I can help others be reconciled to you through the gift of your Son, Jesus.

And we impart this in words not taught by human wisdom but taught by the Spirit, interpreting spiritual truths to those who are spiritual. (1 Cor. 2:13 ESV)

Most weekends, I deliver a message to tens of thousands of people at all of our different Life.Church locations over satellite video. However, I rarely see more than several hundred people in one location at one time. If I saw them all at once, it would freak me out! The first time I ever spoke in front of tens of thousands of people in a huge stadium, I almost lost more than just my voice!

Overwhelmed, I prayed, "Lord, help me to do this. I know I am your chosen instrument to carry your message to these people this day." I felt like I had no right to be there whatsoever, but when I remembered that God had brought me there, then I could step out with authority.

I'm not the best. I'm not a Bible scholar. But God has chosen and appointed me, and I take confidence in this truth. He has called me and I continue to fulfill that calling to the best of my ability. It's not about being a flawless speaker; it's about my faithfulness and what God wants to do through me.

The same is true for you.

Maybe it's not speaking or preaching, but sooner or later he will stretch your boundaries beyond what's comfortable and convenient. You'll be tempted to bail because you're scared or intimidated or unsure of yourself. That's when you pray and remember it's not up to you—it's up to God in you.

Power Lift

As I continue to grow in my faith, Lord, don't let me settle for a comfortable plateau or back away from scary opportunities. You are my authority and I am your ambassador wherever I go today.

Love one another with brotherly affection. Outdo one
another in showing honor. (Rom. 12:10 ESV)

A while back, I treated myself to the sauna after working out at the gym. I had the place to myself until this younger guy walked in. From his facial expression, I could tell he was upset.

We chatted casually, and then I said, "Hey man, it's obvious you're having a bad day, and I don't want to pry, but if you want to talk, I'll listen."

He opened up. He said he'd betrayed his wife and they'd got in a big fight. Fearing his marriage was over, he'd moved out the day before. He said, "I'll never forget my three-year-old daughter, as I'm backing down the driveway crying, 'Daddy don't leave us, don't leave us!'"

At that moment, I realized I was exactly where God wanted me. Trying not to sound like a preacher, I said, "Forgive me if it sounds crazy, but I believe God wants me to tell you to go home and get on your knees, apologize, and start again. I believe God wants you to be the Daddy to that little girl and the husband to your wife."

The guy choked up and said, "I'm not a religious guy at all, but I think you're right. I believe God sent you here to tell me to go home."

I wasn't trying to jump into "pastor mode" and force him to pray and accept Christ there in the sauna; I just listened to God's Spirit and relayed the message I heard. That's what an ambassador does. When you're willing to step out in faith, you will find all kinds of opportunities to represent God.

Where is God calling you to be his representative today?

· · · · · · · · · · · **Power Lift** · · · · · · · · · ·

Lord, today I want to be attuned to the hearts of others so I can represent you
and show them your love.

Great peace have they who love your law, and nothing
can make them stumble. (Ps. 119:165)

I've shared several stories about being nervous, uncomfortable, and intimidated as I've stepped out in faith. But I want you to realize that as you grow in your faith, you will also experience more of God's peace. The tendency to feel anxious may still pop up, but as you pray and rely on God's power, you relax into the security of knowing he's in control. You aren't responsible for how other people respond when you share your testimony of what God's done in your life. You just have to risk sharing it.

And when you do, then you experience God's presence sustaining you. As you know God's peace more and more, then you can stay calm when he stretches you beyond your comfort zone, knowing your security rests with him. It sounds crazy, but sometimes when life gets more stressful, I sleep better because I know the situation is too big for me to handle. Therefore, I'm not even tempted to try and take control. I can trust in my Savior.

And so can you.

If we follow Jesus and obey God's commands, then our feet will remain steadfast and sure. We will not stumble or fall victim to the many worries, fears, and anxieties that try to slow us down. Our peace is certain. Today don't let anyone or anything rob you of the security you have in the Lord.

Power Lift

Dear God, you are my shepherd and I will not fear. Your peace gives me comfort, power, and strength. No one can steal my joy today.

In [God's] strength I can crush an army; with my
God I can scale any wall. (Ps. 18:29 NLT)

Almost everything worthwhile I'm doing today is a result of God helping me overcome a challenge, a problem, opposition, or my doubts. Years ago when I began serving in ministry, I worked for five years at a terrific church. My first year, however, the church board decided I was "too enthusiastic" and should be fired. My first year! I didn't even make it to my one-year anniversary! It's only because my senior pastor, Nick, stood up for me and convinced them to give me another chance that I'm still in ministry today.

Not only did the church board have their reservations about me but so did my denominational leaders. After their screening process for ordination, the group said, "Craig, we're not sure you're called to ministry. Your ideas are just too . . . well, we're just not sure you'd make a good pastor." So they put me "on hold" for a year.

I jumped through their hoops and was finally ordained, only to be declined to start a new church. But God continued to burden my heart for ministry and leadership, and he's the reason I am where I am today. So for as long as I can remember, I've always believed that even if I come up to a wall that's in my way, with my God, we'll go over it, we'll go under it, or we'll put our heads down and go through it. Why? Because today's verse says I can crush an army in God's strength!

What fight do you need to win? With God, all things are possible.

This month is about fighting the good fight—and it starts right now.

. . . . **Power Lift** . . . .

Lord, nothing can stop me from doing what you want me to do! Today I will push through walls with a conquering attitude.

> Fight the good fight for the true faith. Hold tightly to the eternal
> life to which God has called you, which you have declared
> so well before many witnesses. (1 Tim. 6:12 NLT)

If you're a follower of Jesus, then you're also a fighter. In Exodus, we're told: "The LORD is a *warrior*; the LORD is his name" (15:3, italics mine). So if we're created in God's image, then we, too, have this fighter inside us as part of our nature. This is not just a cultural, patriarchal thing. It's a God thing—for all of us, both men and women—inherent to our Creator's design.

And don't forget the greatest warrior who ever lived, Jesus. Surprised? Many of us imagine Christ based on pictures of him, all meek and mild, smiling as children gather at his feet with sheep grazing nearby. But if you look at his life, this picture is incomplete.

The Son of God was not a divine doormat. He was overwhelmed with righteous anger, violently toppling the tables of the money-changers in his Father's temple. He was the scandalous Messiah, willing to buck the Pharisees and their religious establishment. He is the fierce King of Kings whose eyes are like blazing fire and who wears a robe dipped in blood (Rev. 19:13).

Jesus is both the Lamb of God and the Lion of Judah, the Prince of Peace and the Risen Savior, overcoming sin and death once and for all. We must consider all of what the Bible tells us to fully appreciate God's character and Jesus' example. No doubt about it, Jesus was a fighter.

And so are you.

Power Lift

Jesus, I want to be both gentle and defiant, meek as a lamb and fierce as a lion, just like you. Today I will fight whatever stands in the way of growing in my faith.

I have fought the good fight, I have finished the
race, I have kept the faith. (2 Tim. 4:7)

If all this talk about fighting and violence and being a warrior bothers
you, let me just say this: the virtue of strength is determined by how it's
used. If it's used to love and to protect, it's good. Unfortunately, it can
also be used to inflict harm, and that's not consistent with God's character that we see reflected in the Bible. He calls us to fight for what's right.

Warriors are only as worthy as their cause.

Someone without a cause from God is often just an angry person
who doesn't know where to direct their pent-up energy and aggression.
A warrior *with* a cause from God directs that war-like energy in a direction for a greater cause.

Until there's something you're willing to die for, you can't truly live.

You were created to fight for righteousness.

Until you tap into that divine cause, you'll be bored, destructive,
and frustrated. Find something more. I thank God I get to live my divine
cause. I honestly believe I'm on the front lines of the most important
war: the one between heaven and hell. The kingdom of God versus the
kingdom of darkness. My sword is drawn, and I'm willing to die for
the cause to lead people to become fully devoted followers of Christ.
That's not *what I do,* that's *who I am.* It starts with my family, and it
bleeds over to everything I do, anywhere I am.

What are you fighting for?

. . . . **Power Lift** . . . .

Lord, I don't always think of myself as a fighter, but with your power I'm willing to
do battle—for you, your kingdom, and your people.

"The LORD will fight for you while you keep silent." (Ex. 14:14 NASB)

I learned how to fight in the second grade. When I walked home from school one day, I became the school bully's latest target. Technically, Bo Talbot was only one year older than I was, but I suspected his parents kept him out of school for a few years to have him professionally molded by UFC trainers.

Bo grabbed my shirt with one hand, drew his hand back in a fist, and snarled, "Groeschel, are you *gay*?"

Now, since the year was 1975 and I was only eight years old, I wasn't really sure what "gay" meant, so I stammered, "I-I-I'm not sure. C-C-Can I get back to you tomorrow?"

Truth can be a dazzling weapon. Bo was visibly startled and said, "Well, okay. But you *better* tell me tomorrow!" Crisis averted—at least until the next day.

At home I didn't tell my mom about my run-in with Bo, but I did ask, "What does 'gay' mean?"

"Honey," she said calmly, "Gay just means . . . happy."

That made sense to my naïve second-grade mind, even if it seemed like a strange question for a bully like Bo to ask. The next day after school, I found myself cornered by Bo once again. Like actors resuming our roles, he asked the same fateful question: "Craig, are you gay?"

I just grinned broadly, proud to know how to answer. "Sure am. Been gay my whole life. I'm probably the gayest guy you've ever met!"

I don't remember much after that. My very first fight, and I didn't even get a punch in. Being beaten up would have been bad enough. Being beaten up for being "happy" was infinitely worse.

Are you in a spiritual battle? Thankfully, you don't have to fight alone. The Lord will fight for you.

• • • • • • • • • • • **Power Lift** • • • • • • • • • • •

Dear God, thank you for empowering me to fight the battles before me today.

> "But the people who know their God shall stand
> firm and take action." (Dan. 11:32 ESV)

When I stumbled home with Bo's knuckle-prints on my face, my mom was horrified at the violence a bully could inflict on a person. My dad, on the other hand, reacted differently. Instead of consoling me as my mother had, he led me to the garage, which he proceeded to transform into a training facility that Rocky would envy. "Now I'm gonna teach you to fight. You're gonna find this Bo punk and set things right."

For the rest of the weekend, he taught me every trick he knew.

Mom was furious and told Dad, "You're going to get our son hurt. Violence doesn't solve anything!" My dad stood his ground, as calm and resolute as an army general. "You have to trust me, honey. Craig *has* to stand up to this bully. He needs to win this fight, and win it decisively. And he will."

On my way to school Monday, I felt dizzy, my body drenched in nervous energy. Entering the school playground, I saw Bo, marched over, and proceeded to follow my father's directions.

"If you *ever* touch me again, Bo, I . . . will . . . *finish* . . . what you started! Do you understand me?" It was hard to believe that was actually my voice.

Bo stared at me, then laughed and held up his open palms. "Uh . . . Okay, then. I didn't *really* think you were gay anyway."

And just like that, Bo and I became friends. But even if he'd knocked me down again, it wouldn't have mattered because I had stood up to him. I had learned how to fight back.

If your spiritual enemy is trying to push you around, with God's help you can stand your ground.

· · · · · · · · · · · **Power Lift** · · · · · · · · · · · ·

Lord, thank you for teaching me to fight through your power and not my own.

"My grace is sufficient for you, for my power is
made perfect in weakness." (2 Cor. 12:9)

Everybody wants to be strong. But if your physical health and appearance
is all you invest your life in, then you'll miss out on something that lasts
forever—God's kingdom. And you can't fight for God's kingdom using
physical strength alone. The people who are really strong, the women
and men who are world changers, honestly admit their limitations.

Their refrain is "Lord, I'm weak. And I need you."

Being a warrior is not about cockiness and attitude, not about
six-pack abs and CrossFit, not about succeeding in life and winning
everyone's admiration or envy. Being a true warrior is about knowing
the source of true strength. It's about knowing your weaknesses and
turning to God to empower you to be the person he made you to be.

Whether you think about it much or not, your spiritual Enemy
wants to take you out. He's a master at making the strong become weak.
Sometimes he does that by making us comfortable, secure, and safe,
resigned to a mediocre life because it's familiar and doesn't require much
from us. But is that really how you want to live?

On the other hand, God is in the business of making weak people
strong. Your past isn't the most important thing. Your future is. If you
want to live your life—really live it in a bold, passionate, life-giving way
that's contagious—then don't compromise.

Fight. Every. Day.

· · · · · · · · · · · **Power Lift** · · · · · · · · · · ·

God, you know my weaknesses, and I know you can transform them into your
strengths. Today I will rely on your power and not my own to fight the Enemy.

"Be strong and let us fight bravely for our people
and the cities of our God." (2 Sam. 10:12)

Not only does God want you to fight, but he wants to give you a cause greater than yourself. Then, once you love something enough that you're willing to die for it, you'll be set free to live. Fight for a cause greater than yourself. It's in you.

Maybe you're thinking, *I don't know, Craig. I'm laid-back, peaceful, live and let live. I'm not really into that whole fighting thing.* Or you might be thinking, *Yeah, bring it on! I'm tired of feeling like I'm losing a battle wherever I go.* Either way, just remember that ultimately the strongest person is not the one who lifts the most weight, but the one who has the most faith.

Maybe you're in danger of failing financially. Now is the time to fight like your life depends on it. To get control of your budget and align your priorities with your cash flow.

Perhaps you're playing with a lustful fire. You keep returning to images and people and places that excite you but also unleash something you're afraid you can't control.

Your marriage might be hanging by a thread. Determine to never surrender. Use love, patience, and forgiveness. Lay down your life and save your marriage. Maybe your kids are making dangerous decisions.

Learn how to fight with faith, with prayer, and with the Word of God. Then, when your Enemy begins to attack, fight for the righteous cause that God gave you. Draw a line in the sand. Make your Enemy pay. Make sure he gets the message. *Don't cross a warrior. Don't mess with me. God is on my side.*

Power Lift

Dear God, help me to discern where I need to fight today, and then give me the strength I need to win the battle.

> Though we live in the world, we do not wage war as the world does. The weapons we fight with are not the weapons of the world. On the contrary, they have divine power to demolish strongholds. We demolish arguments and every pretension that sets itself up against the knowledge of God, and we take captive every thought to make it obedient to Christ. (2 Cor. 10:3–5)

Where are you weak?

Where are you vulnerable?

When are you most likely to get caught in a trap that could destroy what you treasure most?

Now is a very important moment. Be truthful.

You are only as strong as you are honest.

I want you to pause for a moment and think about when you are most vulnerable. Maybe it's when you travel. You're away from home. Working hard. Feeling lonely. And temptation strikes hard. Perhaps it's when you are bored. Without much going on during a Sunday afternoon, your mind wanders. You're playing on social media. A few clicks later you end up somewhere you shouldn't.

Once you have identified your most vulnerable points, you'll want to put up boundaries. If you don't have a strong wall of defense, it's time to build one. If you have some vulnerable spots in what once resembled a wall, let's close those gaps and eliminate the obvious access points. I'd suggest that if you are even remotely tempted or think you might be vulnerable, plan today to stay out of trouble tomorrow. If you truly want to honor God, living by his Holy Spirit, then it's time to defend your weaknesses.

Why? Because most fights are won or lost before they ever begin.

Power Lift

Search my heart, Lord, and show me where I need to protect my weaknesses. Protect me from the Enemy's attacks. Help me fight before the battle even begins.

But among you there must not be even a hint of sexual immorality. (Eph. 5:3)

Times have changed.

But that doesn't mean our morality should. While all the sexy stuff in our culture may seem normal, that doesn't make it right. No matter how much others try to normalize what God calls sin, normal doesn't make wrong right. As Paul points out in today's verse, there shouldn't even be a *hint* of sexual immorality.

Now, some sites, movies, and pictures may seem obviously immoral. But others may catch you by surprise if you're not careful. Years ago I had teenage boys from my youth group confess that they lusted after department store newspaper ads of models wearing underwear. If that can create lust, surely more suggestive ads do the same.

What about a sexually suggestive YouTube clip or a joke posted on Facebook?

Again, to God—that would likely qualify as a hint.

If this sounds severe, you might be tempted to write me off as a religious fuddy-duddy. That's totally fine. If you don't strive to know and follow Jesus—then fair enough—that's your choice. But you want to live in a way that honors our Savior—if you want to follow Jesus in a sin-saturated, selfie-centered world, then you will have to be different.

You will have to fight.

Our convictions must be guided by God's timeless principles, not the ever-eroding popular opinion of what's now acceptable. We must stand firm in our faith, fighting a battle against the temptations and sinful habits that our Enemy gladly uses to pull us away from knowing God and loving others.

· · · · · · · · · · **Power Lift** · · · · · · · · · · ·

It's so easy to "go with the flow" of the culture around me, Lord. Today sensitize my heart to anything that carries even a hint of immorality and help me resist it.

> For the word of God is alive and active. Sharper than any double-edged sword, it penetrates even to dividing soul and spirit, joints and marrow; it judges the thoughts and attitudes of the heart. (Heb. 4:12)

If we are going to follow Christ with integrity, we must defend our weaknesses and fight the Enemy. While this is nothing new, the prevalence of social media and the internet have created a new battlefield for the old war against temptation and sin.

The Bible is more than clear that we deceive ourselves if we think we can flirt, literally, with lust and not contribute to our souls' destruction. And smartphones, tablets, and laptops make such flirting and lusting easier than ever. All the more reason to be deliberate about how we use technology. Scripture is clear that we must avoid any hint, any flirtation, anything opening up an opportunity to sin.

Oddly, in our culture today, many people want to do just the opposite, seeing how close they can get to trouble without crossing the line. But God's Word teaches us the opposite. Stay as far away from temptation as possible.

I love the way David phrased it in Psalm 16:6 when he said, "The boundary lines have fallen for me in pleasant places." In other words, there are some fences or boundaries God has put in place, and I'm very thankful they are there. The fences keep the good stuff in and the bad stuff out.

The boundaries are there not to confine you but to protect you.

Power Lift

Lord, thank you for the power of your Word in defending and arming myself against the Enemy's temptations.

So then, each of us will give an account of ourselves to God. (Rom. 14:12)

If you are going to love God with all your heart, mind, and soul, you will have to be deliberate about protecting your heart, mind, and soul. That's why to follow Jesus in this selfie-centered, lust-filled world, you'd be wise to set up some boundaries to keep you safe. Before temptation can reach you, find ways to push it farther away.

I'm far from perfect, but let me share with you the defenses I have set up to keep me safe. Rather than simply hoping I have the strength to get out of trouble when temptation knocks, I have decided to do my best to keep temptation from ever getting close to my front door. (As I tell you the things I do, you need to remember these are for me.)

Knowing my weaknesses and vulnerabilities, here's what I do. I've decided to eliminate all temptation (I can think of) on my computer with a tracking software that sends a detailed (and scored) list of every single click I make.

Every. Single. Click.

This weekly report goes to two different men, both of whom have the authority to remove me from my role as pastor. If I didn't have this boundary in place, there might be times that I'd find myself vulnerable. Now that I have no access, I am not ever tempted. I no longer have the option to jump over the edge into an abyss that would wreck my heart, destroy my marriage, and undermine my calling.

Why would I resist a temptation in the future when I have the power to eliminate it today?

Who knows your secrets? How can others help you uphold your boundaries?

• • • • • • • • • • **Power Lift** • • • • • • • • • •

Dear God, I know I'm accountable to you, but I also want to be accountable to others. Help me know who I can trust with my secrets.

Worry weighs a person down; an encouraging word
cheers a person up. (Prov. 12:25 NLT)

We all say we want more peace, but I wonder if we're willing to fight for it. So many people don't even seem to recognize the things we do that often rob us of our God-given peace. Like checking your email obsessively because you're afraid you'll miss something and not be in control of how everyone views you as the hardworking, super-efficient person you are. Like binge-watching TV for hours on end, knowing you're wasting time and avoiding what has to be done. Like working obsessively to avoid painful realities at home.

Here's what many people miss. When you refuse to set limits and to obey God, you're robbing yourself of the peace you so desperately crave. Because even the momentary escape will be followed by waves of guilt. You want to numb the pain, but on the other side of your binge, the pain is still there, often worse. You love the momentary distraction, but then reality screams at you and your responsibilities pile up. You love the thrill of the lust, but the fear of getting caught haunts you and robs you of sleep and peace. Like a person dying of thirst gulping salt water, that which is supposed to satisfy only intensifies the need. So life goes on as usual. More stress. More anxiety. More worries.

And less peace.

The Bible is quite clear about how to cultivate and enjoy God's peace—we must fight to maintain our relationship with him. We spend time with him. We experience his presence.

Fight against the stressful lures of this world. Embrace God's peace available to you today.

Power Lift

Dear God, I really do long for your peace. Give me strength to fight the temptation to look elsewhere for the security and rest only you can provide.

No temptation has overtaken you except what is common to mankind. And God is faithful; he will not let you be tempted beyond what you can bear. But when you are tempted, he will also provide a way out so that you can endure it. (1 Cor. 10:13)

Are you battling an addiction? It might be something dramatic and chronic like an addiction to alcohol that you've been fighting for years. Or, it could be something more subtle, like an online addiction to playing Pokémon for hours on end.

While it's never going to be fun or easy to kick any addiction, you will be surprised how quickly your peace is restored when you surrender it to God. Because if you're serious about pursuing God's healing, then he will meet you where you are.

So if you find yourself overwhelmed with temptation, just remember God is not surprised. He knew what you'd face and has already made a plan to help you find freedom. Don't miss the power of Paul's words in today's verse.

God will provide a way out.

What's your way out? Just like your addiction, your way out is tailor-made just for you. It could be something dramatic or more low-key. It might be confessing to your spouse, your best friend, your small group, or your pastor. It might be deleting an app and making sure you can't get to it again. You might need to see a counselor, visit the doctor, or attend a group. I don't know what you need to do, but God promises he will give you a way out.

Just ask him to show you the way.

· · · · · · · · · · · **Power Lift** · · · · · · · · · · ·

Lord, sometimes I resign myself to struggling with the same old temptations over and over again. I know that you can deliver me. Show me my way out.

Submit yourselves, then, to God. Resist the devil, and he will flee from
you. Come near to God and he will come near to you. (James 4:7–8)

Sometimes we fight and struggle and push against our addictions and
ongoing temptations when we need to surrender—not to their power
over us but to God's power over them. We wouldn't keep falling and
slipping if it were possible to overcome these chronic battles on our own.
But when we quit giving our issues power over us, and instead focus
on our relationship with God, then we give him room to work in us.

If you want to be a man or woman of integrity, then maybe it's
time to submit to God like never before. Maybe that's where your fight
begins. Then with Christ's power, you'll be able to resist the devil and
his temptations. Tragically, so many people do the opposite. They resist
the promptings of God and give in to the temptations of the Evil One.
But that will not be you. And it won't be me.

Instead, we will live with integrity. Because our lives are not about
us. We will not gratify the self-centered lusts of our flesh because we
are born of the Spirit. We will not allow God's loving truth to slide into
the quicksand of popular opinion and allow ourselves to sink into lower
standards. We will guard our peace and not allow others to rob us of
our purpose, passion, and power.

Submit to God.

Resist the devil.

He will flee.

You will overcome.

· · · · · · · · · · · **Power Lift** · · · · · · · · · · · ·

Today I surrender my struggles to you, Lord, and trust your power to help me
overcome them.

"Blessed are those who are persecuted because of righteousness, for theirs is the kingdom of heaven. Blessed are you when people insult you, persecute you and falsely say all kinds of evil against you because of me. Rejoice and be glad, because great is your reward in heaven, for in the same way they persecuted the prophets who were before you." (Matt. 5:10–12)

If you are a believer in Jesus, you don't have to wonder if you will ever be persecuted. You should just know that it comes with the territory.

For years I knew people would criticize me, but I usually only heard about it from a distance. Then one day, I saw it up close and personal. One Saturday morning a young guy, probably in his early twenties, rang our doorbell.

He was a new Christian going door to door to share his faith and invite people to his church. Not wanting to dampen his excitement, I told him I was very involved in my church but didn't tell him I was a pastor. He finally slowed enough to ask me what church I attended. When I told him Life.Church, his face fell. He leaned in and said, "I heard the pastor of Life.Church doesn't preach the truth—you should get out of that church right away!"

And there it was.

I found out that day that you don't have to look for persecution. Sometimes it will knock on your front door. If we follow Jesus, we will be persecuted. That's why I never worry when people persecute me for my faith in Christ. I only worry when they don't.

Power Lift

Lord, help me to expect persecution to come my way when others see me following you. Help me to recognize it as a blessing, allowing it to draw me closer to you.

Be made new in the attitude of your minds. (Eph. 4:23)

One time three teenage boys randomly flipped me off as they drove by and raced ahead—laughing hysterically at how much faster, cooler, and superior they were to poor old geek-dad driving his kids around in a soccer mom's SUV.

Even though I had three of my kids in the car, in that moment something snapped. My foot pressed down on the accelerator and I found myself in hot pursuit. It must have been a full two minutes of full-throttle car chase mayhem (not unlike a car chase you'd see in a guy movie) before I came to my senses and let them go.

Maybe it was catching the look of sheer terror in my daughter's eyes in my rearview mirror. Maybe it was the thought of having to explain to my wife why the kids and I were being held down at police headquarters. Maybe it was remembering that I live in a relatively small town and that I'm a pastor, one who usually doesn't go over ninety miles per hour on the highway (with his kids along) just to teach three punks a lesson.

Maybe it was realizing that I was choosing the wrong battle to fight.

Today make sure you're fighting the right battle and not being distracted by something that ultimately doesn't matter.

Life is too short to carry a grudge. Your calling is too great to waste your energy in anger. God's grace is too powerful to keep to yourself.

• • • • • • • • • • • • **Power Lift** • • • • • • • • • • • •

Father, thank you for your power to renew my mind and keep my attitude focused on loving and serving others, not on seeking revenge.

I do not understand what I do. . . . For I do not do the good I want to do,
but the evil I do not want to do—this I keep on doing. (Rom. 7:15, 19)

I'm as human as the next guy. One minute I'm seeking God in prayer.
The next minute I'm in a very unnecessary argument with my wife. I
can worship passionately at church, only to criticize someone on the
drive home. Occasionally, only by the grace and power of God, I've even
been known to preach a passionate, Spirit-filled message!

But many days I wonder if I'll ever get it right.

Not only is it hard to serve God fully when things are going my
way; it's even harder to be faithful to him when things *don't* go my way.
You likely know what I'm talking about. You try to get ahead financially,
but then your car or your air conditioner or your dishwasher breaks
down, and you slip even farther behind. You work as hard as you can
to get promoted into your dream job, only to get passed over for that
annoying person you can barely stand. More and more it seems that
when you decide to live for God with all your heart, everything bad
breaks loose in your life.

Which makes it really hard to do what you know you want to do.
The more you fight to get things right, the more frustrated you become.
That's why you must remember this simple truth: Jesus has already won
the battle for you. All you have to do is follow his lead.

· · · · · · · · · · · · **Power Lift** · · · · · · · · · · · ·

Today I want to give you control of my life, Lord. I may sometimes struggle with
sin in this life, but I know that you have won the victory once and for all.

For sin shall no longer be your master, because you are
not under the law, but under grace. (Rom. 6:14)

Did you ever read *Superman* as a kid, or at least see one of the movies?
You may remember that his only weakness was Kryptonite, chunks of
rock and debris that came from his home planet, Krypton. In the old
comic books, Kryptonite was originally green and instantly drained
Superman of all his powers. But then some writers got creative and
started coming up with different varieties of Kryptonite. The red variety had random, wacky effects, sometimes causing him to mutate into
animals or insects. The black kind changed his personality and caused
psychological problems. Ultimately, though, they all reduced the Man
of Steel's powers and made him weaker.

That's what sin does to us. Although it takes various colors, shapes,
and sizes, sin saps our strength and shrinks our faith. Some people struggle
with financial sins—greed, gambling, overspending. Others wrestle
with sexual immorality and physical addictions. For some, it might
be controlling their anger or resisting gossip. Or maybe it's struggling
with online idolatry—wasting precious hours envying others on various social media sites.

Regardless of your personal Kryptonite, you don't have to be a
superhero to overcome it. Jesus has already defeated all your sins. He is
the source of your strength no matter what temptation comes your way.

Remember, there is no temptation greater that is than his grace.
When you are weak, he is strong.

● ● ● ● ● ● ● ● ● ● ● **Power Lift** ● ● ● ● ● ● ● ● ● ●

Jesus, help me focus on your power to overcome any temptations that may be
waiting to cross my path today.

Be alert and of sober mind. Your enemy the devil prowls around like a roaring lion looking for someone to devour. (1 Peter 5:8)

About ten o'clock one night, my kids came to tell me that our dog was freaking out outside. "Daddy! We think Sadie has caught something in the back yard!" *Hmm, maybe a cat?* I thought and smiled to myself.

Now you may not know this about me, but cats don't like me (probably because I rarely have anything nice to say about them). And besides, Scripture says that the devil roams around like a lion—linking him directly to the cat family. So the thought of our dog treeing a cat brought a little spark of joy to my otherwise quiet evening.

"I'll go check on her," I said, reassuring them.

Arming myself with my nunchucks and my iPhone flashlight, I headed out for search-and-destroy maneuvers. Once I had assessed the situation, sure enough, Sadie had treed not our neighbor's housecat— but a *bobcat*!

Fortunately, my ninja training kicked in, and before I even realized what was happening, I was back inside my house, with the doors locked and the blinds closed and all the lights on. Then I remembered that Sadie was still out there. Thankfully she survived and lived to hunt wild cats another day.

It's funny now, and maybe I'm exaggerating (just a little). But what's real is the fear I felt in that moment with that beast snarling at me. We need to remember that we have an Enemy every bit as real and lethal as any wild animal. If we're not armed with prayer and God's Word, then we leave ourselves open to a major attack.

Never let down your guard spiritually. Be alert.

Power Lift

Lord, help me to take the Enemy seriously and to remain alert for his snares. Protect me so that I may continue to serve you and grow in my faith.

"God is opposed to the proud, but gives grace
to the humble." (James 4:6 NASB)

Even though both men and women have emotions, we process them
very differently. Generally speaking, women talk, while men *act*. Most
of the time, when a woman is upset about something, she'll talk about
it. (And talk and talk and talk.) Most guys don't usually do that. One
article I read said that men talk on average about 7,000 words a day,
while women say 20,000 words a day—with gusts up to 30,000!

Sometimes when my wife needs to process some difficult emotions,
she'll invite one of her woman friends over to talk (usually for hours).
That works well for her, but I have never in my life had a dude call me
and say, "Hey Craig, could you come over to my house and sit with
me for half a day on my sofa and drink some tea so we can talk?" For
most men, talking doesn't feel like it accomplishes anything. Instead
"doing something" does.

The problem most of us face, women as well as men, is that we
often allow our emotions to determine our actions. When we let our
feelings call the shots, we're much more likely to cave to temptation.
We sin, which only makes us feel worse and gives women more to talk
about and men more to do something about.

While being emotion-driven often leads us to do the ungodly thing,
being Spirit-led *never* does. If you truly want to do what's right, letting
your emotions take over will rarely get you the outcome you want.

Feel what you feel, but do what God wants you to do.

• • • • • • • • • • • • **Power Lift** • • • • • • • • • • • •

Lord, give me the strength to be obedient today no matter how I may feel when
things go wrong.

Pride goes before destruction, a haughty spirit before a fall. (Prov. 16:18)

So many of us try to define ourselves by our accomplishments, to find our worth in what we've done, instead of in whom we belong to. We want to let our achievements, our victories, our trophies, our wins to define us instead of acknowledging God as the source of all good things in our lives. We want to take the credit and be known as a winner, a leader, someone who "has it all together."

And when things are going well, which usually means going the way we want them to go, life feels great. We have enough money in the bank, our home stays clean, our spouse is devoted, and our kids are healthy and happy. When it's all going great, we feel like we're the source. We want to take credit.

The problem is pride, and pride can be intoxicating. But the hangover is inevitable. We're human; we have many limitations; we must rely on God. When we lose sight of our identity and start suffering spiritual amnesia, we often feel like we're drowning in our emotions. And it's not just the storms of anger and pride that can capsize us. On the surface, we can appear calm and in control, even as an emotional riptide pulls us under into the depths of despair.

If we want to defeat pride, then we must remain humble and dependent on God. When we fight pride, we're growing in humility.

Where does God want you to grow in humility today?

· · · · · · · · · · · **Power Lift** · · · · · · · · ·

Lord, thank you for reminding me that I have nothing except for you. May all I do bring glory to you, not to me.

> "Come to me, all you who are weary and burdened,
> and I will give you rest." (Matt. 11:28)

A few Mondays ago I walked lifelessly into my office, feeling hungover from preaching all weekend long. While I was certainly exhausted from weeks of nose-to-the-grindstone work, it was all the things coming up next that consumed my thoughts.

I had seven more weekends to preach before having a weekend off, six ministry trips, our annual three-day all-staff event, too many meetings to count, and oh, yeah—a book to complete. After just glancing at my to-do list, I felt paralyzed, frozen in fear. Certainly I couldn't do it all. No one could. Resisting my emotions, I tried to fight back the tears. My emotions won. The tears flowed against my will.

I was exhausted.

That stress you're feeling isn't necessarily just from physical exertion. It's more like you feel the weight of your responsibilities—being there for family and friends, never wanting to let anybody down, living up to your parents' expectations, earning enough to pay all the bills. You try to be strong for everybody, the provider, the glue holding everyone's lives together. Maybe you even feel like your life makes all of their lives possible. If you're carrying that kind of burden, no wonder you're exhausted. Acknowledging it is the first step in overcoming it.

Let God lift that load off your shoulders.

You can't do it alone.

He is with you all the way.

Power Lift

Dear God, as my day unfolds, I often feel overwhelmed by all my responsibilities and the many demands on my time and energy. I can't, but you can. Show me the way.

"Take my yoke upon you and learn from me, for I am gentle and humble in heart, and you will find rest for your souls. For my yoke is easy and my burden is light." (Matt. 11:29–30)

When we're exhausted, the last thing we feel like doing is fighting. Like a boxer who has been knocked to the mat, we can't catch our breath, let alone stand up and swing at our opponent again. We're tired and overwhelmed. We begin to feel like it doesn't matter whether we get up again or not. We always seem to get knocked down again. Another unexpected bill, a sick kid, more work for less pay. Life is relentless.

But you're not alone. If you feel empty, low, or defeated, God wants to revive your strength. And as odd as it sounds, sometimes you have to fight for it.

When culture screams at you, "More is always better," remind yourself that less is often more. The moment life gives you more than you can handle, train yourself to stop, pause, breathe deeply, and take whatever burdens you straight to Jesus.

Jesus told us to "learn from him." Sure he ministered to people faithfully. Of course he was available, willing to drop everything to meet a need. But he also took significant breaks. He rose early to seek his father. He broke away from the crowds to spend time alone. He experienced extended periods seeking deep rest for his soul.

Not only does your body need a break but so does your soul. Maybe it's time to slow the pace. Breathe deeply. And enjoy his presence. You may feel like you simply can't. Don't make excuses. You can make excuses or you can make progress, but you can't make both. Fight for it. It's worth the fight.

You may not feel like you can afford to rest. I'd argue you can't afford not to.

Power Lift

When I can't keep going, Lord, I know you revive me and give me rest. You sustain my spirit, strengthen my body, and calm my mind. Thank you for letting me rest in you.

"Repent, then, and turn to God, so that your sins may be wiped out,
that times of refreshing may come from the Lord." (Acts 3:19)

All of us have done things we wish we could undo. Take text messages, for example. Once you click Send, there's no getting it back, so you have to be really careful what you say. I travel sometimes for work, but Amy and I keep in constant touch by texting. Because we're married—and *only* because we're married (Heb. 13:4)—sometimes we like to throw in a little Song of Solomon love action, if you know what I mean.

One evening, she had texted me about us going for a walk in a vineyard together or something saucy like that, so when I got back to my room at about eleven o'clock, I texted her back how much I love her flock of sheep. Only it was kind of racier than that. Okay, *a lot* racier.

Unfortunately, just as I hit Send, I noticed that I hadn't replied to the right conversation. I had two open conversations with Amy: our private one and a group text from earlier in the day. I had just texted a very romantic message to a group of my wife's friends!

So there I was, in full panic mode, staring at my phone when it rang.

"Oh, hi, babe. I was just thinking about you."

"Do you realize what you just did?"

"Yes, I do!"

Don't worry—no one will ever know what was in those texts. We had dinner with each of those couples in nice restaurants, and we paid for their meals to bribe them to secrecy.

You cannot unsend.

You cannot undo past mistakes.

But you can repent.

Father God, I'm so grateful that your mercy has no limits. When I fail, you always forgive me and welcome me home.

> Then Samson reached toward the two central pillars on which
> the temple stood. Bracing himself against them, his right hand
> on the one and his left hand on the other. (Judg. 16:29)

Remember Samson? The strong man with the famous haircut at the hands of the beautiful but devious Delilah? If you know his story well (or go read it in Judges 13–16), then you know he made some big mistakes. He let his vanity, pride, and male ego get in the way of his commitment to God. But even after he blew it, Samson did what he could to overcome his weaknesses. He may have felt defeated, but he wasn't through fighting—not yet.

The same is true for you. Even in the midst of your failures, God can use you. No matter how many times you've messed up, if you're not dead, you're not done. There's more in you.

Maybe you're thinking, "But Craig, you don't know all the stuff I've done. I've made *so many* mistakes." Haven't we all? Those chapters from your past just add new dimensions of redemption to your story. And if you're reading this, then your story isn't over.

God isn't finished with you.

You're not finished with you either. Do you have some pillars in your life that you need to push down? Pillars that are holding up what's been ruling you, oppressing you, tormenting you? What are they? Give every pillar a name—then with God's power, knock them down.

Don't go down without a fight.

Remember, God will fight alongside you.

· · · · · · · · · · · · **Power Lift** · · · · · · · · · · · ·

God, sometimes I get discouraged and want to give up the fight. Thank you for never giving up on me. You are the author and finisher of my faith—and my story isn't over yet.

"What good is it for someone to gain the whole
world, yet forfeit their soul?" (Mark 8:36)

When my son Bookie was only a toddler, I saw him jumping and squeal-ing with joy on our front porch. "My fwend! My fwend!" he shouted exuberantly, twisting and turning with delight.

As I looked where he was pointing, I saw what appeared to be a baby toy, maybe a plastic rattle or an action figure left by one of the older kids, on the edge of the porch. However, when I got closer, I noticed his "fwend" started squirming and making noise—it was a baby rattle-snake! I almost knocked Bookie silly getting him out of the way so I could "take care" of his little fwend.

I will never forget that moment, partially because it was both cute and dangerous at the same time. But it also offers a picture of how we often relate to something we think we need, something we'll love, something we can't live without. Harmless enough at first, it eventu-ally causes great harm in our lives. We're searching for something to meet our needs, only to be seduced by our dependence on a counterfeit that can hurt our souls.

Nothing is worth getting between you and your growing passion for loving God. Stay in the fight. Don't be deceived by your own heart. Focus on God's instead.

Power Lift

Lord, I often chase after things that I hope will fulfill me, only to be disappointed when they don't. Remind me that you are the only one who can fill the longing in my heart.

If you suffer as a Christian, do not be ashamed, but praise God that you bear that name. (1 Peter 4:16)

I remember when someone wrote a pretty negative article about our church and me. Within minutes the hateful comments started rolling in. Even though I pray for thick skin and a soft heart, it seemed my skin was way too thin and my heart was nowhere near soft toward these hateful people.

By God's grace, I had a flight to another city later in the day. Once our flight took off, I didn't have access to what people were saying. (Remember when planes didn't have Wi-Fi?) We climbed higher and higher into the air, and as I ascended toward the heavens, everyone and everything on earth looked so much smaller.

For some reason, I felt closer to God above the clouds, and the problems on earth seemed small and distant. That's when it dawned on me. If I'm earthly minded and self-centered, I will always feel the sting of critical people. But if I'm close to God and my life is his, then by faith, I can rise like an ascending plane above the smaller-minded critics.

If you are facing criticism (or when you do), turn to God. Expect criticism. Endure it. And by his power, embrace it. Do not be shocked when persecution comes. And take it even another step. Embrace it. Rejoice that in some small ways you suffer with and for the one who suffered for you.

Power Lift

Jesus, help me to follow your example and to expect criticism, knowing that others often won't understand when I live for you.

"So do not corrupt yourselves by making an idol in any form—whether of a man or a woman, an animal on the ground, a bird in the sky, a small animal that scurries along the ground, or a fish in the deepest sea. And when you look up into the sky and see the sun, moon, and stars—all the forces of heaven—don't be seduced into worshiping them." (Deut. 4:16–19 NLT)

In today's passage, we see God dealing with a specific problem. His children were distracted and probably a little desperate, so they started worshiping golden calves, cedar poles, statues, the moon, and the sun.

Those objects sound irrelevant and even silly to us—having no bearing on modern-day life. And yet today, our pursuits and the things that get the majority of our time, money, and attention are no more worthy of worship. For instance, we have a generation still being seduced by our social standing. How many followers do we have? How many likes did we get?

Still resisting the possibility that you're idolizing technology? Think of it this way. Someone said idolatry is making a good thing an ultimate thing. Idolatry is taking something, anything, and making it bigger than it should be in our lives.

Maybe for you it's a girlfriend or boyfriend, a husband or a wife, an obsession with a celebrity or a sports team. It could be a certain job or an impressive title. A corner office or your own company expense account. It might be a certain amount of money in the bank or the perfect tropical vacation.

How have you filled in this blank most of your life? If only I had [blank], then I would be happy and fulfilled. Were you aware this was replacing God in your life? How should you handle this idol?

Power Lift

Lord, I don't want anything to come between us. You are my God, and idols can never compare.

"Whoever wants to be my disciple must deny themselves
and take up their cross and follow me." (Matt. 16:24)

Did you know that the majority of what we do on social media pertains to us? Just like the latest tweet I sent. I care about my tweet way more than anyone else's. (Jesus might have said to love other people's tweets as you love your own, but I don't think so. I'll keep working on that.)

Think about the whole notion of selfies for a minute, a phenomenon that still fascinates and repulses me in equal measure, like some roadside accident on the information superhighway. I'm not even sure if the word selfie existed a decade ago. Yet in 2013, Oxford Dictionaries crowned it as their Word of the Year. Out of almost nowhere, selfies have become an obsession for so many.

Everywhere we go—the office, home, church, the gym—we're encouraged to take a selfie. It's almost like we have to prove that we really did brush our teeth, lift that barbell, or wash the car, so we take a selfie to prove it. We're the selfie-proclaimed star of our own daily reality show.

Our culture says show yourself. Update your status. Pin your latest pic.
Jesus said deny yourself.

If someone looked at your Facebook page, your Instagram photos, or your most recent tweets or snaps, what would they see? Would they see a humble, others-focused, Christ-centered disciple? Or would they see something less than who Christ has called you to be?

Power Lift

Dear Lord, I know I get caught up in my own little world and focus too much on myself. Give me a soft heart willing to put others first.

"Love your enemies, do good to those who hate you, bless those
who curse you, pray for those who mistreat you." (Luke 6:27–28)

Jesus taught us to pray for our enemies. I don't know about you, but that
is one of the most difficult of his commands for me to obey. Cursing
our enemies would be natural; praying for them is supernatural.

This never felt truer than years ago when our family discovered that
a man I'll call Max had molested my little sister. Lisa was in the sixth
grade when this very sick man groomed her along with other young girls
before he robbed them of their innocence. Any type of abuse is horrible
and heartbreaking. What Max did to these precious young girls is still
gut-wrenching to think about.

To be honest, I would rather have beaten Max than prayed for him.
But because our family took God's Word seriously, we knew we would
want to work toward forgiving him. It wouldn't be easy. It would take
a lot of time and faith. And for me, it would start with prayer.

At first, all I could pray was, "God do something to Max." As you
can tell, my prayer was very open ended. Secretly I hoped God would
"do something" to punish him for his sins. Over time, my prayers pro-
gressed. I managed to barely utter the words, "Bless him."

Through months of personal searching and seeking God, our family
made the faith decision to forgive this man for the unthinkable—just
as Christ had forgiven us.

Although for a while I didn't know if our prayers had any impact
on Max, they did on us. And I learned that our prayers for others may
or may not change them. But they will always change us.

• • • • • • • • • • • **Power Lift** • • • • • • • • • • •

God, give me the strength to forgive those who have hurt me the deepest.

> By the grace God has given me, I laid a foundation as
> a wise builder, and someone else is building on it. But
> each one should build with care. (1 Cor. 3:10)

I've learned the hard way that I'm never as strong as I think I am. Like you, I'm a work in progress, often taking two steps forward and three steps back. Sometimes I can be the most self-disciplined person you've ever met, a ninja warrior of self-control. I can go a year without eating pizza, hamburgers, junk food, and desserts with no problem at all. But when someone cuts me off on the road, then all my self-discipline goes out the window in a flash.

Knowing how quickly I'm capable of failing, I'm never going to say for a second I'm above any sin. I'm as human as everyone else. Truth be told, we all are. We're all capable of falling short in any way at any time, and we have to recognize our weaknesses and defend ourselves against attacks from the Enemy. Acknowledging your weakness is the first step toward true strength. You are only as strong as you are honest, and if you really want to rely on God, then you must not deceive yourself about your flaws.

This month we're going to focus on building—a secure defense system against sin, habits pleasing to God, and stronger relationships, including forgiveness and restoration. Like a house that's being renovated, some parts have to be torn down before the new design can take shape. You are God's masterpiece, even when you can't see the transformation.

Power Lift

Lord, thank you for tearing down the old sinful ways in my heart and building a strong foundation anchored on you and your Word.

> For whoever keeps the whole law and yet stumbles at just
> one point is guilty of breaking all of it. (James 2:10)

I'm not proud of this, but before I was a Christian, I used to shoplift occasionally. In college, my buddy Stan and I even made a sport of it. At the end of spring semester, Mother's Day was approaching, and I asked Mom what she wanted. She said she needed a pair of women's running shorts, so Stan and I went to the top-of-the-line premiere store for women's fashion, Montgomery Ward, to make the hit.

There I found the perfect pair of shorts for my mom. I hid behind one of those big round clothing racks and slipped them into my bag, relishing this sick rush of adrenaline. Then I casually walked out of the store and headed into the mall to meet Stan. Just as I reached the food court, suddenly someone grabbed my arm from behind—a security guy.

I was busted right there on the spot. It was a horrible, traumatic event, but it got my attention, reminding me that no one was above the law. I started seeing myself differently and wanted to be a better person. Seriously, what kind of guy steals his mom's Mother's Day present? By the grace of Jesus, I'm not the same person I was then.

We have all sinned against God, and we deserve death. The good news is, because of the grace of God, he doesn't have to give us what we deserve. You're not who you used to be.

What does God need to change in you?

. . . . **Power Lift** . . . .

Father, when the Enemy tries to taunt me with reminders of my past, let me stand strong in your power, as a new creation, your child saved by faith in your Son, Jesus Christ.

The LORD confides in those who fear him; he makes his covenant known to them. My eyes are ever on the LORD, for only he will release my feet from the snare. (Ps. 25:14–15)

My family once was pet-sitting a friend's hamster. One night, and we still have absolutely no idea how, Houdini the hamster escaped his escape-proof home and was loose in our house. Unfortunately, we had traps set in various places for mice. I'm sure you can tell this story doesn't have a happy ending. The furry guy is in a better place now. At least that's what we're telling ourselves.

If you're not paying attention, you can find yourself caught in the Enemy's snares the same way. One minute you're scrolling through Facebook, enjoying seeing pictures of your old friend's Hawaiian vacation, and the next you're resenting the fact that your day at the waterpark with your kids can't compare. Next thing you know, there's an empty Doritos bag next to the empty pint of Cherry Garcia ice cream.

When we focus on what we don't have, especially if we compare ourselves to others who seem to have what we want, then we're walking into a trap. Instead, we must keep our eyes on the Lord, knowing that he guides our steps and will lead us around the minefield of comparison, envy, and covetousness planned by the Enemy. God always provides a way through those traps, but we have to focus on him.

Today avoid the Enemy's snares by keeping your eyes on God and his abundant blessings in your life.

Power Lift

Jesus, I'm not taking my eyes off you today. You are my shepherd and you will guide me safely through the temptations waiting ahead of me.

It is for freedom that Christ has set us free. Stand firm, then, and do not
let yourselves be burdened again by a yoke of slavery. (Gal. 5:1)

If you watch fireworks today, let them remind you of the source of your
greatest liberty.

We celebrate our country's freedom today, but if you're following Jesus, then every day should be your Independence Day. All those
yucky things you've done in the past have been washed away. You're no
longer held captive by your sin and selfishness. You're a new person, a
child of God who is becoming more and more like Christ every day.

And that's nothing you did for yourself. You're saved by grace,
through faith and not by works. By the grace of God and by believing
that what Jesus did on the cross was enough, you're set free. He ransomed
you with his death, paying your penalty for you, an overwhelming debt
that you could never pay yourself.

You're not made right with God by going to church. You're not
made right with God by being a church member. You're not made right
with God by giving money. You're not made right with God by helping little old ladies cross the street. You're not made right with God by
being a nice person. You're not made right with God by getting rid of
bad stuff. You're not made right with God by refusing to gossip about
the other moms in the school carpool. You're not made right with God
by being a religious person.

You're made right with God by grace through faith.

You've been set free from the burden of sin.

● ● ● ● ● ● ● ● ● ● ● **Power Lift** ● ● ● ● ● ● ● ● ● ● ●

Thank you, Lord, for the gift of salvation and the freedom I have through Christ.
Today help me to overcome any struggle by remembering the source of my
freedom.

Therefore, there is now no condemnation for those
who are in Christ Jesus. (Rom. 8:1)

Years ago, I began saving my money and buying small houses to fix up and rent out. While I was always looking for a bargain fixer-upper, I could tell that some of these places were only one step away from being condemned by the city and torn down. You know the kind of places I'm talking about. The ones that look like haunted houses, with boarded-up windows and sinking foundations, places you wouldn't want to be inside during the daytime let alone at night.

These condemned houses usually sat vacant, decaying and falling into further disrepair, waiting until they could be destroyed or demolished. These sites are sad remnants of their former glory, when they were new, strong, and beautiful. When shopping for properties, I knew that no matter how hard I worked, these homes were beyond repair.

Sometimes we treat ourselves like an old house that has been condemned instead of like a new home that God has renovated and restored. Through our faith in Christ, God forgives us, loves us, and brings us new life. What's old has passed away; he is doing a new thing in us. Often we don't live this way, though. Instead we create an enormous challenge by continuing to condemn ourselves even after God has forgiven us.

There's no way your standard can be higher than God's perfect holiness. It's time you realize what God is building in you, rather than what you continue to try to tear down. Through the power of Jesus Christ, you have been given the ultimate foundation for true transformation.

Power Lift

Sometimes I feel so ashamed and focused on my sins, Lord. Thank you for your grace and mercy, the cornerstones of my faith in you.

> Do not offer any part of yourself to sin as an instrument of
> wickedness, but rather offer yourselves to God as those who have
> been brought from death to life; and offer every part of yourself
> to him as an instrument of righteousness. (Rom. 6:13)

We have to recognize that we don't have the potential of eternal life because we're good—we have it because God is good. We can't change on our own power any more than we could build a new house with our bare hands. We change because we yield our lives into the hands of God, the master builder, the author and finisher of our faith.

If you've accepted the free gift of salvation through Christ, the foundation for your new life is already in place. There's nothing you can do to make him love you more, and there's no sin you can commit that can make him love you less, because he loves you. God is love. Love is not what God does; it's who he is.

Because he loves you so much, he sent Jesus, who did not consider equality with God something to be grasped but humbled himself and became nothing, taking on the form of a servant. Even being obedient to death on the cross. It's hard to grasp this kind of humility and servant-heartedness.

While you were still a sinner, Christ died for you.

Now that you're forgiven, you can live for him.

Power Lift

Jesus, I can't fully comprehend the sacrifice you made for me. Today I offer myself to you as your instrument of righteousness, grace, and love for those around me.

> I waited patiently for the Lord; he turned to me and heard my cry.
> He lifted me out of the slimy pit, out of the mud and mire; he set my
> feet on a rock and gave me a firm place to stand. (Ps. 40:1–2)

All of us, unfortunately, at one time or another, fall short and let ourselves, God, and other people down. Even today, I'm still haunted by the first time I preached and failed miserably. When I was only twenty-two years old, my pastor took a chance and brought me on staff at his church. He also gave me my first opportunity to preach a real Sunday-morning sermon before the entire congregation, the most terrifying and humbling experience of my life to that point.

With all the other pastors sitting in these big, fancy throne-like chairs behind me, I stood up front to deliver the sermon. Finally, my nerves settled and I thought maybe this would be okay. I said, "What you need to know is that God knew you before you were born," which brought several amens from the congregation. So I kept going: "God knew you before your mama knew your daddy," which once again brought several amens. Having gained momentum, I couldn't stop myself: "And God even knew you before you were an itch in your daddy's pants!"

You could've heard a pin drop.

No one said amen.

I went too far, and from there I never recovered in that sermon. By God's grace, my pastor let me preach again. Despite one of my most embarrassing moments, God built on my mistakes and used me for his kingdom.

He will do the same for you.

· · · · · · · · · · · · **Power Lift** · · · · · · · · · ·

Lord, I am not only the mistakes I have made—I am a trophy of your glory.

"I am the Lord, the God of all mankind. Is anything
too hard for me?" (Jer. 32:27)

There's a lot of pressure to strive for perfection in our culture today. Whether you're baking a birthday cake or earning a college degree, leading a meeting at work or teaching a Sunday school class, you want to get it right. You want to do your best, and if you're honest with yourself, you want to impress those around you.

When you focus only on achieving such goals as a reflection of your identity and self-worth, then the pressure builds. You replay what you said in the meeting over and over again, thinking about what you should have said differently. You hide the sunken cake in the trash and pick up one from the grocery store. And as these various demands compete for your time, energy, and attention, the pressure builds and you begin to feel overwhelmed.

Obviously, God wants you to do your best—but so much of what we take on isn't from him. Instead, it's a list of what we want to do to prove to ourselves and others that we're capable, talented, strong, smart, cool, and therefore worthy. But this is a house of cards waiting to fall whenever we don't do it all perfectly, which means most of the time.

If life's demands feel too hard for you, consider why you're doing what you're doing. Is it from God or from your own desire for personal validation?

• • • • • • • • • • • **Power Lift** • • • • • • • • • • • •

Thank you, Lord, that today I don't have to do it all. When life feels too hard for me, I can rest knowing that nothing is too hard for you.

Take delight in the LORD, and he will give you
the desires of your heart. (Ps. 37:4)

Some days you wake up and wonder how you ended up where you are in your life. You remember when you were younger and had a dream. You always thought, "One day I'm going to pursue that dream and I'm going to go for it and I'm going to take the chance." You may have believed God gave you this dream and that he would provide the path you needed to reach this divinely appointed destination.

But when you look at your life now, it feels like you went off road and into a wilderness of distractions and diversions. Now you're in a place where it seems like the ability to pursue that dream has passed you, and you feel like a failure because you thought by this point in your life you would be doing something different, something better, something more significant, something more meaningful. Then one day you just looked up and you were nowhere close to where you thought you would be, where you thought God would lead you.

No matter how disappointed you feel, or how far away you seem from your expectations from long ago, don't give up on your dream. If God has planted it in your heart, then he will lead you there, blazing a trail marked by his glory. No matter how painful or impossible it seems, keep walking by faith.

· · · · · · · · · · · **Power Lift** · · · · · · · · · ·

Today, Lord, I will take the next step and trust you for where we're going and how I'll get there.

> As far as the east is from the west, so far has he removed
> our transgressions from us. (Ps. 103:12)

Knowing the origin of a sinful struggle can be helpful but doesn't necessarily make it any easier to overcome. The first time I saw pornography, I was in the fifth grade. My buddy Steven had found his dad's stash of *Playboy* magazines, so he invited me over after school. Thumbing through those pages, I didn't even know why I liked what I was seeing there.

It just intrigued me and I felt this rush of adrenaline and it was so exciting. At the same time, I felt such guilt. I felt so dark and so dirty. It only got worse when I went home and saw my mom. She was like, "Oh, son. I love you. You're such a good kid." I was thinking, *No! I'm horrible. I've been looking at Miss February for hours.* I felt so bad.

I prayed for God to forgive me and promised never to do it again—until the next day after school when Steven invited me over to check out March and April. For a long time, I struggled with the lustful desires those images ignited and felt like I would never overcome the shame, guilt, and burden of being this horrible person.

But after becoming a Christian, I realized that when I focus on the problem, I only give it more power to invade my thoughts and lure me into familiar temptations. Instead, I focus on Christ and the way he has overcome the power of sin and death in my life. Yes, I understand how this struggle started in my life, but greater still, I understand how it ends.

· · · · · · · · · · · **Power Lift** · · · · · · · · · · · ·

Jesus, I am no longer bound by the old struggles and temptations because you have defeated sin once and for all.

> Set a guard, O Lᴏʀᴅ, over my mouth; keep watch
> over the door of my lips! (Ps. 141:3 ESV)

Do you ever look back on conversations you've had and think, "Man, I can't believe I said that!" or, "Wow, I thought I was being so funny, but it backfired big time. I really hurt my friend"? Most of us have plenty of cringe-worthy moments that we wish we could take back. Sometimes we speak without thinking first, and other times we don't realize the way our words reveal the motives of our hearts.

If you want to build stronger relationships with those around you, then you will have to ask God to guide your words. I love today's verse because it gives me comfort to imagine God placing a guard beside my lips to prevent me from saying things that don't honor the Lord.

He's committed to helping us control what we say when we focus on him and his Word. If you ask God to help you with what you say, then you can relax and trust that his Spirit will guide you. There might be a second where you pause to think about the impact your next words will have on the person hearing them. Or you may not talk nearly as much as you once did. Remember, our words communicate more than what they're literally saying. They reveal who's in control of our heart.

. . . . **Power Lift** . . . .

Lord, I know that you want me to bless and build up others with my words. Guard my lips and give me your power to control what I say.

Carry each other's burdens, and in this way you
will fulfill the law of Christ. (Gal. 6:2)

Recently Amy and I got away for the weekend, so I planned a romantic dinner at a nice restaurant. We had just been seated when a lady at another table gave us that "Hey! You're our pastor" look. I tried to avoid eye contact at first, using the excuse that I was just focusing on my beautiful wife. But then Amy noticed this woman glancing over at us too. She sort of smiled and said hi, and then the other woman did the same and came over to talk to us.

As it turned out, we knew this woman from church, but she had moved away awhile back. We chatted and caught up, and then we said, "Hey, you know, we're about to order. Do you want to sit down and talk for a couple of minutes?"

We started talking, and the next thing I knew, our food came just as this woman opened up about some really hard struggles in her life. She kept apologizing and offering to leave, and part of me wanted to say, "It's so good to see you. We'll keep praying for you" so I could get on with date night. But I knew that's not what Jesus would do, nor would it be what my wife wanted.

We hadn't planned to spend those two hours talking with this lady, listening, praying with her, crying a little bit. But later Amy and I agreed that time with her had been the most important part of our entire weekend.

● ● ● ● ● ● ● ● ● ● ● **Power Lift** ● ● ● ● ● ● ● ● ● ● ●

Jesus, I want to let go of my plans so that I can be present for the needs of others. Today help me to put other people ahead of myself.

Each of you should use whatever gift you have received to serve others,
as faithful stewards of God's grace in its various forms. (1 Peter 4:10)

My wife, Amy, loves serving people anytime she can. Awhile back, she
had a good friend who was going through a tough postpartum depression.
This woman had just had her fifth child and felt totally overwhelmed,
clothes piling up and the house looking like a bomb had hit it.

Amy decided she wanted to get a babysitter for our own kids so she
could go spend an entire day cleaning her friend's house. I said, "Babe,
that's a great idea, but instead of paying a babysitter, let's just pay someone else to go clean your friend's house."

My wife looked at me funny and said, "No, I have to do this. I want
to give this to my friend. I'm sorry if you don't understand."

I sighed and said, "Okay, do what you've got to do. Pay the babysitter and go ahead."

Later when she returned from spending the day at her friend's,
Amy had the most amazing look in her eyes. She said, "My friend was
blown away! She was so happy and that made me so happy, and then
she started crying, so I started crying." Hearing her talk about it, I
almost started crying too!

Your compassion not only blesses others, but it blesses you as well.
Every time you ignore an opportunity to serve someone else, you miss an
opportunity for God to use you and bless you. Don't miss out on what
God wants to do in you when you serve the needs of others.

. . . . **Power Lift** . . . .

Dear Jesus, you left your glory in heaven to come to earth as a humble servant.
Give me the strength and humility to serve others in the same way.

Praise the Lord, my soul, and forget not all his benefits—who
forgives all your sins and heals all your diseases. (Ps. 103:2–3)

When I was growing up, it seemed like every adult I knew smoked cigarettes. I never realized the effect it had on me until I went away to college. After being away for several weeks, when I came back home, I thought, "Man, this place smells like smoke! Wow, I never noticed that before." Then I kind of got used to it again and didn't think about it until I got back to my dorm Sunday night.

When I walked into my dorm room, my roommate said, "Dude, get out of here! That's rank! Where have you been—inside a chimney?"

Then it dawned on me. For the past eighteen years, I'd lived in this smoke-filled environment and didn't realize the toll it had taken on me. I had been breathing in this secondhand smoke, this poison, and it was affecting me and I didn't even know it.

So often our culture affects our souls the same way. We breathe in secondhand toxins that infiltrate our minds and hearts and make us sluggish. After a while we don't realize it and are just going with the flow, doing what everyone else around us is doing, not what God wants us to do.

If you want to build a stronger relationship with Christ, you have to live apart. You have to follow his ways and not the crowd. You have to recognize the impact that those around you are having on your faith.

• • • • • • • • • • • • **Power Lift** • • • • • • • • • • •

Father, thank you for calling me to a life that's set apart from the world. Today help me see the ways I have been affected by spiritual pollution.

Truly my soul finds rest in God; my salvation comes from him. (Ps. 62:1)

Some months I get tired just looking ahead at my schedule. I'm guessing you might occasionally feel the same way. Work deadlines loom. A kid gets sick. You've got company coming to town. The dishes need doing. The yard needs mowing. And let's not even talk about how bad the closets look. With kids' activities taking over, social media to manage, and financial pressure looming, it's no wonder so many of us feel stressed.

Whenever I face a grueling season, I always try to make sure I eat healthy, keep working out when I can, and get decent sleep. That last one can be tough because my body gets exhausted, but my mind keeps turning, thinking, and planning. But I know that if my body doesn't get good rest, I'm not nearly as productive, not to mention a lot grouchier.

But I've also discovered that my soul needs rest too. Have you ever considered that your soul needs rest on a regular basis just like your body? It's true. And there's only one place our souls can find rest: in God's holy presence.

If you're feeling exhausted by all of life's demands, then hit pause for a moment. Before you burn out or give in to some temptation that promises comfort, still your soul before God. Let his Spirit breathe new life into your heart, your mind, your body. Today let your soul breathe again.

• • • • • • • • • • • **Power Lift** • • • • • • • • • • •

Lord, my soul finds rest in you alone. Refresh me with your Spirit and renew my strength with your power.

Be strong and take heart, all you who hope in the Lord. (Ps. 31:24)

Working out has always been fun for me. Setting goals helps me feel like I'm making progress. If I'm improving in one area of life, it makes me feel like I can improve in others.

One rare time Amy came on a workout with me. For some reason, I thought I'd impress her with my growing strength. (Truthfully, she doesn't care at all about my muscles, but I like to pretend she does).

Prepping to dazzle her with my strength, I put more weight on the bar than normal, thinking my record-breaking set would wow her into cheers and kisses. Lying on the bench, I carefully gripped the bar, placing my hands in the precise spot. I inhaled deeply, paused for dramatic effect, exhaled deeply, then lifted the bar off the rack.

One . . . the first rep was easy. Two . . . still easy. Three . . . Four . . . Five . . . It started to get more difficult. Undeterred, I pressed on. Six . . . Seven . . . Eight . . . Now it was dangerously difficult. Nine . . . This should have been my last rep. But I told myself one more would knock her socks off. And that's when the bar—boom! collapsed on my chest. Trying to impress my wife, I had pushed too far.

Sometimes we overestimate what we can do. We try to carry more than we are designed to carry. That's why every step of the way, we need a strength greater than our own.

God's power is greater than your own. Tap into his strength today.

• • • • • • • • • • **Power Lift** • • • • • • • • • • •

I sometimes take on too much, Lord, rushing in to impress others instead of waiting on you to guide and direct me. Today I will rely on your strength instead of my own.

Wait for the LORD; be strong and take heart and wait for the LORD. (Ps. 27:14)

My wife is not the only person I've tried to impress at the gym. For years, I've worked out with my buddy I call Paco. (It's a rule that a good friend has to have a nickname or he's not a good friend.)

At the end of our workout, sometimes we will do a "burn out," a set when we do light weights to the point of exhaustion. So one day we decided to close out the session by bench-pressing an embarrassingly light weight. I went first and started out with ease. One . . . two . . . three . . . four . . . sixteen . . . seventeen . . . still relatively easy, no sweat.

After about twenty-five reps, I hit the wall. Suddenly it felt like I was trying to bench press four hundred pounds instead of forty. Paco, doing his job, cheered me on, "Come on, Groesch! Don't quit! Get ten more! You can do it! It's all you, man!"

Then he started counting off the final ten, spotting me carefully. "One . . . you got this. Two . . . Don't quit. Three . . . keep going." And that's when I gave in and let go of the bar. And shockingly it kept moving. Paco kept lifting the bar up and down for me, not even noticing I'd stopped lifting. My spotter was doing all the work! When I reached the end of my strength, he took over.

God is way better than my workout partner. When we are weak and at our end, he sustains us. His strength is made perfect in our weakness.

• • • • • • • • • • • • • **Power Lift** • • • • • • • • • • • •

Lord, sometimes I feel like I can't keep going and don't know how I'll make it through my day. Thank you for "spotting" me at those times and filling me with your power.

> One thing I ask from the Lord, this only do I seek: that I may dwell
> in the house of the Lord all the days of my life, to gaze on the
> beauty of the Lord and to seek him in his temple. (Ps. 27:4)

One of the secrets of growth is something I call "consistent variety." To get better at anything, we must be consistent. Successful people do consistently what normal people do only occasionally.

If you want to get closer to God, consistently seek him. If you want to get healthy, consistently eat right. If you want to see your marriage improve, consistently treat your spouse with respect. Consistency matters. But so does variety.

For example, if you go to the gym consistently but only do the same exercises, your muscles will get used to it and your improvement will quickly diminish. It's important to work out regularly, but you also have to change your workouts.

The same is true in your relationships. You will want to encourage those you love. But if you just say the same thing again and again, it won't mean as much. We must find creative ways to encourage and show our love.

When seeking God, we should pursue him daily. But don't just pray the same thing. Or even read the Bible in the same way. Consider praying in a different place. Read a different version of the Bible. Worship if you normally don't or find some new music that draws you to God.

To grow spiritually, make sure you consistently seek Christ, but mix it up. Today stretch your spiritual muscles and experience him in a fresh new way.

Power Lift

Forgive me, God, when I get stuck in a rut and keep approaching you the same way over and over again. Surprise me today with new ways of experiencing you.

"If you are faithful in little things, you will be faithful in large
ones. But if you are dishonest in little things, you won't be
honest with greater responsibilities." (Luke 16:10 NLT)

Over the years, since our church meets in many places, we've built dozens of different facilities. I distinctly remember building the first one. It was a 30,000-square-foot building that would seat about 600 people in one service. This was more than four times the size of the space we had been meeting in. I couldn't wait to move into a gigantic building.

When the builders finally poured the foundation, I was so excited to walk the property. But when I arrived, I was crushed. It looked ridiculously tiny. Did they make a mistake? Where was the rest of the building? This couldn't be it.

Then with each step in the building process, the facility that looked so small seemed to magically grow. Once they framed it in, it looked a bit better. Then when walls started to go up, it seemed to grow again. And when we finally put furniture into the finished space, what had seemed so small was transformed into a nice, big, incredible facility.

If you are laying a foundation toward a better life, don't be discouraged. What seems small today can grow into something significant in the future. Stay faithful today and watch as God does more over time than you can imagine.

· · · · · · · · · · **Power Lift** · · · · · · · · · ·

I want to be faithful in the small things, Lord, trusting you to give me more opportunities and responsibilities as I grow stronger.

And God is able to bless you abundantly, so that in all things at all times, having all that you need, you will abound in every good work. (2 Cor. 9:8)

One day my son came into my office at home while I was trying to hang a framed picture someone had just given me. Rather than go to the garage to get a hammer, I had taken off my shoe and was trying to drive the nail with it. "Hey, buddy," I said. "What's up?"

"I just heard you pounding on the wall and thought you needed help," he said.

I nodded and said, "Thanks, but I'm good. Just trying to hang this picture." In the meantime, I dropped the nail because my running shoe was not providing enough force and resistance to drive it into the wall.

"Here, try this," my son said, taking off his boot and handing it to me. I tried to use the heel of his boot, which was smaller and harder than my shoe, to drive in the nail. Still didn't work. As I looked around my office for something else to use—stapler? bowling trophy? paperweight my daughter made me?—my wife walked in, smiled at us both, and without saying a word, handed me a hammer.

Needless to say, the right tool at the right time makes a huge difference. God sometimes wants us to be creative and improvise. But sometimes the right tool is there in front of us, just waiting for us to use it.

Today you're equipped with the right tools to complete whatever God is building in your life.

• • • • • • • • • • **Power Lift** • • • • • • • • • •

You provide all I need, Lord. Thank you for your resources and the abundance of blessings you give me each day.

> You need to persevere so that when you have done the will of
> God, you will receive what he has promised. (Heb. 10:36)

For years our family has gone to the lake with close friends. About a half mile from the house, there is what must be one of the steepest climbs in Oklahoma. This road has an incline that feels as steep as the highest level on the treadmill at the gym.

Every time we get about half an hour into the climb, several walkers always begin to talk about quitting. Every step is painful. Looking up, it seems like we will never reach the top. Step after step, the climb feels impossible to finish.

About that time, inevitably someone turns around and looks back. Wow! Every time it's shocking just how far we've already come. The view is always stunning, and it's always worth it. The progress we've made renews our passion to finish. There may be a long way to go, but we've come so far.

If you have been working at something for a long time and don't feel like you will ever hit your goal, take a moment and pause. Look back. You might have traveled farther than you thought. Take note of all that God has already done. Embrace all the progress you've made. And celebrate that God isn't finished with you yet!

. . . . **Power Lift** . . . .

When my day gets steep, Lord, and I want to give up, thank you for giving me a second wind and the power to keep going.

But for that very reason I was shown mercy so that in me, the worst of sinners, Christ Jesus might display his immense patience as an example for those who would believe in him and receive eternal life. (1 Tim. 1:16)

Years ago a mentor told me something that I've never forgotten. I was in my midtwenties at the time, disappointed that I wasn't doing "more" and "bigger" things. I had big dreams but was still doing small things.

That's when my wise friend told me, "You will very likely overestimate what you can do in the short run. But you will vastly underestimate what God will do through a lifetime of faithfulness." I've come back to the wisdom of his words many times.

Maybe you feel discouraged right now. You would like to do more. Be more. Have more. Maybe the words of my mentor might encourage you.

It's so easy to be disappointed with where we are in life. But God is still working on you. If you are not where you want to be or doing what you want to do, be encouraged. You really don't have any idea what God can do when you keep showing up and doing what's right. God loves when his kids are faithful. When you are faithful with a little, God will bless you with more.

Stay in the game. Do what you know God wants you to do. Don't give up. Do everything with excellence. Work as if you are working unto the Lord. And over time, God will reward your faithfulness. One day you will be shocked at what God has done through a lifetime of your faithfulness.

· · · · · · · · · · · · **Power Lift** · · · · · · · · · · · ·

I get discouraged, God, when I don't see the kind of spiritual growth I want in my life. Please give me patience today and help me to remain faithful with all that you have given me.

For in this hope we were saved. But hope that is seen is no hope at all. Who hopes for what they already have? But if we hope for what we do not yet have, we wait for it patiently. (Rom. 8:24–25)

Sometimes life can be so discouraging. You have a clear vision of where you would like to be, but you can't seem to get there. You know who you would love to become, but the journey just doesn't seem possible.

Whenever I feel overwhelmed, I try to remind myself simply to do one thing that will move me toward the goal. Just one thing.

Think about it. Can you run a marathon today? Probably not. But can you walk a mile today? Sure. If you can walk a mile today, then you might be able to walk two tomorrow. Before long, you are growing in endurance. Within months you may be running five or ten miles a day, and the journey toward a marathon is on its way.

The same is true with your weight. Can you lose twenty pounds by Friday? It's not likely. But can you say no to dessert? Of course. Can you exercise three times this week? Yes—if you put your mind to it. Can you do little things each day that will help you shed the pounds over time? No doubt about it.

If there is something you hope to accomplish, tell yourself, "I will do the things today that will enable me to do tomorrow what I can't do today." God will help you achieve your goal. One step at a time.

Power Lift

I'm overwhelmed sometimes, Lord, and feel like I'll never reach my goals. Today I know you will encourage me and give me the strength to take my next step.

The Lord will fulfill his purpose for me; your steadfast love, O Lord,
endures forever. Do not forsake the work of your hands. (Ps. 138:8 ESV)

Because I travel frequently, I get to see most of the major cities in our
country. No matter how successful or dynamic a city's downtown area
may be, I almost always see at least a few buildings that have clearly
been abandoned. Their glass windows stare back at me like vacant eyes,
looking down upon the graffiti and trash continually accumulating
around their foundations.

Many of these sites aren't even that old. I can tell that only a few
years ago these monoliths were the pride and joy of some new builder,
business owner, or company. For whatever reason, though, they now
sit empty and abandoned.

Inner-city office buildings aren't the only things that people vacate
and leave behind. It might be our families, our jobs, our pasts that we've
tried to move away from, often for good reasons. Nonetheless, those
vacancies echo inside us as the emotional scars remain.

The good news is that God not only heals our wounds, but he will
never abandon us. He has promised to be with us always. He's not going
to suddenly leave us in the lurch, orphaned and alone. He's our Father,
and he loves us, pursues us, and cares for us.

• • • • • • • • • • **Power Lift** • • • • • • • • • • • •

Thank you, Father, for promising never to abandon me. Your love provides the
foundation of security I need today to face anything that's ahead.

> Do not let the sun go down while you are still angry, and
> do not give the devil a foothold. (Eph. 4:26–27)

I hate painting our house. And even more, I hate the fact that it has to be painted again and again every few years. We don't always get a lot of snow in Oklahoma where I live, but we get plenty of rain, wind, hail, and sleet. The weather chips away at my beautiful paint job, wearing away the layer of protection it provides for the layers beneath. And when it's not bad weather stripping it away, the sun is beating down on it and fading away the color.

Anger has that kind of friction on our faith. Just as Jesus became angry and did not sin, we're called to express righteous anger appropriately. But so much of my anger isn't righteous—and I don't always express it appropriately. Instead I want to yell at the guy who tweeted the snarky comment about our church, or I want to bump the little sports car that just took my parking spot at the mall.

But that's not very Christlike.

So I try to practice patience and compassion and let go of my anger. Because if I don't, I know it will strip away my faith, one layer at a time, leaving me cold and vulnerable to the Enemy's weapons. I don't want to give the Enemy an opportunity to pour gasoline on my temper.

When you feel the anger rising inside of you, how do you usually handle it? Are you giving the devil a foothold? Or are you using your anger as a way to draw closer to God and depend on him?

Power Lift

There are so many things that get my blood boiling, Lord. Give me your patience and strength to remain focused on you and your peace.

Walk with the wise and become wise, for a companion
of fools suffers harm. (Prov. 13:20)

Someone said, "Show me your friends and you'll show me your future."
This important truth draws on biblical wisdom, and I'm sure you've seen
it in your life too. From past adventures I've shared in previous entries,
you'll recall that friends of mine like Steven (his dad had the *Playboys*)
and Stan (my accomplice in the debacle known as The Great Running
Shorts Heist) weren't doing me any favors. And believe me, there were
numerous others, such as frat brothers and tennis teammates from college, who weren't concerned in the least about my relationship with God.

Today, though, one concern about our friendships is summed up
by a recent conversation I had with a college-aged woman from our
church. She said, "I have over 700 Facebook friends, over 500 people
who regularly check my daily pics on Instagram, and almost 1,000
who follow me on Twitter. And yet I don't have anyone to grab coffee
or go shopping with me. Despite how many people I know online, I'm,
well, really lonely."

From my experience, when I'm lonely, I'm more susceptible to
temptation. For example, I'm more likely to feel sorry for myself and
justify eating donuts and not working out. But I don't always realize
that's what I'm feeling until it's too late. After all, with all this constant
connectivity, how could I be lonely?

Show me your friends—your real friends, not just virtual—and
you'll show me your future.

• • • • • • • • • • • **Power Lift** • • • • • • • • • • •

Lord, I do feel lonely sometimes and know that I need to build deeper friendships
with people who love and seek you as much as I do. Today point me toward
someone I can befriend.

The godly give good advice to their friends; the
wicked lead them astray. (Prov. 12:26 NLT)

What do you do when you realize you're feeling lonely? Most of us text
a friend, post an update, retweet a favorite line, or share an old favorite
photo. If we're feeling really creative, we'll surf for items to pin to our
page on Pinterest or make a new YouTube video. We might take a picture of our homemade chocolate chip cookies and share on Snapchat.
Or edit some video footage for a meme to post on Vine.

Then when several of our friends (or several dozen, or several hundred) respond with their approval, their comments, their adoration of
that cute picture of how we dressed up the cat, we feel better about ourselves. The only problem is we're still lonely. We've only been distracted
for a moment by all the online affirmation.

Sociologists call this addiction to instant affirmation "deferred
loneliness." We're trying to meet some short-term need, but in the process, we're deferring some deeper, longer-term need. But the tradeoff
is that we're deferring our longing for intimacy. We keep pushing that
feeling of loneliness into the future, putting off dealing with the root
of our problem. Our addiction to instant gratification is changing how
we frame our relationships.

We're living for likes, but we're longing for love. Thankfully, God
has something so much better for us. Reach out and show his love today.
When you give it, you'll be even more likely to receive it back.

. . . . **Power Lift** . . . .

Dear God, I know I need friends in my life, trustworthy believers who love me
enough both to encourage me and to challenge me. Today help me be that kind
of friend to others.

"For where two or three gather in my name, there am I with them." (Matt. 18:20)

When you're in a large worship service with hundreds or even thousands of other people, it can feel wonderful to be a part of something bigger than yourself. But it's also easy to be invisible, to shake hands with a few greeters, smile at the ushers, and leave without having had any meaningful connection with other human beings.

This is why we urge everyone in our church to be committed to a small group with whom they can do life. It's not only for the support and fellowship but also for their spiritual growth and development. If you really want to build a deeper faith as well as richer relationships, then sharing life in a community of other Christ-followers is fundamental.

Why? Because the Bible promises us that whenever we come together with other believers in the name of Jesus, we will experience the very real presence of Christ in a supernatural way. Does that mean you can't experience his presence when you're alone? Absolutely not! You can. It's just that there's something more, something special, something powerful that happens when we come together with other believers to seek God.

When you join hands with someone, when you join your faith together, and you go before God on his throne, you experience the power and presence of God together in a very real way (Heb. 4:14–16). Something powerful happens when we join together with other believers and we lift up holy hands before our God to worship him (Ps. 22:3).

Something heavenly happens when we join with other believers, open up God's Word, and, as believers have done for centuries, read his Word aloud together.

There is power in presence.

· · · · · · · · · · · **Power Lift** · · · · · · · · · · ·

Today I pray that you would direct me to the right group of people with whom I can share my life, my faith, and my heart.

Since we live by the Spirit, let us keep in step with the Spirit. (Gal. 5:25)

For years my wife has walked behind me. Not because I want her to or asked her to but simply because my legs are longer than hers. We'll be walking along, talking, and then after a bit she'll drift a half-step behind me, and I assume she's slowing down to help one of our kids if they're with us or to catch her breath. By the time I notice she's not there anymore, I'm a considerable distance away.

I've learned to slow down and to be more deliberate about walking alongside her. Maybe you've had this problem with your spouse or another friend. If you've ever had a running buddy or a group you go hiking with, you know it can be tough to find a pace that fits everyone's body size and fitness level. But it's definitely more fun and more relational (and my wife might say more respectful) to keep stride with the people you care most about. After all, that's the whole point of going someplace together, right?

Fortunately, God's Spirit allows us to catch up to him when we fall behind, stumble and grumble, or lose our focus. We can relax knowing that God waits on us and allows us to get in sync with his timing.

Today stay in step with God, trusting him for your relational rhythm.

· · · · · · · · · · · **Power Lift** · · · · · · · · · · ·

Lord, help me keep pace with you today, not rushing ahead or lingering behind. Thank you for staying with me each step of the way.

"Enter through the narrow gate. For wide is the gate and broad is the road that leads to destruction, and many enter through it. But small is the gate and narrow the road that leads to life, and only a few find it." (Matt 7:13–14)

The first time I remember encountering today's passage, I was leading a Bible study for a group of guys in my fraternity. You may recall that I started this group as a PR move to change our bad-boy reputation. You know, sort of the thought that if a fraternity is hosting a Bible study, they can't be all bad. The only problem was that I was not yet a Christian!

So when I came to this statement by Jesus, I hit a major wall. What in the world did he mean? It sure sounded like he was saying that the majority of people will go with the flow and take the route everyone else is taking, even though it leads to destruction. However, his followers aren't like everybody else. They will take a more challenging passage through the narrow gate. And waiting for them on the other side is new life.

Jesus' words shook me up, planting seeds that later led to my getting on my knees on a campus softball field and inviting him into my heart as the Lord of my life. But I've never forgotten the wonder, fear, and longing I felt when I first considered what it means to follow Christ and enter through the narrow gate.

What direction are you traveling right now? Are you on the twelve-lane interstate to destruction? Or on the narrow path toward God?

Power Lift

I'm committed to following you, Lord, even when I don't always understand where you're taking me or how I'll get there. Today I want to follow you through that narrow gate that leads to new life.

"I have loved you with an everlasting love." (Jer. 31:3)

It's hard to make sense of all the tragic events unfolding in our nation and world today. When others seem motivated by hatred, greed, and prejudice to the point where they're consumed by violence and evil, it's difficult to know how to respond. In light of natural disasters and life-ending tragedies, people often ask me, "Why would God allow such suffering and devastation to take place? How could this be part of his plan? How can I trust him when he lets things like this happen?"

Because I'm a pastor, people expect me to have answers that make sense or feel right, but my responses might not be what they want to hear. The simple answer is that God gives us the power to choose how we live our lives. It has been this way since creation, when Adam and Eve exercised their gift of free will by disobeying God and choosing their own way. Ever since, we've been living in a world filled with the consequences of sinful choices and willful disobedience.

If left unchecked, our selfishness becomes a cancer. It's only through the grace of God and the power of Christ that we can be transformed. Our lives on this side of heaven will always include pain and suffering. But God loves us so much that he sacrificed his Son in order to provide the cure for our sinful condition.

• • • • • • • • • • • • **Power Lift** • • • • • • • • • • • •

So often, Lord, I can't understand the suffering taking place in the world today. Yet I know that you're in control and that your love is truly everlasting. I will trust in you.

> "I know that my redeemer lives, and that in the end
> he will stand on the earth." (Job 19:25)

My wife and I often remember our wedding anniversaries in different ways. What I recall as an awesome, romantic time to celebrate how long we've been together, she sees as a milestone of God's faithfulness in keeping us together another year. We do agree, however, that anniversaries are important times of remembrance.

"We remember" is also a phrase I see frequently with pictures posted by people on the anniversary of 9/11 or on 4/19 here in Oklahoma. It's a way to honor those loved ones we lost, the first responders who served fearlessly, and those who gave to help rebuild. Many are tempted to focus on remembering the negative—the senseless violence of such attacks.

But others, with a different filter, are able to find the good in their memories of those events. They recall the selfless sacrifices made by numerous men and women, the unity and faith of our nation, and the generosity of support and resources to facilitate healing.

From my experience, how you remember something usually depends on what you believe about God. While we're tempted to allow our fear, confusion, and anger to consume us, if we focus on God's sovereignty, then we know that there's more than what we experienced or what we remember. Our God redeems even our greatest losses and most painful disappointments.

Power Lift

Thank you, Lord, for the way you transform the trials in my life into your trophies. Even though I can't always understand, I know that you are at work for my good.

Come and see the works of God, Who is awesome in His deeds toward
the sons of men. He turned the sea into dry land; they passed through
the river on foot; There let us rejoice in Him! (Ps. 66:5–6 NASB)

Over a quarter of a century ago, Amy and I returned early from our honeymoon. We had planned a full seven-day trip to San Antonio. However, when we ran out of money on day five, we simply got in our car and drove home. Even though it was shorter than we hoped, it was still more than we could have dreamed.

Unfortunately, our dream melted when we arrived home. On a 100-plus-degree day, we arrived at our house to discover the air conditioning was not working. With no money to fix it until payday, we felt desperate and cornered, not to mention sweaty and hot. That's when Amy asked me if I thought I should pray for our AC.

Pray? For an *air conditioner*? Well, with no money and no better options, I decided it was worth a try.

To this day, I remember looking over my shoulder to make sure no neighbors were watching when I laid hands on our broken window unit. In the Bible we're told in James to "lay hands on the sick," so this seemed reasonable to me.

In the middle of the prayer—I'm not kidding—the AC suddenly clicked on and cool air shot out the vents! We were almost too shocked to remember to thank God, which I know was a big problem with the people of Israel. It only took them three days to start grumbling after God parted the Red Sea and delivered them from slavery in Egypt.

Don't forget to remember what God has done for you.

. . . . **Power Lift** . . . .

Lord, I never want to forget your faithfulness and goodness. Thank you for the times you have provided, healed, and blessed my life.

The memory of the righteous is blessed, But the name
of the wicked will rot. (Prov. 10:7 NASB)

When I was in the fourth grade, I had a crush on my older neighbor, Missy. Every time she came over to the house, my heart would beat faster, I'd try to stand a bit taller, and I'd do my best not to say something stupid and embarrassing.

So you can only imagine the horror I felt when she picked up my dad's athletic cup that he'd left lying out after his big softball game the night before. If you aren't familiar with sports protective gear, a "cup" is a triangular piece of plastic that fits around a guy's . . . well, you can figure it out. It's also got small holes situated evenly apart, likely to "let things breathe." I guess you could say it looks a bit like an oxygen mask. And unfortunately, that's exactly what Missy thought when she innocently picked it up.

"What's this?" she asked. Then it dawned on her, or so she thought. "Oh, I know what this is!" she said enthusiastically, raising the cup rapidly toward her nose.

N-o-o-o-o-o! Time stood still. There was nothing I could do to stop it from happening.

She inhaled deeply and exhaled completely into my dad's cup. Then she put it down and continued in small-talk conversation. Obviously, I never told her what happened.

When I remember that moment, I can only conclude that if you don't know the purpose of a thing, all you can do is misuse it. Always remember, you exist to glorify God. In whatever you do today, do it for his glory.

Power Lift

Today I will remember that I'm created in your image, God, and created for your glory.

> For we are God's handiwork, created in Christ Jesus to do good works, which God prepared in advance for us to do. (Eph. 2:10)

I've seen a bumper sticker on several cars that makes me chuckle every time. It simply says, "God don't make no junk!" (Ironically, it seems like every time I see this bumper sticker, it's *always* on an old clunker.) But it's true: when you're in Christ, God don't make no junk!

You are the masterpiece of God, created for the Master's purpose. The reason it's important for you to believe this is because when you know who you are, you'll know what to do. Otherwise, you might be tempted to accept the labels others stick on you and settle for much less.

You are special in Christ, the Master's creation, created for the Master's purpose. The Greek word translated as "masterpiece" here in Ephesians 2:10 is *poiema* (POY-ay-muh). To be "God's *poiema*" literally means to be "a work made by God." Because we derive our English word "poem" from this word, I like to think of us as his beautiful poems.

In Christ, your life should be a poetic statement of God's glory. The master artisan designs each of our lives to join and interlock to create a big picture, a giant living tapestry, woven of people. Sometimes, from where you're standing, you might not be able to see where you fit. But if you can take a step back and look at it from his perspective, you can see the overall masterpiece, the perfect workmanship of God.

Power Lift

God, help me to remember that I'm your masterpiece, as unique and beautiful as a poem. I am not who others say I am but who you say I am. My identity rests in you.

You are not your own; you were bought at a price. (1 Cor. 6:19–20)

When my wife, Amy, was a teenager, her dad told her the same phrase again and again. Before going out on the weekends with friends, Amy's dad knew there would be plenty of opportunities to do the wrong things. So before she would leave the house, her wise dad would always say, "Remember who you are."

Amy's dad knew that Amy had a strong faith in Christ. Because of what Christ did for Amy, her life was not her own. She belonged to Christ. He was hers. And she was his.

So many voices try to tell us otherwise. *You aren't worthy. You are a failure. You are pathetic.*

Whenever you find yourself battling against any kind of temptation, remember who you are. You are a child of God. You were purchased with the blood of Jesus. You are not your own. You belong to him.

Because you are his, he will never leave you. You will never be alone. God is for you. God's spirit dwells within you. Christ's power is available to you.

Don't let anyone or anything steal your true identity in Christ.

Remember who you are.

Remember *whose* you are.

• • • • • • • • • • **Power Lift** • • • • • • • • • •

Jesus, I know you've defeated the power of sin in my life once and for all. I'm a new creation and am becoming more like you every day. When I'm tempted to slip back into sinful habits, remind me who I am in you.

> No, in all these things we are more than conquerors
> through him who loved us. (Rom 8:37)

Today I played my thirteen-year-old son, Stephen, in checkers. Before I tell you how the game ended, you need to know that Stephen is two grades ahead in math, and that's because it's as far ahead as experts agree is wise to allow him to go. In other words, he's crazy smart.

Several moves into the game, I made a mistake. Just one, but it was crucial. Stephen pounced on my misstep and that was all she wrote. Although I put up the best fight I had, I never stood a chance. By the end of the game, I had only jumped him once as he beamed at me. I wouldn't want him to know, but to say he crushed me would be an understatement.

Sometimes in life it feels like we are being trampled by our Enemy. But the truth is, with Christ, we are "more than conquerors." This three-word, power-packed phrase comes from the Greek word *hupernikao*. This word means to vanquish beyond recognition, to gain a decisive victory. It means exceedingly more than to conquer. It's like David defeating Goliath. It's like Gideon besting the Midianites. It's like Jesus conquering the devil. And yes, it's like what Stephen did to me in checkers.

If you are facing something that is more than you can handle, remember, you are not alone. With Christ, you are more than a conqueror.

. . . . **Power Lift** . . . .

Even when I feel defeated and discouraged, Lord, I know that my victory remains strong in you.

> We demolish arguments and every pretension that sets itself
> up against the knowledge of God. (2 Cor. 10:5)

It's way too easy to live with a victim mindset. I know because I've been there. When our church was about eleven years old, we seemed to hit a massive wall. Whatever we tried, we couldn't seem to make any real spiritual progress.

Before long, I honestly felt like I had lost the church that I loved. Instead of leading with faith, I led with fear. I was consumed with the fear that our best days were behind us.

If you are honest, you might occasionally (or often) recognize victim thinking in your own life. It's easy to recognize because it usually starts with "I can't," "I won't," "I always," "I never."

You know how it goes. I can't lose weight. I'm always depressed. I just can't change. I always struggle financially. I just can't get ahead.

The story I told myself during the tough season at church was, "I just don't have what it takes to make the changes." Thankfully, God got ahold of me. With his help, I realized that I was telling myself a lie. He was with me. He would empower me. He would help me lead the church to where he wanted it to be.

Remember, you are more than a conqueror. So fight with a conquering attitude. Believe Jesus will help you change. Empower you to overcome. Give you the strength to win the battle.

Faith-filled attitudes lead to faith-filled actions. Godly beliefs lead to godly behavior. You are not a victim. With Christ, you are a victor.

Power Lift

I am not a victim of my circumstances, Lord, but a victor through the power of Christ. Today help me live like a child of the King.

"Truly I tell you, if you have faith as small as a mustard seed, you can say to this mountain, 'Move from here to there,' and it will move. Nothing will be impossible for you." (Matt. 17:20)

When the car breaks down, the kids need school clothes, and your boss demands more overtime without additional pay, it's easy to struggle in our faith. Before long, we replay old and unproductive messages in our minds: *You'll never have all you need. You aren't good enough. You don't have what it takes. God doesn't hear your prayer. God doesn't really care about you.*

If you feel like your faith is fading, don't freak out. Remember, Jesus said if you just have the faith of a mustard seed—think of how small that is, like a grain of sand—you can move a mountain. Surely it's no coincidence that the mustard seed is one of the smallest seeds, probably the smallest known during the first century.

Jesus must have known that we would often feel that our faith is stretched to the breaking point. Sometimes I'm like the man in Scripture who said, "I do believe, but help me overcome my unbelief!" (Mark 9:24 NLT).

If you are praying for a miracle, even one that feels small or unimportant to anyone else (remember that AC I told you about?), then keep the faith. If you are praying for someone to be saved, continue believing. If you are trusting God to restore your marriage, don't stop. If you are begging God to help you change, wake up every day and continue to seek him.

Don't forget, it's not the size of your faith that matters.

It's the size of your God.

And with him, all things are possible.

• • • • • • • • • • • **Power Lift** • • • • • • • • • • •

Lord, I want to focus on the way you can do anything. Despite whatever obstacles I encounter today, I will believe and trust in you.

For we live by faith, not by sight. (2 Cor. 5:7)

A few weeks ago, I told you about one of the toughest seasons in my life. When I was in my midtwenties, I was rejected for ordination as a pastor. My first time before the board of overseers, they explained that my ideas were too radical, my approach too unorthodox, and my passion was simply "over the top." So instead of ordaining me with my class of peers, they put me on a one-year probation. After another year of seminary, they would re-evaluate my potential to become an ordained pastor.

I distinctly remember driving home, sobbing in my little red Geo Prism. Now, there is crying and there is ugly crying. I was unquestionably in ugly-snot-flinging-barely-breathing-ugly-crying mode. I felt like my whole life, everything I had lived for, was being stripped from me.

That's when I sensed the unmistakable presence of God. In that moment, I heard the words inside my heart, "You are not who others say you are. You are who I say you are. And I say you are called to serve me in ministry." And that was all I needed. People's opinions didn't matter. God's assurance was all I needed.

Whenever you feel down or discouraged, remember, you are not who others say you are. You are not even what you think you are. You are who God says you are.

And he says you belong to him.

You have his Spirit.

And you can do whatever he calls you to do by his power.

Power Lift

When others doubt me, God, it hurts, and sometimes I want to give up. But then I remember all that you have done for me and what you have called me to do. I am yours—use me, Lord, no matter what anyone else may say.

> And we know that in all things God works for the good of those who love
> him, who have been called according to his purpose. (Rom. 8:28)

Even as you are reading these words on this very page, God is shaping you.

You may not see it, you may not understand it, you may not be able to imagine how what you're going through could be redeemed.

But it can.

What does this verse promise us? In how many things? *All things!* Does all things include the good things? Yes! Does all things include the bad things? Yes! Does all things include things you are glad happened? Yes! Does all things include things you wish had never happened? Yes! In *all things*, God works for the good.

So here's another question: Does this verse apply to everybody? Actually, no. This verse makes it really clear that God works in all things to bring about good *for those who love him*, and *who have been called according to his purpose.*

The good news is, you love him. I know you do or you wouldn't be reading a devotion all the way to August tenth!

Because you are in Christ, you are a masterpiece created for the Master's purpose. He is the Potter. You are the clay. He's working all things for your good. Whatever you are going through today, thank God that he already knew it would happen and that he will use it to shape you into who he wants you to become.

Nothing is wasted with God.

Power Lift

I love you, Lord, and I will serve you even when I experience life's losses and daily disappointments.

Remember the wonders he has done, his miracles, and
the judgments he pronounced. (1 Chron. 16:12)

Unfortunately, God doesn't always do exactly what we hope he will do, does he? For every miraculous air-conditioning miracle, I know as many or more stories of prayers that seem to go unanswered.

Even as I'm writing this, I still pray every day for my daughter's knee. Almost three years ago, she went to find one of her siblings in class at church and she slipped on a wet floor. This simple accident caused more pain and heartache than we could have ever predicted.

My once passionate dancer suddenly had to stop pursuing her dream—without knowing if it will ever return. After consulting with the best doctors, trying surgery and the latest treatments, spending countless hours and dollars in physical therapy, and praying more prayers than a Cubs fan, Anna still has pain in her knee.

Seemingly unanswered prayers might make you somewhat unsure of God's presence, his power, or his involvement. But just because you don't see him doesn't mean that he's not there. Just because he doesn't do what you want doesn't mean that he doesn't care. And just because you don't understand the plan doesn't mean that God doesn't have a purpose.

If you are facing something you don't understand, choose to trust God. Remember all he has done for you. His ways are higher than our ways. And he is always good.

Power Lift

Dear God, some things in my life just don't make sense right now. But I trust you and know your heart. You are a good God and all good things come from you.

> "My grace is sufficient for you, for my power is made perfect in weakness." Therefore I will boast all the more gladly about my weaknesses, so that Christ's power may rest on me. (2 Cor. 12:9)

The apostle Paul was as faithful to God as anyone I've ever read about or known. He was imprisoned again and again for his bold preaching about Christ. He was stoned for loving Jesus (and I'm not talking about the recreational kind). He was shipwrecked, bitten by snakes, beaten and left for dead—all because of his unwavering obedience to Christ.

This guy wrote a huge portion of the New Testament, started churches everywhere he went, and had heavenly visions. So when Paul prayed, you would think God would do about anything for him. We actually see one time when the opposite is true.

Paul begged God again and again to remove a thorn from him. We are not sure what this thorn was. Some experts guess it was an eye problem, arthritis, headaches, depression, or spiritual opposition. Although we don't exactly know what the "thorn" was, we do know God said no.

Instead of simply answering this prayer, God had another plan. God was going to teach Paul that his grace was enough. God's presence was sufficient for Paul.

Prayer isn't just asking God to do what we want him to do. It's also knowing him.

Ultimately, prayer reminds us that we are not in control and keeps us close to the one who is.

Power Lift

I don't understand your ways all the time, Lord, especially when my prayers seem to go unanswered. Help me to be as patient and accepting as Paul so that Christ's power may rest on me too.

> "For I know the plans I have for you," declares the Lord, "plans to prosper you and not to harm you, plans to give you hope and a future." (Jer. 29:11)

In the early years of our church, we were blessed to see tremendous growth. After finally constructing our first real church building, it wasn't long before it was packed to capacity with multiple services.

While that is what most would call a "good problem," it was still a problem. Week after week, we consistently turned people away, unable to fit them into the building. With as much faith as I could muster, I asked God to provide. Surely he would speak to multiple wealthy people who could give enough to help us build something bigger.

But the more we prayed, the more we sensed God wasn't going to do what we were asking him to do. It was only after this sense of disappointment that God answered our prayers in a very different way. Once I finally started to surrender my will, our team had an idea. *What if, instead of doing church at one building, we did church in two locations?*

This idea opened the door to enable us to reach tens of thousands of more people than I ever dreamed possible. What seemed like a no from God was more of a redirecting from him. That's when I learned that true prayer isn't about getting our will, but surrendering our will.

Whatever you are facing, don't be afraid to ask for what you want. But don't forget to remind yourself that our good God knows best.

Power Lift

Dear Father, you really do know best, and even when it might not be what I asked for, I will trust in you and your perfect will.

If we confess our sins, he is faithful and just and will forgive us
our sins and purify us from all unrighteousness. (1 John 1:9)

When I was a senior in high school, my buddy Jimmy quietly signaled me during a test. "Psssst, Craig," he whispered. Then when the teacher wasn't looking, he passed me a note.

Mild panic set in. Jimmy wanted my "help" on our test, to put it nicely. The truth is he wanted me to *cheat*. While I certainly didn't want to do the wrong thing, mostly out of fear of getting caught. I also didn't want to let down my close buddy.

So without seriously contemplating the potential negative consequences, I robotically gave him the answers he needed. When the teacher's back was turned, I handed the sheet back to him. Unfortunately, our handoff wasn't quick enough.

Jimmy fumbled the paper and dropped it between our rows the exact moment the teacher turned around. We were busted red-handed.

Within the hour, both my mom and dad were with me in the principal's office. While they agreed with the school's punishment, they didn't yell at me or require extra discipline. When I acknowledged my sin completely, without any excuse, and asked for their forgiveness, I was shocked when they said, "You are forgiven."

That was it. No questions. No qualifications. No lecture. And they never mentioned it again. In that moment, I think I got a glimpse into what our God is like. When he forgives, he forgives freely, fully, and permanently.

You are forgiven when you confess your sins to God. Remember that.

Power Lift

It's tough, Lord, to get through the day without recognizing I blew it somewhere along the way. Thank you for your grace and mercy. Thank you that I am forgiven.

You, God, are my God, earnestly I seek you; I thirst for you, my whole being longs for you, in a dry and parched land where there is no water. (Ps. 63:1)

They call them the "dog days" of summer, those weeks when the temperatures soar and make it impossible to enjoy being outside for long. The air scorches our nostrils, the heat burns our skin, and the pavement sizzles beneath our feet. You know cooler weather will come eventually, but in the meantime, you're sweating buckets.

Sometimes our spiritual lives feel this way, dry and desolate, without any rain from heaven in sight. We feel alone and rejected, misunderstood and isolated. We feel afraid and wonder how we got to this place—and how long it will last.

I didn't think my life was going to turn out like this, we lament. *I didn't think I'd be at this place in my life right now. I feel stuck and unable to move forward. Everyone around me seems to be enjoying their lives, but I don't know how I'll ever experience God's joy and peace again. My heart is like a parched desert.*

You want to talk to someone, but you're not sure who will understand. While talking to other believers can be encouraging, only God can provide you with the Living Water your soul craves. Nothing else will satisfy you.

Cry out to God when your soul feels dry. He will refresh you and satisfy the deep longing within.

Power Lift

God, I don't even know what to pray when I start feeling dry and stuck in a rut. Meet me where I am today, Lord. Refresh my spirit and revive my faith.

"Anyone who wants to be first must be the very
last, and the servant of all." (Mark 9:35)

Like a lot of people, I can be really competitive. Sometimes my wife tells me it's a "guy thing," but I believe we all want to do our best and finish first. We want to know how we're doing compared to our peers, partly so we can set new goals and strive even harder for future growth.

Each year, various sources compile lists of the most influential, the wealthiest, and the most admired. Even within Christian circles, it's hard to escape the comparison mindset and ask someone, "How big is your church?"

There's an annual list of the biggest and fastest-growing churches in America each year, but I realized early in my ministry that I shouldn't participate. Because if our church was included, then I would think, "Man, I can't believe that church over there is number eight—I know we're bigger than they are. And that number-one church better get ready to move aside—we're closing in." These lists aren't bad. For me, though, they lead into temptation to become prideful, boastful, and focused on numbers instead of changed lives.

Jesus' example reminds us that being first is all about being last and putting others before ourselves. In our competitive, selfie-obsessed world, it's not easy to adopt a servant mindset. But it's the only way to become more like Christ and reach others for God's kingdom.

- - - - - - - - - - - **Power Lift** - - - - - - - - - -

Jesus, thank you for demonstrating what it means to put other people before myself. Forgive me when I start comparing and competing and lose sight of your humility and grace. Give me strength to be first by being last.

So David triumphed over the Philistine with a sling and a stone; without a sword in his hand he struck down the Philistine and killed him. (1 Sam. 17:50)

As the father of both daughters and sons, I learned quickly that the movies *Rocky* and Disney's *Cinderella* have more in common than I realized. Both main characters are big-hearted, hard-working, and good-natured, willing to do whatever it takes to achieve their goals even when the odds are overwhelmingly stacked against them. One loses her shoe at the royal ball, and the other loses his teeth in the boxing ring.

But in the end, they both win.

All of us, kids as well as adults, love to see an underdog triumph against adversity and reach their dreams. These heroes give us hope that we can keep fighting and overcome the same kinds of obstacles in our own lives.

One of my favorite underdogs of all time was a young shepherd boy who refused to back down. Faced with a giant bully who was mocking not just David's family and nation, but David's God, this fearless kid wasn't about to run away from a fight. Goliath had already killed many of the Israelites, which only made him more outrageously obnoxious. But David wasn't scared to take on this enemy, despite the difference in their size, age, and experience.

Using his knowledge and skill from protecting his sheep from bears and lions, David refused to use conventional weapons and instead took his slingshot and left the giant face-planted in the ground. You have the same power, faith, and courage available to you through Christ.

Don't forget, just like David, you are a giant-slayer.

· · · · · · · · · · · **Power Lift** · · · · · · · · · ·

Dear God, today help me remember that you give me all I need to overcome the giant obstacles in my life.

I will praise you as long as I live, and in your name
I will lift up my hands. (Ps. 63:4)

When I became a follower of Christ, I was in college, and as I've shared with you, it sort of happened by accident. I had started this Bible study with my frat brothers to improve our image. I had been given a Bible by a man from the Gideons visiting campus. And I had no clue what I was doing. I would close our sessions with, "And God, please protect us as we go out partying this weekend. Keep us safe when we get drunk. Don't let any of our girlfriends get pregnant." Seriously, that was my prayer.

Then one day I was reading the Bible and stumbled across a passage in Ephesians (2:8–9) that flat-out said that we are saved by the grace of God and not by our works. This news hit me like a ton of bricks. Right then, I left my room and went out to an empty softball field, all by myself, knelt down before God and gave him my whole life.

Feeling God's presence, I automatically lifted my hands. Keep in mind, I grew up in a traditional church, where the only time I raised my hand was in Sunday school to ask permission to go to the bathroom. But there on the field, I was so overcome with the joy of the Lord, I had to worship.

Never forget to praise God for how he has saved you from your sins and given you a new life.

Power Lift

Lord, I'm so grateful for how you've saved me from my sins. Today I will praise you throughout the day, remembering your grace and mercy, celebrating your goodness.

"You intended to harm me, but God intended it for good to accomplish what is now being done, the saving of many lives." (Gen. 50:20)

The first time I visited Australia, I couldn't wait to try out an authentic boomerang. Originally a hunting weapon of the indigenous Aboriginal people, boomerangs also became popular as a toy and a souvenir from a trip Down Under. So when I held that L-shaped piece of carved wood in my hand, I was curious to see if it could really be thrown so that it would return back to me. With the help of an expert guide, I saw that boomerang whiz through the air and come back to us.

Others like to call it "karma," but the Bible makes it clear that what we give to others affects what we end up receiving for ourselves. While other people can intend to harm us, God protects us and transforms our suffering into Christ's glory, reversing the outcome expected by those who harmed us. We're never going to enjoy experiencing pain, disappointment, and rejection, but we're comforted knowing that they won't destroy us.

God uses everything—even the devastatingly hard moments—to strengthen, equip, and transform all that comes our way. Even when life throws you a curve ball, you can trust that God will turn it into a boomerang and use it for our good.

Power Lift

I don't always understand certain painful events in my life, Lord, but I know you will use them for my good and for your glory.

When he saw the crowds, he had compassion on them, because they
were harassed and helpless, like sheep without a shepherd. (Matt. 9:36)

You will always have an excuse to justify not getting involved in other
people's lives. When you see someone in need, just get ready for that
conversation in your head because you will always have an excuse. "I
wish I could help, but I'm running late. And I don't know these people.
I've got so much going on already. What if I helped them out today
and they turned out to be super needy? Plus, I just don't have time for
anymore ongoing relationships."

Sound familiar? Yes, we're all so busy with hectic schedules and
lots of demands on our time, energy, and resources. Yes, it's inconvenient and means letting go of our plans and agenda. Yes, it's what Jesus
did over and over again—seeing others in need and loving them, healing them, helping them, listening to them.

The conversation in your head will likely keep playing, but to say
that we care and yet not act is not to care at all. And we are called to
care so deeply that we have to act. Jesus never turned away from anyone who needed him.

Compassion often will interrupt your schedule. So ask yourself,
do you want to be on time to your next appointment? Or do you want
to be more like Jesus?

· · · · · · · · · · · **Power Lift** · · · · · · · · · · · ·

I get so busy, Lord, that I often overlook the people who are hurting around me.
Today give me eyes to see the needs of others instead of focusing on my own
agenda.

Come near to God and he will come near to you. (James 4:8)

I have a confession to make, one that shocked the women in our church: I don't go crazy over babies. I'm not proud of this. I wish it were different, but I prefer to look at them from afar. If I have to look at someone's baby, I've trained myself to smile and say, "Oh, what a baby!" But that's all. I don't want to hold babies, rock babies, or talk baby-talk to babies. They just aren't that cute and interesting to me—and I'm including my own children in that assessment!

But the moment my babies sat up, rolled a ball toward me, or said, "Da-da!" I went crazy, because I love toddlers. They're learning so much so fast, doing the Frankenstein walk as they bump into things, and mimicking every sound they hear. So around toddlers, I'm the biggest bowl of Jell-O you've ever seen.

Knowing how I melt so easily when I see my kids lift their hands toward me to be picked up, I can just imagine the love of our heavenly Father. There's no loving father on earth who would reject the outstretched hands of his child, and our Abba Father loves when we lift our hands toward him. When our hands move toward God, I believe his heart moves toward us. He loves when we lift up our hands to worship him.

God loves to hold us close when we move closer to him.

• • • • • • • • • • **Power Lift** • • • • • • • • • •

I'm so glad I can call you my Father in addition to calling you my God. Today I lift my hands in praise to you!

As we have opportunity, let us do good to all people, especially
to those who belong to the family of believers. (Gal. 6:10)

Before I became a Christian, I used to think doing good meant always
being polite to strangers, saying the right thing, and always trying to
help those in need. I basically thought it meant knowing what to do
in every situation and doing it perfectly. Not just trying to be the best,
but coming darn close no matter what you were doing.

Later I learned this is not what serving God and others requires.
We're never going to be perfect in this lifetime. There's no competition
among us as believers. God has gifted each of us uniquely, and when we
each give our best, it often looks different for different people.

Doing good simply refers to following the example set by Jesus and
living in a way that reflects God's love, grace, and generosity. It means
following the Golden Rule and treating other people the same way you
want to be treated. It's your attitude of compassion, acceptance, and
kindness that demonstrates God's love in action.

There's no perfect way to get through your day. And the good news
is you don't have to be perfect. You only have to love God with all your
heart, mind, and soul. Out of this pursuit of him, you will naturally
display God's love for them.

Power Lift

So often I want to do good works for others but end up pressuring myself to do
them perfectly. Today Lord, give me power to love others as I have been loved.

Lift up your hands in the sanctuary and praise the LORD. (Ps. 134:2)

Throughout history, uplifted hands have usually signaled one of two things. First, they're used to indicate victory. You're at a sporting event, and even if you're not religious, if your team scores the winning goal, touchdown, or basket, then what do you do? You pump your fists in the air, high-five all those sitting nearby, and cheer until you're hoarse. One time I went to an Oklahoma City Thunder game, and my hands were up and down so much I was sore the next day. When you're winning, you raise your hands in triumph.

However, if someone jumps out in front of you in a dark alley and puts a gun in your face, the gesture is the same, but the meaning conveys almost the exact opposite. You say, "Don't shoot! I surrender." Raised hands, especially with your palms forward, indicate that you won't resist. Instead of balling your hands into fists, blocking your face, and preparing to fight, upraised hands signal your willingness to give in.

When you raise your hands, it can mean victory or it can mean surrender. However, in the presence of God, it means both, simultaneously. At the exact moment when you surrender to him, then you find victory in him. Remember that with God, submitting to him is the greatest victory you'll ever experience.

Power Lift

Lord, today I raise my hands and yield to you, but I also praise you for loving me so much that you were willing to die on the cross. Thank you, Jesus.

Clap your hands, all peoples! Shout to God with
loud songs of joy! (Ps. 47:1 ESV)

Here's the problem with many Christians today: they're underjoyed.
We should be the most overjoyed people around, and yet some of us
look underwhelmed by the Good News of what God has done for us
through Christ. We forget all that God has done for us. We lose sight
of the joy to be found by walking with God on a daily basis.

When I'm looking around the church during a service while we're
worshiping, I'm amazed at how many people look like they're delivering a eulogy rather than singing an upbeat worship song. Sure, we all
have our tough days, but week after week, so many believers don't look
like they know the joy of the Lord.

If you're overjoyed, then tell your face! Show it with a smile. Let
other people around you know. Being a follower of Jesus, you should be
full of more joy than anybody else in the world. It doesn't matter how
bad life gets—you've got the promise of eternity. You've got a God with
you, a God who's working in all things to bring about good to those
who love him and are called according to his purpose, a God who is
greater, who is ever-present, all-knowing, and all-powerful.

Don't settle for living underjoyed today. Instead, smile and let
your attitude reflect the wellspring inside you that delights in the Lord.
When others see you, make them take notice and say, "Wow, that has
to be one of the happiest people I've ever met!"

Be overjoyed you have a Savior.

• • • • • • • • • • • **Power Lift** • • • • • • • • • • •

I get so caught up in the crazy busyness of each day, Lord, that I lose sight of
the big picture and all you've done for me. Today help me remember that you are
the source of my eternal joy.

Rejoice always, pray continually, give thanks in all circumstances;
for this is God's will for you in Christ Jesus. (1 Thess. 5:16–18)

I saw an article recently in which some psychologists studied the relationship between gratitude and joy. Their study was apparently one of many that confirm what the Bible has told us for centuries. When we stop focusing on what we lack and instead concentrate on what we have, then we feel grateful and experience joy. Stopping to count your blessings reminds us that God has given us more than we realize.

Our culture tells us to buy more and spend more if we want to be content. But in this continual consumer mindset, nothing is ever enough. We're told we should always want more stuff. But it's not more stuff that gives us joy. It's realizing and appreciating what we've already received: a loving family, our health, food to eat, our home, a sense of humor, and so many other blessings we tend to take for granted.

As you go through your day, pay special attention to all that you're thankful for: a hot cup of coffee, the kindness of a family member, the support of a friend, a kind word from a stranger. Give God thanks for blessing you so abundantly.

Power Lift

Sometimes I grumble and complain, God, and yet I know I have so many blessings in my life. Forgive me when I forget to recognize them and to thank you for all the many gifts you bless me with each day.

> The world and its desires pass away, but whoever does
> the will of God lives forever. (1 John 2:17)

When I officiated my first funeral, I came to the part at the end of the graveside service. Pastors always say, "Ashes to ashes, dust to dust." So I uttered the famous lines. Forgetting what came next, I improvised. Thinking it would be funny, I said, "Ashes to ashes, dust to dust, sure hope this coffin doesn't rust."

I thought it was funny. No one else did. Maybe it's because death is no laughing matter. But our culture certainly seems fascinated with life after death, details about heaven, and what happens after our bodies here on earth expire. In so many movies, TV shows, and books, favorite characters frequently and miraculously seem to come back from the dead. In soap operas it became such a clichéd device that viewers knew that any character who died would likely return a few months down the road.

Sometimes I worry that these depictions of death make it seem temporary, reversible, or trivial. Because the reality remains that our time here on earth is limited. Our bodies will eventually die. However, if we've trusted Christ as our Savior, then we will have eternal life with him and our heavenly Father. While we don't know exactly what this will be like, we're told there will be no more tears, no more sorrow, no more worries.

Whether you live to be one hundred, or you're called home sooner, you can rest in the security of knowing where and how you'll spend eternity. Remember: Heaven is your home, now and forever. Earth is not your home. Today make the most of the time the Lord has given you.

Power Lift

Dear God, help me make my time here on earth count for you and your kingdom. I'm so grateful for my purpose and for the promise of eternal life afterward.

> But let all who take refuge in you rejoice; let them ever sing for
> joy, and spread your protection over them, that those who love
> your name may exult in you. For you bless the righteous, O Lord;
> you cover him with favor as with a shield. (Ps. 5:11–12 ESV)

When my kids were small, I always loved how they celebrated my birthday. They would get so excited and couldn't wait for me to open their presents, which was often something they had made. I remember when my daughter Joy was about ten, she had worked so hard—probably for days—to make the perfect gift for me, something she knew I would just love. She was like, "Daddy! Daddy! Daddy! Look what I got to make for you!" She seemed absolutely overjoyed that she got to give me something.

What she and my other kids didn't realize was that my joy was in seeing their joy! Sure, I loved their macaroni pictures and string art, their finger-paintings and tie holders. But what I loved more was seeing them want to honor, celebrate, and love on me.

I suspect God must feel this way when we open our hearts in worship to him. When we fully realize all he's done for us and our heart overflows with gratitude, we are so blessed! There's nothing we can give him to show how we feel except our hearts. What a blessing that we get to be known by the God of the Universe and love him back.

Today remember what a privilege it is to love and serve your heavenly Father.

Power Lift

Lord, I give you all my praise and worship! Your deeds are wonderful and mighty. Your lovingkindness has no limits. Thank you for being such an awesome God and for saving me from my sin.

The Lord is faithful, and he will strengthen you and
protect you from the evil one. (2 Thess. 3:3)

Evil has many faces, and you might not recognize it when it's directly in front of you. The devil likes to disguise himself and attempt to befriend us, to seduce us, to trick us into thinking he's there to help us. Nothing could be further from the truth. He wants to destroy us. Even after we're saved, our Enemy would like nothing better than to derail our faith and undermine our joy, purpose, and peace.

When you face trials and temptations, you can lose sight of what's really going on. You begin to doubt God's goodness and your faith wavers. You stop praying and close your Bible. Church seems like less of a priority, and other people only annoy you. During these times, the Enemy wants to use our feelings of fear, uncertainty, and anger to pull us away from God.

All the more reason we must remain vigilant and focused on God. Our power comes from the Lord, and he will see us through whatever we may be facing. Never forget that the Enemy is out to get you, to push you down, and to take you out of the race of faith.

Your faith isn't determined by what you feel. Acknowledge your emotions without dwelling on them and giving them power to control your decisions and actions. No matter how frustrated you are, trust in God's power to help you handle what's ahead.

Power Lift

Lord, give me the strength I need to face what's ahead. Protect me from the Enemy and keep my faith strong.

I glory in Christ Jesus in my service to God. (Rom. 15:17)

Sometimes when I'm doing something I know I was created to do, I sense God's pleasure bubbling up within me. Whether it's preaching or leading a meeting with my team, even just helping my kids get through some problem they're facing, I'll catch myself feeling this sense of happiness, the joy of fulfilling my God-given purpose.

When was the last time you experienced this kind of sensation, the feeling you were doing something so significant, so personal, so uniquely what you were made for? It could've been cooking a meal for your family or completing a report at work, balancing the tires for a customer or helping a friend with her makeup. Your joy might come from painting, writing, baking, teaching, coaching, counseling—whatever it is, do it to the best of your ability for the glory of God.

Our Father has gifted each of us with diverse and personalized abilities. And when we use them and grow in our ability to serve others with them, we can rest assured he's pleased with us. This is the secret to true contentment, the abundant life Jesus told us he came to bring. Your joy will be made complete as you fulfill your purpose, reflect his glory, and advance God's kingdom.

Power Lift

Thank you, God, for the unique ways you've created me. I want to glorify you by the way I use my gifts to serve others.

*Great peace have they who love your law, and nothing
can make them stumble. (Ps. 119:165)*

When I'm anxious and upset, my body shows it. Whether I'm running away from bobcats hiding beside our driveway after dark or about to let loose on the guy who took my parking spot at the mall, I feel the adrenaline kick in and my body prepare for "flight or fight."

If you've ever been in a car accident, fight at school, or confrontation with the office bully, then you know what I'm talking about. Anytime you're facing a perceived threat or imminent risk of danger, then you can literally lose your balance. Your body feels disoriented as you react and make split-second decisions about what to do in the heat of the moment.

While your body may still react this way, you can know the peace of the Lord even amidst your scariest situations. When you trust in God's sovereignty, you experience the peace that passes understanding. Your security is in God. You don't have to get worried, upset, and stressed figuring out how to fight your way into—or run away from—your future.

If you follow Jesus and obey God's commands, then your feet will remain steadfast and sure. You won't stumble and fall victim to the weight of worries and anxieties that try to crush us. Your future is certain. Today don't let anyone rob you of the peace of the Lord.

Power Lift

With you as my rock-solid foundation, Lord, I know I have nothing to fear. Your peace gives me comfort, security, and strength. Nothing can steal my joy today.

Light in a messenger's eyes brings joy to the heart, and
good news gives health to the bones. (Prov. 15:30)

Ever have one of those phone calls in the middle of the night? You
know, the kind that you know must be bad news before you answer it.
Or maybe it's that sick feeling in the pit of your stomach when you see
the return address on certain letters in your mailbox or particular subject lines in your emails.

Fortunately, the news is not always as bad as we think it will be—
or even bad at all. I especially love it when the news is good. That text
that came in was just a friend reminding me that he's praying for me.
The phone call was just one of the kids asking to extend her curfew.
The letter wasn't a bill but simply an overview of your account.

Sometimes I think we forget to share our good news with others.
But we definitely need to share it now more than ever. We hear plenty
of negative stories, horrific headlines, and depressing sound bites from
the 24/7 news cycles. We get jaded and forget about all the amazing
things God is doing in millions of lives around the world.

Good news is a gift to be shared. Today remember to let the people
you care about know what the Lord's been doing for you. Ask them to
share in your joy and celebrate your blessings.

Power Lift

Dear God, allow me to be a messenger of your good news, bringing grace and
life to all those around me.

> But he was pierced for our transgressions, he was crushed
> for our iniquities; the punishment that brought us peace was
> on him, and by his wounds we are healed. (Isa. 53:5)

Years ago it only took a quick hug from Amy or me to make our children feel better. For really serious injuries, which usually meant the ones involving blood from a scraped knee or cut finger, we had to bring out the bandages and say a prayer. In a day or two, their wounds had usually healed and we didn't have to worry about them again until the next fall, bike accident, or playground tussle.

As a pastor ministering to adults, however, I quickly realized we all carry chronic wounds and tender scars from more complex injuries and incidents. These don't heal overnight. These internal wounds to our soul stay with us, slow us down, and sometimes color all the choices we make. The brutal words from a parent, the unspeakable betrayal from someone we trusted, the harsh disappointment in our marriage—these tend to linger and require God's healing power to help us forgive those who let us down and move on.

But we can be healed. Jesus, too, knew what it meant to bear both physical pain as well as the emotional and mental anguish of suffering the offenses of others. Having lived without ever sinning, Christ chose to bear the burden of our sins through his excruciating death on the cross.

This month is about overcoming our wounds, our fears, our doubts and worries, all the obstacles, big and small, that often hinder our faith. Today ask God to heal all those hurts that still linger from your past.

Power Lift

Thank you, Jesus, for bearing my sins on the cross so that I can be healed from my wounds and have eternal life.

The Lord knows how to rescue the godly from trials. (2 Peter 2:9)

Whether it's the latest Star Wars installment, yet another superhero flick, a fictional mother searching for her child, or the true story of a prisoner of war from WWII, I love to see the good guys win. In a messed up world where injustice and senseless violence assault us daily, I suspect we all enjoy seeing a next-to-impossible situation resolved so that good triumphs over evil. The galaxy gets saved, the world restored to order, the kid gets home safely, and the prisoners are set free. Even if we can't see it yet in our own lives, there's hope for the future.

These movies and stories also inspire us and encourage us to be strong and resilient, unstoppable and undefeated. We can be those heroes who refuse to give up and somehow make it happen. And usually we're told we can do it by ourselves.

But no matter how strong we are, ultimately we all face limitations. There's only one source for true, limitless power: faith in our God. Jesus left the glory of heaven and the presence of his Father to go "under cover" on earth and live and die as a man. He rescued us from the greatest evil in existence and overcame the power of sin in our lives once and for all.

Bask in the knowledge that you have been rescued and redeemed by the love of your Father and the sacrifice of his Son. With their power, you can overcome anything!

Power Lift

Jesus, you rescued me from the power of sin and death in my life so that I can have life and fulfill my purpose. Today I will overcome all temptations and obstacles in the power of your name.

"For I am the LORD your God who takes hold of your right hand
and says to you, Do not fear; I will help you." (Isa. 41:13)

I loved the old Popeye cartoons. You know, Popeye the Sailor Man? It was clear he was our hero and Brutus was his natural enemy, threatening to harm poor Olive Oil, the love of Popeye's life. Every episode, after Brutus' taunting and bullying, Popeye reached the point where "that's all I can standz, and I can't standz no more." Out came his can of spinach, down it went, and suddenly his muscles were popping and fists were flying. Brutus didn't stand a chance!

I'm convinced we occasionally need to choose a "Popeye moment." When the Enemy attacks and we keep struggling, we need to "draw a line in the sand" and have a showdown. That's all we can stand, and it's time to change.

What fight are you facing today? Are you overworking, missing what's most important in life? Are you battling an addiction and telling yourself it's not that big of a deal? Are you putting off a conversation, hoping the problem will solve itself? Are you making excuses as to why you can't drop the pounds, making jokes about it to help relieve your pain?

Maybe it's time to stop. Make a decision. Enough is enough. It's time to change. The good news is your strength doesn't come from a can of spinach. Yours comes from our God. His power is available to you. His strength dwells within you. His spirit will help you do what you can't do on your own.

Power Lift

That's it, Lord. I'm tired of fighting temptation and giving in more times than I can count. Help me change—and help me change now!

> Finally, dear brothers and sisters, we urge you in the name of the Lord Jesus to live in a way that pleases God, as we have taught you. (1 Thess. 4:1 NLT)

Growing up in the eighties, I enjoyed not only really cool music but really cool fashion. If you had a pair of Levi's and a colored knit Izod with the collar popped, you had a real shot at the cool table in the cafeteria.

Unfortunately, Izod shirts were crazy expensive. And because our family couldn't fit one into our budget, I was exiled to the unpopular table. That was, until my mom got creative. At a garage sale, she found a pair of used Izod socks, each sporting a perfect little green alligator—the much-coveted symbol of potential popularity.

Mom purchased two label-less knit shirts, cut off the socks' gators, and sewed them onto the shirts. Voila! Instant fake Izods. The plan would have worked if she hadn't sewed them slightly crooked and in the wrong place, something the authentic-Izod kids immediately discovered and ridiculed me for.

Now that we're grown up, not much has changed. We still feel immense pressure to fit in. But we have to remember that God didn't call us to fit in; he called us to stand out. Becoming obsessed with what people think about you is the quickest way to forget what God thinks about you.

Whatever you do today, live for an audience of one. If God is pleased with you, it doesn't matter what people think about you.

Power Lift

Lord, I don't care what others think of me as long as I please you. Thank you for loving me and giving me the power to overcome my need to please those around me.

Catch for us the foxes, the little foxes that ruin the vineyards,
our vineyards that are in bloom. (Song of Songs 2:15)

Recently at church we were attempting to record an important video message for our services. Several camera guys had worked hard to create the perfect set in a small confined studio. The backdrop perfectly complimented the communication theme, and the lights were strategically placed.

After reviewing our carefully constructed plan, the director said, "Take One . . . and rolling." At his cue, I started talking confidently into the camera. Within a couple seconds, a fly buzzed by, so the director said, "Cut!" not wanting the fly in the shot.

A few minutes later, we started "Take Two." As if on cue, I was barely into my second line when the annoying fly zoomed back into the shot. After several failed attempts to shoot one scene, all halted by this cunning fly, we changed our strategy. Instead of trying to shoot the clip, we decided to try to kill the fly!

Talk about slapstick comedy; for probably close to an hour, a roomful of people swatted, clapped, slapped, and swooshed after one stupid fly. None of us were able to make the kill. So we finally admitted defeat, packed up the gear, and called it a day.

It's still hard to believe that one small fly kept us from reaching our goal. But truthfully, it's often the small distractions that hurt us the most. Perhaps today you are distracted by ongoing worry, another's offense, a looming project, financial pressure, or a broken gadget.

Remember, it's just a small thing. Don't let the small things keep you from pursuing the big things.

Power Lift

Today I will keep my eyes on you, Lord, and not get distracted by the little flies buzzing in my life.

"In this world you will have trouble. But take heart! I
have overcome the world." (John 16:33)

It's really hard not to look at our friends' status updates and latest posted photos and not be envious. Their grass looks so much greener than our latest, tired retweet. We think, "If I only had a job like they have, then I could go on those kind of trips too. If my spouse were as understanding as theirs, then our marriage would be just as great. If I'd finished my degree, then I would be on track for that promotion."

If only, if only, if only.

When we live conditionally, comparing and envying what everyone around us seems to have that we don't, then we're setting ourselves up for frustration and not faith. Living in the "if only" moments requires us to hit Pause and overlook all that God has given us in the present. Instead of embracing the many blessings we have and the stewardship they require, we spin our wheels and feel discouraged by our perceived inadequacies.

The truth is that you have everything you need for right now. God provides, equips, and empowers you and won't call you to something you're not ready to handle. You often won't feel ready, but you are. Jesus has overcome the world, including your own tendency to envy others rather than give thanks for what you have.

Power Lift

Help me resist the temptations to live conditionally, Lord. I'm so grateful to have all I need today and for the confidence that you've already overcome all I'm facing.

This is the day the LORD has made. We will rejoice
and be glad in it. (Ps. 118:24 NLT)

For too much of my life, I've lived with a "when-then" mindset. I used to wake up thinking, one day when I'm married, then life will be fun. One day when we have our first child, that will be the best. When our baby is walking, then life will really be amazing. When our kid is out of diapers, then we will have more money each month!

Every stage of life seemed to have a "when-then." Then one day it finally dawned on me: I was wishing my present days away. My present season never seemed to be that perfect one I had once hoped, prayed, and expected it to be. I always felt that whatever was coming next held the promise of something better.

When I hit midlife, I realized that more than half my life had likely passed. Why in the world would I keep wishing it away?

Today is the only day I know I have. This is the day the Lord has made. I will rejoice in it. Embrace it. Enjoy it. Savor it.

What is your current "when-then"? What are you waiting on to fully embrace the life you have today? Look around you. Ask God to make you fully present, completely engaged with the people you see. Take a few minutes longer with your kids. Don't see them as interruptions, see them as blessings.

Remember today is the day you were hoping for in the past. Thank God for it.

Power Lift

Lord, you have given me so much, and I thank you for the abundant blessings I have right now, today. Only you know the future, and I can relax knowing you are with me always.

This is the LORD's doing; It is marvelous in our eyes. (Ps. 118:23 NASB)

Life can be so serious, right? Bills to pay. Chores to complete. Projects to finish. Kids to raise. It's hard to enjoy today when it's all flying by you at a hundred miles per minute. You have to stay focused and prepared for what's next—which doesn't leave much room for joy.

Years ago a mentor challenged me. "Craig," he asked in a heartfelt way, "why are you so serious all the time? When are you going to take time to smell the roses? Seize the day? Embrace the moment?" If you are a Type A kind of person, you may be able to relate. He said, "Why don't you plan something *spontaneous*?"

His question seemed to be an oxymoron. How do you plan something spontaneous? He explained to me that people who lean toward responsibility over enjoyment often need to plan fun. I knew what he meant.

Are you like this? Are you more worried than carefree? Do you plan to achieve more than you plan to enjoy?

If so, maybe it's time for some planned spontaneity. Decide today to drive a different way to work. Grab someone for a coffee in the middle of an otherwise stressful day. Take an afternoon walk, and walk extra slowly. Call a friend and grab cheap tickets to a game—tonight. Play cards with your kids before making them do homework. Grab a banana split on the way home from church.

If you are often overwhelmed with doing what's right, remember that sometimes what's right is also what's fun.

Power Lift

Dear God, you are in control, and today I can loosen my grip and experience the joy of spontaneous fun.

You are my hiding place; you will protect me from trouble and surround me with songs of deliverance. (Ps. 32:7)

Each year in Oklahoma, we average more than fifty tornados, typically resulting in multiple fatalities. As you would imagine, we're trained and prepared for the kind of severe weather that often produces those twisters. We conduct drills regularly—in our homes, schools, businesses, even churches. If you live here, you learn quickly how to look for a safe place and take shelter.

Our lives often feel just as unpredictable and dangerous. Our circumstances can change overnight, relationships fracture and break, and unimaginable obstacles crash into us. If only it were as easy as looking for a storm shelter like the ones we have in Oklahoma.

Where do you go when you're overwhelmed, weary, anxious, afraid, and unsettled? What's the first thing you do when you see trouble headed your way?

God is our shield and protector, our rock and our shelter. No matter what calamity, natural disaster, personal crisis, or devastating loss we face, we can run to him. When you pray and spend time alone with him, you create a safe place where you can always return.

Because we live in a sinful, fallen world, you can be sure that you will face trials, temptations, and tragedies. But God will always be your hiding place. The winds of change and attacks of the Enemy cannot harm you there in his arms. He wants to hold you close and remind you of his power, strength, and sovereignty.

Let him.

Power Lift

Lord, thank you for being my rock, my hiding place. I am so grateful for having a safe place in your arms. When storms come my way, I will run to you.

A cheerful heart is good medicine, but a crushed
spirit dries up the bones. (Prov. 17:22)

Years ago I was talking with my son Sam, who was about six at the time. With my kids I often intentionally asked fun, even silly, questions before gradually moving onto more important ones. You know, what's your favorite animal in the world and why? What's your favorite kind of ice cream? If you could go anywhere, where would you want to go?

Sam and I were in the middle of one such fun conversation when I shifted it toward the future. "Hey, buddy, what do you want to be when you grow up?"

"I want to be what you are, Dad!"

My heart about burst with love and pride. How amazing that my son already thought about being a pastor. I tried not to show my excitement and said, "So, you want to minister and start a church someday?"

"Well, that's not exactly what I was thinking," Sam replied innocently. "I just want to be what you are—the best dad in the world."

I know, it sounds too much like a Hallmark moment, and it was. As long as I live, I will forever cherish his little face looking so lovingly into mine as he said those words. That small flash in time is with me always.

The longer I live, the more I realize that our best life exists in embracing the small moments. If you look carefully, you might find your own special moment to grasp today.

Seize it. Enjoy it. Embrace it. Thank God for it.

Power Lift

I treasure those precious moments, Lord, when you surprise me with love, joy, and affection. They will sustain me and help me overcome any doubts I may face today.

No one who hopes in you will ever be put to shame, but shame will
come on those who are treacherous without cause. (Ps. 25:3)

This date is one weighted with painful images, deep sadness, and rec-
ollections of where you were and what you were doing when terrible
acts of terrorism struck our nation. Believe it or not, I was in midair
on a flight to Chicago when we suddenly made an emergency landing
in St. Louis instead.

On that 9/11, it was a Tuesday morning, and most people were
going about their lives like they would on any other weekday—going
to work, carpooling to school, cleaning the house, meeting with team
members, making lunch plans. And then, suddenly and dramatically,
our world changed.

On this day I'm reminded that things we assume are permanent
can fall down around us. It can happen to nations and, of course, it
seems to happen more noticeably on a personal level. We take our health
for granted until we get the doctor's test results back. We assume we'll
grow old with our spouses until the terrible betrayal. We anticipate
advancing in our jobs and then overnight get handed a pink slip for no
discernable reason.

So much of what we put our hope in on a daily basis is far more
fragile than we realize. As believers, we know that the only eternal,
bedrock basis for our faith is in God. He is the same yesterday, today,
and tomorrow. He never changes and never gives up on us. No matter
what happened, is about to happen, or ever will happen, God is faithful.

Power Lift

Lord, I lift up the many people who may be remembering loved ones and griev-
ing today. Remind them of your presence and the hope we always have in you.

Each of you should give what you have decided in your heart to give, not reluctantly or under compulsion, for God loves a cheerful giver. (2 Cor. 9:7)

On a mission trip to Honduras, our host introduced our team to a sweet older woman. Even though she was shockingly poor, evidently many looked to her as a leader and spiritual influence in this small impoverished community.

The lady was ecstatic that we there to help. She had prayed for years that God would send people to help empower her neighbors to get jobs and begin to build lives that would matter. When we arrived at her hut, I was reminded again of how blessed we are in America. Not only did she not have running water or electricity, but the floor was dirt and the walls were made of scraps.

We sat down on logs for lunch. This precious woman beamed as she served me meat. Glancing around, I noticed that no one else, including her, had meat on their plates. I asked our host who explained to me that she had heard I hadn't had meat in a while. This was true, but only because Amy was in a vegetarian phase (which thankfully passed as quickly as it came).

Our host explained that she wanted to honor me with meat and had saved her money for quite some time to bless me with something should could not even afford for herself. I sat stunned. Speechless. And shaken. How could someone with so little give so extravagantly to someone who has so much?

As you have been blessed, God wants you to be a blessing to others.

Power Lift

Lord, I have so much and yet often still want more and overlook those in need around me. Pierce through my selfishness and help me overcome my excuses so I can give generously and joyfully.

Now you are Christ's body, and individually members of it. (1 Cor. 12:27 NASB)

When my kids were younger, I walked in on them playing with their stuffed animals. Bobby the teddy bear was preaching to the polar bear, the bunny, and the raccoon. (I guess preachers' kids play a bit differently than others.)

When I asked what they were doing, they exclaimed, "We are playing church!" At that moment, it hit me. How many adults do the same thing? Not with stuffed toys, but with grown lives. They go to church occasionally on Sundays, but their lives are not that different on Mondays. They sing songs while at church, but rarely worship otherwise. They give whatever money they have on them at the time but refuse to tithe or commit to giving consistently.

As Jesus followers, we must avoid the temptation of playing church. We must remember that technically, we don't go to church. We *are* the church. That's an important distinction.

When we realize that we don't go to church, we stop looking for a church to meet our needs. Instead we realize that we are the church and we are here to meet the needs of the world.

Today as you go to work, interact with friends, attend a class, or do whatever your day has in store, remember—you are a member of Christ's church. You are called to be an ambassador, a heavenly representative. You are the salt of the earth. You are the light of this world. Let your light shine brightly in all you do.

Power Lift

I am so grateful to be part of the body of Christ, and I never want to "play church." All I have is yours, Jesus, and I want to love, serve, and bless others as your representative.

Faith is confidence in what we hope for and assurance
about what we do not see. (Heb. 11:1)

Bridges have always freaked me out a little. Just think about it. You're driving thousands of feet above some very deep, dark, dangerous body of water. What if the steel cables broke? Or a concrete column suddenly crumbled? There you'd be, trapped under tons of water and rubble.

Can you imagine what it would be like if our bridges were invisible? "Yeah, Craig, just keep driving until you get to the riverbank—it won't look like there's anything there, but you just can't see it. So just keep driving, straight off the edge, and that bridge will support you until you get to the other side." Is that a crossing you'd be willing to make?

Of course, that's often what it feels like to step out in faith and follow God. We can't see where our second step is, we're not sure where he's leading us, and we don't know how we'll get there. We can trust him and be sure of our hope in him. But it still gets scary sometimes, like that weird kind of vertigo you get seeing how far the plunge is in your peripheral vision as you drive across a huge bridge.

Overcome your fear of spiritual heights today and take the next step. Trust God to show you the way.

Power Lift

Thank you, Lord, for the way you remain so faithful to me. Even when I'm afraid, you empower me to step forward in faith. I can take that next step today because you have gone before me.

> The one who does not love does not know God,
> for God is love. (1 John 4:8 NASB)

Growing up, I was a serious baseball fan. One of my favorite players was Kansas City Royals' third baseman, George Brett. His 3,154 career base hits topped any other third baseman in history. And in 1980, Brett almost batted .400, finishing the season at a modern-day record of .390. In case you're not into baseball, that's an amazing record.

As a fan, I knew all about my hero, but I didn't *know* him. Until one day in college, I was playing in Kansas City for the National Collegiate Tennis Championship. Walking by a nice outdoor restaurant, I glanced up, and live and in the flesh—there he was. George Brett was eating a burger. Wow, I thought, he even eats hamburgers.

Without hesitation, I approached him and spurted off all the stats I knew about him. One of his buddies, obviously used to strangers like me approaching, tried to encourage me to leave, but George stopped him. "You know all that about me?" he said. "Why don't you sit down for a minute and tell me about you?"

And that's how I got to know George Brett.

So many people know "about God" but don't really know him. They may attend a church, know some Bible verses, and even have a cross tattoo. But they don't know him intimately. There is a big difference between knowing about someone and truly knowing him.

Today take time to get to know him better. Seek God. Listen for his voice. Open your heart to his Word. He wants to show himself to you. He wants you to know him as he knows you.

· · · · · · · · · · · **Power Lift** · · · · · · · · · · ·

Lord, I'm grateful that you are a personal God and want me to know you, not just worship and serve you. Draw me closer to you so I can know you even better.

"I am the good shepherd; I know my sheep and
my sheep know me." (John 10:14)

Indecision is often a huge barrier in our faith.

Making decisions can be so draining. What school should I go to? Should I break up with this person I'm dating or try to work things out? Should I take this job or stay where I am? Should I buy a new car or put more money into this old one?

It's encouraging to know that Jesus wants to speak to us. In John 10, Jesus shows us who he is—the Good Shepherd. The good news is that the Good Shepherd speaks. And not only does he speak, but the sheep know his voice.

If you need to make a decision, remember that Jesus wants to speak to you, and he does this in a number of ways. He will speak to you through his Word. He may speak through people. He might speak through circumstances. He could nudge you with his Spirit.

I always try to remember that the Good Shepherd guides the sheep. His job is to guide. My job is to follow.

When you are trying to make a decision for direction in your life, tell Jesus, "If you guide me, I will follow. Wherever you lead, I will go."

Power Lift

I will listen for your voice today, Lord, and will follow where you lead me. Give me wisdom, discernment, and peace as I seek to make decisions that will always honor you.

> Therefore confess your sins to each other and pray for each other so that you may be healed. The prayer of a righteous person is powerful and effective. (James 5:16)

One evening I got held up at a church meeting later than planned. We already had company over, and Amy texted me, "Get home as fast as possible and grab some ice cream for the brownies. Hurry!"

Rushing out of the building, I drove quickly to the nearest grocery store. Not wanting to slow down to visit with others, I put my phone to my head and acted like I was talking to someone. Surely that would discourage people from wanting to chat.

My plan worked flawlessly until someone tried to stop me, "Pastor Craig, can I talk to you? It will only take a minute." Forgive me if this sounds harsh, but "it will only take a minute" generally means I'm about to tell you my life story. Under normal circumstances, I would be blessed to stay and talk, but I felt pressure from Amy to be home fast!

So without thinking, I said, "I'm sorry" and pointed to my phone, implying that I was in a conversation. And that's when my phone rang.

Busted.

It's so easy to rationalize sin in our lives. We often have what we think is a good excuse. Ask yourself today, is there something I've been doing that is displeasing to God? Have I told myself it's okay even though it's really wrong?

Confess it. Repent. Be forgiven. And be changed.

Power Lift

I often rationalize my sins, Lord, and try to justify them as being an exception. Thank you for being quick and merciful to forgive whenever I confess to you.

Many are the plans in the mind of a man, but it is the purpose
of the LORD that will stand. (Prov. 19:21 ESV)

Our family just returned from a great trip to the beach. We had all four of our kids who live at home and our two married daughters with their husbands. What's most exciting to me is that they all wanted to be together.

To be honest, this didn't happen by accident. My good friend and pastor Andy Stanley once talked about what success was to him as a dad. He said he wanted to parent his children so that when they were older they would want to spend time as a family. That was the prize.

If you don't have kids, then think about what kind of parent you want to be if God opens that door. If you have children, ask yourself, "Am I creating an environment that my children will want to come back to when they don't have to?"

Amy and I have not been perfect as parents. We have made too many mistakes to count. But at this point, we rejoice knowing that for one week, our whole family wanted to be together. When I texted Andy to tell him thanks, he sent me this exact response: "How blessed you are that your family wants to be together. If you don't have it at this stage, you can't get it. Congratulations!"

That's the prize.

Do something today that will lead you to the prize you want in the future.

Power Lift

Dear God, give me wisdom about how to love my family well and draw us closer together and closer to you. Let me invest in our future together right now.

"When he, the Spirit of truth, comes, he will guide you into all the truth. He will not speak on his own; he will speak only what he hears, and he will tell you what is yet to come." (John 16:13)

Time used to drive me crazy. There was never enough of it! I'd be doing one thing, mentally thinking ahead to what was next and how to get through it as quickly as possible. And if I was in a meeting and someone was taking too long (according to my internal efficiency clock) to make their point, then I about came unglued.

As I've gotten older, however, I've remembered something my grandmother used to tell me, "Don't look ahead too far and wish your life away." She knew that a lot can happen in the future that we never see coming. We can only focus on what God has given us to do today. We must try to make the most of our time, but ultimately, we're most contented when we align ourselves with God's timing.

Most people assume that if they could predict the future, then they would have an easy, carefree life. They could make millions off the stock market, know which winning teams to support, and prepare perfectly for tomorrow's weather. But I suspect if we really saw the future the way God sees it, we would be terrified and overwhelmed by having too much to handle.

Rest in the security of God's power and presence. He is sovereign and has the future in control. He gave us his Spirit to help guide us through tough times. Tomorrow holds nothing that God is not already holding.

Power Lift

I trust you, Lord, with my today, tomorrow, next week, next month, and next year. Because you are for me, it doesn't matter who might be against me.

As iron sharpens iron, so one person sharpens another. (Prov. 27:17)

One day Amy approached me and said, "Okay, I just have to tell you something." I could tell that she had put a lot of thought into this. She was obviously annoyed, but didn't want to hurt my feelings.

"When you preach," she explained, "your hands are so distracting." Then she showed me exactly what I do. "It looks like you're carrying a box." She told me that everyone laughed about this. Not in a mean way—just in a would-someone-please-help-him-stop-so-we-can-concentrate-on-the-message way.

At first I was upset, but I took her words to heart because I know how much she loves me. So I watched a couple videos of myself. And she was right. My hands looked like I continually grasped an imaginary box, like I was continually lifting it from one side of the stage to another. So I decided—I'd put the box down.

There is a common saying: We don't know what we don't know. So often we are blind to our faults and shortcomings. A truth from a trusted friend is an absolute treasure.

A wise person seeks advice from close and trusted friends. Have you sought wisdom from those around you? Have you invited and welcomed feedback? Is there something others have been trying to tell you that you haven't opened your heart to hear? Listen to those who love you.

Power Lift

Father, I'm grateful for friends and loved ones I can trust. Thank you for the ways they sharpen me and draw me closer to you.

Whether you turn to the right or to the left, your ears will hear a voice
behind you, saying, "This is the way; walk in it." (Isa. 30:21)

Like most kids, ours often had bad dreams and worried about monsters under the bed. Even when they didn't get up and rush into our bedroom, our kids would often wake us with their restlessness. Amy especially had that kind of super-powered hearing that new mothers have, the kind that can recognize their baby's cry from across a crowded nursery or anywhere in their house. It's funny because it probably took my superpowers longer to develop, but I can remember being up front and preaching at church and hearing one of my kids cry outside the auditorium.

It works the same way with our children's ability to recognize our voices. Sometimes just a whispered, comforting prayer or lullaby was the only thing needed to overcome a nightmare or heal a scraped knee. In crowded situations, like the mall at Christmas and amusement parks in the summer, our kids learned that they better be able to focus in on their parents' voices if they wanted to keep up.

As God's children, we need to hear our Father's voice and receive reassurance of his love, protection, and guidance. And it also gives me comfort to know that he hears each of our voices, unique and distinct from all his other sons and daughters.

God hears your prayers. Listen for his voice today.

Power Lift

Lord, you hear my prayers and come to my aid. Thank you for listening and responding whenever I cry out to you.

And he said: "Truly I tell you, unless you change and become like little children, you will never enter the kingdom of heaven." (Matt. 18:3)

It's hard to believe, but I'm a grandfather. Yes, I feel way too young to be a "Pops." I'm ridiculously excited to be one of those fun granddads who delights, spoils, challenges, and inspires their grandkids. I'm not ashamed to talk baby talk (even though, as I shared earlier, I'm not that crazy about babies) and will change a diaper if I absolutely have to.

I know there's something humbling and amazing and awe-inspiring about being around a baby, then a toddler, then a child. Their innocence, their honesty, their sense of curiosity and adventure, their uncomplicated love and devoted attention—all those qualities and more remind me of today's verse.

Being Pops to a new little boy reminds me that I need to be like him even as he begins maturing and becoming like me. I want that sense of wonder and possibility, that appreciation for beauty and joy in all the daily things we adults take for granted. I long to have that kind of unquestioning faith that trusts and obeys what my Father tells me.

Today let your heart become like a child's. Seek God without all the issues that often clutter our faith as adults. Just love him. Trust him.

Power Lift

Abba Father, I am your child and I trust you completely. Lead me, guide me, and protect me as I grow in my faith.

You visit the earth and cause it to overflow; You greatly enrich
it; The stream of God is full of water; You prepare their grain,
for thus You prepare the earth. (Ps. 65:9 NASB)

Shortly after Amy and I were married, our next door neighbor's little daughter came for one of her regular visits. Rachel was probably six years old at the time, and after giving me her usual big hug, she looked over her shoulder at my front yard and innocently observed, "My daddy says you have the worst yard on the whole block." And the she ran off to find Amy and play.

I had to laugh, knowing she didn't intend to insult me. But she—or should I say her dad—was correct. Our yard didn't look good. Part of it didn't have much grass at all, and the whole thing was choked with weeds. And it didn't help living next to Rachel's dad—the guy who'd won the "lawn of the month" award for something like seventy-nine months straight.

Amy suggested I seek out his advice, and he had plenty to offer. Who knew there was a right time to fertilize? And a two-week window in which to overseed? No one had ever told me anything about winter rye. And watering regularly seemed way too expensive for our starter budget. But all of these were required to grow and maintain a beautiful yard.

The same is true in your relationship with God. If you want to know him intimately, it requires time in prayer, worship, seeking God in his Word, and fellowship with other believers. It requires devoted attention.

· · · · · · · · · · · **Power Lift** · · · · · · · · · ·

Too often when I get busy, Lord, my relationship with you slips. Forgive me when I overlook doing what's required to grow in my faith. Keep me rooted in your love for me.

There is a time for everything, and a season for every
activity under the heavens. (Eccl. 3:1)

After taking my neighbor's advice, I've been working to perfect these yard principles for years. Finally, we have made some significant progress. Though we haven't won an award, we are quite proud of our yard. God gets most of the credit, but we have worked with it to do our part to make it beautiful.

If you drove up our long driveway, you would likely admire it. That is until you get to the part right outside our front door. Since we live in the woods, we don't have a back yard. You could say we have a back forest, but not a yard. The only usable place to play soccer is right in the front. So we put up two small goals and let the kids go at it. The only problem is—there is a huge dead spot.

For so long, the dead spot bothered me. Then one day I realized I would soon miss it. I recognized that when the mini soccer field finally "healed," it would signal our kids being out of the house. And then I would miss these days when they were home, laughing and playing in the yard.

Is there something you're complaining about today that you will soon miss in the future? Try to focus on what matters most and see the good in everything. It's amazing how a different attitude can help you move from not liking something to loving it.

Power Lift

Lord, help me to let go of insignificant frustrations today so that I can focus on what—and who—matters most to me.

*I have chosen the way of faithfulness; I have set
my heart on your laws. (Ps. 119:30)*

Recently I talked to a lady at my son's soccer game who has been battling some health issues. She explained how she was close to God years ago and used to be very involved in our church. But when she started going through the "fire" with so many serious physical ailments, she questioned why God would allow it.

"How could I worship a God that I couldn't trust?" she asked me, slightly embarrassed as she fought back tears.

Her question hits at the heart of one of life's biggest decisions. Will we trust that God is good even when life is not? Our response to pain and challenges will determine so much about our future. If we decide to trust, we will grow in our faith, deepen in intimacy, and be conformed to the image of Christ. But if we allow our hearts to drift, we'll wake up one day drowning in doubts, buried in burdens, and feeling far from the only one who can help us heal.

If you want to overcome your doubts, then trust God by faith. Continue to worship him, obey him, and seek him. Even when you can't understand why he would allow you to experience what you're going through, count on him to redeem it for your good and for his kingdom.

The way you respond to life's challenges today will determine the strength of your faith tomorrow.

Power Lift

Father, I want to believe in your ability to redeem even the hardest moments of my life. Today I will trust in you and walk by faith and not by sight.

Trust in the Lord with all your heart and lean not on your own understanding;
In all your ways submit to him, and he will make your paths straight. Do
not be wise in your own eyes; fear the Lord and shun evil. (Prov. 3:5–7)

I distinctly remember sitting in church as a kid, bored as usual. That particular Sunday I had already drawn a Superman picture all over the offering envelope. We had just finished verse 4 of the obligatory hymns. Our pastor took the pulpit and started preaching.

But something suddenly didn't seem right. I had walked into church that morning fully convinced that God was real. And then while I was sitting there listening to the sermon, questions flooded my mind: *What if all this God stuff isn't true? What if we are just imagining that there is a God? What if there is a God—but he's not the one that we are worshiping at this church? What if everyone here is just believing they're Christians because that's what most Americans are conditioned to believe? After all, I used to believe in Santa Claus, the Easter Bunny, and the Tooth Fairy, and look where that got me.*

Don't get me wrong: I still *wanted* to believe in God—it just got more difficult. The dam of my childhood acceptance gave way to curiosity (and much later I would learn, cognitive development) that forced me to consider what was true for myself.

Many people are afraid to doubt. But our honest doubts can often become foundational to a genuine faith. Acknowledge your doubts before God and ask him to meet you in the midst of them.

Power Lift

Who am I to doubt you, Lord? Forgive me for not being able to trust you sometimes. Today I will bring my doubts before you even as I continue to follow you.

He leads me in paths of righteousness for his name's sake. (Ps. 23:3 ESV)

I've always been proud of my last name. My father and grandparents clearly enjoyed maintaining the strong, proud reputation of our name, which they had inherited from preceding generations. Groeschel is a good German name, derived from the German word *grosch*, a kind of gold or silver coin. There's a good chance that my name originally reflected the occupation of my ancestors as either bankers, merchants, or moneylenders.

Do you know the meaning of your family name? Throughout history, in virtually every culture, names carry enormous significance. They reveal something about where we've come from and how we got where we are now. They display family occupational history, trigger generational stories, and reflect personal qualities and characteristics.

In the Bible we find dozens of different names for God, each reflecting a different aspect of his glorious character. Consider how we address him as Jehovah, the Great I AM, the Lord Almighty, Emmanuel, El Shaddai, and many more. Each of these emphasizes a particular quality he's known for: his mercy, his generosity, his protection, his patience, his omniscience, his sovereignty.

If you want to overcome your doubts and grow closer to God, learning his names can deepen your faith. Your Father wants you to know him. Today call him by a name that reflects your greatest need right now.

Power Lift

There's so much about you, Lord, that I still don't know and may never know in this life. But I give you thanks and praise for the many wonderful ways you reveal yourself.

If I rise on the wings of the dawn, if I settle on the far side of the sea, even there
your hand will guide me, your right hand will hold me fast. (Ps. 139:9–10)

As I shared earlier, every summer our family goes to the lake with our
close friends. It's in a remote area and is one of the most beautiful, serene
places I know. And the fact that there's no Wi-Fi or phone towers nearby
only makes it that much better.

I confess: I have a hard time unplugging when I'm on vacation or
having family time. I figure one little peek, one quick text, one short
email won't hurt; plus it will save me so much time later when I'm back
and trying to catch up. But like popcorn, one text becomes an entire
back-and-forth conversation, one email becomes three, and pretty soon,
I might as well be working.

I'm working on this. And honestly, the way technology and social
media has become a constant, 24/7 presence in our lives, the more I
know I need to unplug. I need face-to-face time with my wife and kids,
real fellowship with friends. Time alone to pray, think, read God's Word,
and think some more. Time to go on a walk or read a book without
glancing at my phone every five seconds.

Even as I'm learning to unplug more often, I've become more grateful that God never unplugs from us. He's always available. He never
leaves us. He may seem silent or may not be speaking to us in the way we
want or can hear, but we can trust he's there. God never leaves our side.

. . . . **Power Lift** . . . .

Wherever I go or whatever I do, nothing can separate me from you, Lord. Thank
you for being there for me all the time.

> "Put your finger here; see my hands. Reach out your hand and
> put it into my side. Stop doubting and believe." (John 20:27)

Wanting proof is nothing new. Even if you don't know much about the Bible, chances are you've heard of doubting Thomas. It's interesting to me that there are only twelve verses in Scripture that mention Thomas, and yet he's been labeled for centuries as one of the world's biggest doubters, when in reality, that was only a very small portion of his story.

The rest of Thomas's story gives us hard evidence that great doubters can become people of great faith. After Jesus died on the cross and rose from the dead, Thomas said he wouldn't believe it unless he could see proof that the risen Christ was the same Master he'd known before the crucifixion. Instead of Jesus' getting mad at him and casting him aside for his lack of faith, Jesus gave Thomas exactly what he needed to believe.

Maybe you can relate to Thomas's longing for certainty at this season of your life. You don't understand everything about God. Some things in life don't add up to you at this point. You have questions. Lingering doubts. Some spiritual reservations. You may even be committed to following Jesus, yet you still hold back part of yourself, wondering if God really has your best interests at heart.

Thomas learned there's a difference between believing in and believing. Thomas believed in Jesus. But once he touched his Lord, once he had his questions answered, once the tension was resolved, Thomas no longer just believed in Jesus. He *believed* him.

Power Lift

Lord, I release my doubts and choose by faith to believe you are who you say who are. Thank you for helping me move past my doubts as I grow closer to you.

"In my distress I called to the LORD, and he answered
me . . . When my life was ebbing away, I remembered you,
LORD, and my prayer rose to you." (Jonah 2:2, 7)

I've been married for over twenty-six years now, and as I've grown in my wisdom as a husband, I've learned an important lesson about how to respond when Amy's upset. Most of the time when my wife tells me about her problems and struggles, she doesn't want me to fix them—she just wants me to care about what she's experiencing. Once I realized she didn't want me to brainstorm solutions or tell her how to fix her problems, it took a lot of pressure off. She just wanted me to listen with my heart and care that she was hurting.

And Amy is not the only one who wants to be heard in the midst of life's struggles—we all do. It's only human to want to be comforted and assured that everything will be okay when life seems to turn upside down. It's what we did naturally as little kids, and while we learn to hide it and defend our hearts as adults, we still want to feel like our pain matters to someone. I'm convinced we long to believe it matters to God. Even if he doesn't answer our prayer the way we want or when we want, if we believe he hears us, then we will continue to trust him.

Today know without a doubt that your Father in heaven hears your prayers. He's listening. And he cares. What matters to you matters to him.

Power Lift

I'm so grateful, God, that you hear my heart even when I don't have the words to express what I'm feeling. I praise you today for loving me so well.

I appeal to you, brothers and sisters, in the name of our Lord Jesus Christ, that all of you agree with one another in what you say and that there be no divisions among you, but that you be perfectly united in mind and thought. (1 Cor. 1:10)

The first time I heard you could have a personal relationship with God, those words shocked me. I knew you could believe in God. I knew you could fear God. I knew you could worship him. But I had never realized that you could know God in a close, personal relationship.

While I'm always grateful for that discovery, I soon realized God wants us to have something more than just a personal relationship with him. Instead it's even better to have a *shared* relationship with him. While we can obviously know and experience God alone, I believe we can experience him more fully with other believers.

If you are worshiping, you might be able to worship God even more effectively when you do it with others. If you are celebrating God's goodness, wouldn't you agree it's more meaningful when you celebrate with people you love? And when you are hurting, for some reason having others nearby seems to ease the pain.

So instead of just seeking to know God by yourself, commit to pursue him with others. Maybe it's in your small group. Maybe it's with a close and trusted friend. Maybe it's with people from your church.

This month is all about connecting—with God but also with others. Today don't settle for just knowing God from your perspective—experience the richness of Christ-centered community.

. . . . **Power Lift** . . . .

Thank you, God, for the many other believers in my life. As you call us to love, challenge, and encourage one another, help us to reflect your character to others.

Therefore if you have any encouragement from being united with Christ, if any comfort from his love, if any common sharing in the Spirit, if any tenderness and compassion, then make my joy complete by being like-minded, having the same love, being one in spirit and of one mind. (Phil. 2:1–2)

Events like 9/11, the Oklahoma City bombing, and Hurricane Katrina grab our attention and force us to wrestle with what we believe and why we believe it. They compel so many people to return to their faith and to seek God because there's nowhere else to turn.

In times like these, as the body of Christ, we not only comfort and console those reeling from unexpected losses, but we also offer them real hope. By meeting their needs for food, water, medicine, and shelter, we can show tangible evidence of our love, concern, and connection with them.

But we must also keep in mind that we don't have to wait until some tragedy occurs to serve those around us with the same compassionate, intentional focus. There's no reason to wait until we share a major loss to come together as a community. We can demonstrate the love of Christ to our neighbors without any reason other than God's desire to help those in need, comfort the hurting, and set free those enslaved by addiction.

I'm convinced this is the essence of obedience: loving one another. United in our faith and the Spirit of God, we are stronger than any of us could be as individuals. God's presence lives among us as we reflect his generosity, grace, and glory. We are transformed and blessed as we give from our grateful hearts.

Power Lift

I want to connect with other people, Lord, and serve them with your love. Help me to unite with my brothers and sisters in Christ so that others will know the love of Jesus in their lives.

> They all joined together constantly in prayer, along with the women
> and Mary the mother of Jesus, and with his brothers. (Acts 1:14)

Have you noticed the massive difference between praying *for* someone and praying *with* someone? Praying for someone is powerful, meaningful, and special. Praying with someone is all that—and so much more.

For example, if I'm hurting and you send me a text, "Praying for ya," that will mean a lot to me. If I've got a big presentation to make at work and you lean over and tell me you prayed for me earlier in the morning, I'll be sincerely grateful. If I've got a decision to make and you remind me that you will pray before you go to sleep, I will find confidence in your promise.

But you could do more than just pray for me. You could choose to pray with me. If I'm hurting and you stop what you are doing and grab my hands to pray, that prayer just went to another level. If we are on a call and you stop the conversation and say, "Can we pray right now?" It's likely my faith will be moved in a significant way.

Sure, praying with someone can feel awkward. At times praying with others might even be intimidating. But once you start, I can assure you that you will sense God's presence and the words will begin to flow.

If the opportunity presents itself, consider taking prayer to the next level. Don't just pray for someone. Pray with them.

Power Lift

I'm so grateful for the many other people who pray for me, Lord. Today I want to spend a few minutes lifting them up even as I look forward to the next time we can pray together.

OCTOBER 4

Gracious words are a honeycomb, sweet to the soul
and healing to the bones. (Prov. 16:24)

You've probably figured out by now that I have quite a sweet tooth. Donuts are my Achilles' heel. Someone thinks they're doing a good deed by dropping off a couple dozen Krispy Kremes to our church office. They're often still warm with all that sugary glaze glistening, their fresh-fried smell wafting down the hall to me. My temptation isn't limited to donuts either. Cake is a perennial winner, along with anything chocolate.

But I've learned there's actually something sweeter and much healthier than any dessert or treat: gracious words. When someone encourages me with a sincere compliment, a favorite verse, or an unexpected text, I feel so good inside. I'm reminded that I'm not alone in my struggles. I'm encouraged to try harder and to keep my eyes on Christ. And I'm inspired to share the power of positive words by telling others how much I appreciate them, how much they mean to me, what I see God doing in their lives.

Our gracious words are better than donuts. Sweet, warm, and satisfying, they have the power to resolve conflicts, heal wounds, and nourish our souls. Your words matter. Make encouraging others with your words a priority, sharing God's goodness with everyone you encounter.

Power Lift

Dear God, I want to speak sweet, life-giving words to those around me. I want others to experience your love and grace when they hear my voice today.

"For where two or three gather in my name, there am I with them." (Matt. 18:20)

For years, Amy wanted me to pray with her every day. It wasn't that I was opposed to it, I just didn't do it. I could give you a list of the reasons I used to rationalize my apathetic approach to our shared prayers: She prayed too long. She wanted to pray about things that I'd already prayed about. Besides, I preferred to pray alone.

After years of making excuses, somehow God changed my heart. Instead of my list of reasons for avoiding prayer with my best friend, I asked myself why on earth I wouldn't pray with her. The list was even longer than my excuses. I wouldn't pray if I didn't want to experience God together. Or to see him move in our family's lives. Or to grow closer to one another. Or to daily depend on our Savior as one. Or to be more vulnerable to temptation. And the list went on and on.

Now I wouldn't want to miss a day of praying with her. To be clear, we don't have long, fancy, drawn-out prayer meetings. We just grab hands before I leave for the office and talk to God about whatever is going on.

Consider making prayer with someone else a daily part of your life. If you are married, your spouse is an obvious choice. If you have children, you could always pray with them. It might be a close Christian friend from work or someone from church.

Always pray. Try not to always pray alone.

· · · · · · · · · · · **Power Lift** · · · · · · · · · · · ·

It's a privilege to talk with you each day, Lord. Help me to see those opportunities when I can share our conversation with other brothers and sisters in Christ.

And whatever you do, whether in word or deed, do it all in the name of the Lord Jesus, giving thanks to God the Father through him. (Col. 3:17)

When political candidates run for office, the media is relentless in comparing what they say with past facts about their behavior. Reporters know that voters are looking for leaders who are consistent in their beliefs and in their behavior. We want to be able to trust that once a candidate is elected, he or she will do what they said they're going to do.

Whether we realize it or not, we are all held to this same standard. We may not be running for office, but others notice how our words line up with our actions. As followers of Christ, we want to make sure we "walk the talk" and do more than just give lip service to our faith. There's nothing more disheartening to see than a person who claims to know Jesus doing something that's obviously opposite of his example.

As a pastor I get tired of people telling me to be careful what I say or do in public. While I appreciate their intention (most of the time), I also stress to them that they are held to the same standards. Yes, we all say and do things we wish we could take back. But God calls all of us to be doers of his Word and not hearers only.

Today let others know you follow Jesus by what you say and what you do.

Power Lift

Jesus, I want to reflect your example in all that I think, say, and do today. Give me your power to live with integrity so others can see God's glory shining through.

With all prayer and petition pray at all times in the Spirit,
and with this in view, be on the alert with all perseverance
and petition for all the saints. (Eph. 6:18 NASB)

Early in my relationship with God, I wanted to pray for others but wasn't always sure how. Then I heard someone offer a small idea that helped me experience a massive prayer breakthrough. My friend simply suggested that I ask God who to pray for. And then ask God to guide me in prayer. That was it. *Who?* And then *What?*

So I tried. I found a quiet place where I wouldn't be distracted and told God that I wanted to seek him and pray for some people, but I didn't know who needed his touch or presence. Within a split second, a close friend from high school that I hadn't seen in over two years popped into my mind. Then I asked God, "What should I pray?" Immediately, I began praying that my friend would be drawn closer to God.

Wrapping up, I then had another person pop into mind: a lady I had worked with in years past. So I prayed for her and for her family and for her marriage, which I knew had been strained for some time.

While I normally find it difficult to pray for five minutes without being distracted, that day more than a half hour flew by before I knew what had happened.

Today spend some time with God. Ask him "Who?" and "What?" and then start praying.

• • • • • • • • • • **Power Lift** • • • • • • • • • •

Reveal the people you want me to pray for today, Lord, and show me how I can best lift them and their needs up to you.

Let your conversation be always full of grace, seasoned with salt,
so that you may know how to answer everyone. (Col. 4:6)

Recently another family invited ours over for a meal to fellowship and get better acquainted. They treated us like royalty and we enjoyed a delicious meal. And because I had already seen a picture-perfect chocolate cake on the counter, I had made sure to save room for a small slice. After the first forkful was in my mouth, I was so glad I did.

And I was also glad I had a full glass of iced tea beside me. The cake was chocolate but was also flavored with smoky chipotle chiles. The combination was delicious together, just the right balance of sweet and savory, but not at all what I expected.

Our response to others often needs to be more like that cake. While gracious words can be as sweet as honey, our words also need a little spice sometimes. Without the right seasoning, our words, just like our food, get bland, predictable, and too easily digested. But when we speak the truth of God's Word with a loving, compassionate heart, we can expect others to take notice.

In those moments, our conversations become not only encouraging but also challenging. Others see that we care about them and want God's best for them, but they also experience an edge that convicts, motivates, and inspires them to more. When we're willing to indicate the holiness of God's standards as well as his loving mercy, then we offer the life-changing taste of the gospel.

Power Lift

Today, Lord, let my speech be flavored with the salt of truth as well as the sweetness of your love.

May the God who gives endurance and encouragement give you the same
attitude of mind toward each other that Christ Jesus had. (Rom. 15:5)

A few years ago, a family in our church experienced the unexpected
death of their precious little girl. Driving over to their house, I tried
to prepare my heart. What would I say? How could I comfort them? I
wanted to be so strong and comforting for these dear people but feared
I wouldn't be able to control my own sadness. So I prayed and asked
God to direct everything I would say or do.

After knocking on the door, I breathed deeply and walked in.
When I saw the dad across the room, he immediately rose to his feet
and moved toward me. With his full weight, he collapsed on me. Before
I could stop it, I started crying with him. All I could do was hold him
as we sobbed together.

For quite some time, I held him. Then we sat together and no one
spoke. Not a word. When I left, I got in the car and felt like a massive
failure. I didn't say anything to comfort this family.

A few days later I received the most touching note. It was from
both the mom and dad who gushed about how much my visit had ministered to them. It was then I realized that presence is more powerful
than words. Just being there, together, was all that mattered.

Today recognize that you don't have to say the right thing to make
a big difference. Sometimes you just have to be present.

Power Lift

Allow me to comfort others, Lord, just by sharing their burdens today. Help me to
show them your heart through my presence in the midst of their struggle.

> Finally, brothers, whatever is true, whatever is honorable,
> whatever is just, whatever is pure, whatever is lovely, whatever
> is commendable, if there is any excellence, if there is anything
> worthy of praise, think about these things. (Phil. 4:8 ESV)

Not long ago, I planned to take Amy to the movies for our date night. So many friends had recommended a new comedy that had just released, and I thought it would be a perfect choice. Reviews online were mixed, but I didn't read in-depth so I could avoid spoilers.

We got a sitter, bought our tickets, and were happily munching popcorn when the lights went down and the movie started. We lasted about ten minutes. At the risk of sounding like an old fuddy-duddy, I was so upset by what I saw and heard in just that short amount of time. Graphic violence and death were trivialized, and sexual jokes flew faster than the f-bombs coming out of the actors' mouths.

Our culture encourages us to accept graphic language and violent images as no big deal. We're encouraged to be openminded about sex and accept pornographic scenes as commonplace. Human suffering, prejudiced behavior, and evil are punchlines.

More than ever, if you want to follow Jesus, you must be willing to take a stand for what's right, what's true, and what's good. Once you see something, it's in your head forever. Once you hear something, it continues to echo in your mind.

Stop letting others poison you. Instead dwell on the goodness of God: his Word, his creation, and the amazing changes at work in the lives around you.

Power Lift

Give me wisdom and discernment, Lord, so that I'm willing to protect my mind, my heart, and my body from harmful words and images.

Therefore encourage one another and build each other up. (1 Thess. 5:11)

One of the most spiritual things you can do is encourage someone. We are told to encourage one another every day so that sin's deceitfulness doesn't harden our hearts. While it's always meaningful to encourage someone after they've done a good job, scored a goal, or gotten a really cool new haircut, it's even more important to encourage someone spiritually.

Imagine how God might use you to encourage someone to press on when they feel like giving up. Or how God might help someone's marriage as you tell them how you've overcome the same problem in yours. Think about how much of a difference you could make to someone who is down by telling them who they are in Christ.

Sometimes you can literally be a voice of hope. You can be the difference between someone quitting or staying in the game. Between someone giving in or continuing the fight. From someone continuing to hate or choosing to forgive. Between someone losing it or finding real peace, contentment, and joy.

Be watchful. Be prayerful. Be ready. You may walk by someone at work who seems fine, but is in real pain. You may talk to someone by text that puts up a good front, but really needs someone to listen. You might encounter a total stranger, and one word of encouragement might make a big difference.

You have no idea what God might do in someone else's life through one simple act of encouragement. Be available to him today.

Power Lift

Use me today, God, to bless those around me. Direct me to the one person who needs encouragement the most.

> Set an example for the believers in speech, in conduct,
> in love, in faith, and in purity. (1 Tim. 4:12)

Now more than ever, others see and hear you more than you realize. Whether intended or not, a careless comment, thoughtless tweet, or prideful status update can give others a negative impression—or worse, hurt their perception of God in some way. While our culture encourages everyone to broadcast their lives on social media as a personal reality show, we would often be more impactful to think before we click.

It's tempting, too, with so many people posting, tweeting, and commenting, to think that it's no big deal what you say, post, or pin. But keep in mind that hundreds, even thousands, of people may base their understanding of the gospel on what they see reflected in your online presence.

I'm not encouraging you to be artificial and sprinkle a bunch of phrases like "God bless you!" and "To God be the glory!" all over social media. I'm just hoping you realize that when we connect online, we're communicating who we are and what we believe. Just as we make mistakes in real life, we will also misstep with technology. But when you're mindful of all who see you online, you can think twice before posting.

Today ask God for wisdom about how to reflect him with your online presence.

Power Lift

Jesus, you're my perfect role model and best example. Remind me today to reflect you in all that I say and do—both in person and online.

Finally, all of you, be like-minded, be sympathetic, love one
another, be compassionate and humble. (1 Peter 3:8)

One Sunday after church, I was greeting people in the lobby. This young girl came walking slowly toward me. From her body language, I could tell that she was struggling. Her head hung low, shoulders slumped. She looked like she was carrying the weight of the world.

Since I meet a lot of people at church, it's not easy to learn all their names. It's important to me, but I wish I were better at remembering. I had only talked to this girl one time before so I scrambled to try and remember her name. "Melanie!" I blurted out, praying I had it right. "I'm so glad to see you!"

She stopped in her tracks. *Oh, no! Did I get it right? Did I miss it horribly?*

Then her face lit up with gratitude. "How did you remember my name?"

As we chatted, she eventually explained her current struggle. After losing her mom, dropping out of school, and being betrayed by her best friend, she wondered why she should keep living.

But the fact that I called her by name apparently made a difference. I explained to her that God knows her name and he cares about her more than she could ever imagine. She listened, hanging on every word, and I could tell she believed it. I made sure to follow up with her.

Make it a goal today to call everyone by their name. You'll be surprised what a difference it can make.

Power Lift

Lord, you call me by name, and I want to do the same with others today. Help me to focus on seeing them with my heart and not just my eyes.

Better one handful with tranquility than two handfuls
with toil and chasing after the wind. (Eccl. 4:6)

Growing up, I learned that if one is good, two must be better. If one dollar is good, two is better. If one Izod shirt is good, two are better. When I was probably in my midteens, I went to the movies with several buddies. Practicing my theory, I assumed if one roll of candy was good, then two would rock.

So during the show, I sat there and ate two rolls of Spree candies, those little brightly colored, chewy disks. And two was better—until I vomited them up right there on the theater floor. To this day, those friends still tease me about my ultimate "technicolor yawn"!

After growing in my relationship with Christ, I've discovered that less is often more. Jesus told us clearly that life does not consist in the abundance of your possessions. That's why I want less stuff and more friends. Less stuff and more time with family. Less stuff and more experiences to remember and enjoy.

Those who are most blessed are not those who have the most but those who need the least. Your life is too valuable, your calling too great, and your God too good to waste your life on things that don't matter.

Better is one handful and children you know and love. Better one handful with intimate friends. Better one handful and simple vacation memories. Better one handful and a good marriage. Better one handful and passion for Jesus.

Don't forget, less is often more.

Power Lift

Instead of always chasing after more, Lord, today help me to focus on quality and not quantity—of my time with you, in my relationships, and with my work.

Do not repay evil with evil or insult with insult. On the contrary,
repay evil with blessing, because to this you were called
so that you may inherit a blessing. (1 Peter 3:9)

Have you ever noticed that so much of how we connect with others relies on an attitude of give-and-take? If the waitress is friendly and provides great service, then we leave her a good tip. If we need a favor from a friend, then we better treat them well and expect to return the favor to them at some point. If a coworker needs help putting her report together, then she better be prepared to share the credit and help out the next time we need her.

On the other hand, the same mindset seems to apply to negative behavior. If our neighbor snubs us, then we're tempted to ignore them back. If someone spreads gossip about us at church, then we won't likely be friendly to them the next time our paths cross. It seems natural to practice the art of retaliation and assume that's just how we survive being in relationship with so many different people.

Jesus didn't operate this way because it's not his Father's way. God wants his children treating everyone with kindness, generosity, mercy, and love no matter how they might treat us. Yes, turning the other cheek or showing grace to someone who doesn't deserve it doesn't make sense—but that's the whole point! Grace disrupts people's expectations. It breaks them out of their cycle of action-and-reaction and forces them to consider God at work.

Today shock someone with the love of Christ by responding with blessing when they show the opposite.

Power Lift

I've received your grace in abundance, Lord, and want to reflect your love and mercy to all I encounter today—whether I think they deserve it or not.

> Wisdom, like an inheritance, is a good thing and
> benefits those who see the sun. (Eccl. 7:11)

My parents always wanted to know where I would be and who I would be with when I was growing up. They always said I would be known by the company I keep. I knew what they meant, but it wasn't until I was a parent myself that I fully believed them. Suddenly, like many "helicopter parents," I wanted to know who my kids were with and what they were doing. And it wasn't nearly as easy as I thought it would be.

On one hand, I wanted them to be loving, kind, and accepting toward all their peers and classmates. On the other, I wanted them to develop discernment about who was trustworthy and who was not. So I tried to teach them about patterns of behavior, what it means when someone does what they say they will do, and about seeking God for wisdom.

Even as adults, we often overlook seeking God's wisdom regarding the people we should invest our time in. Some are obvious, like our families, coworkers, and certain friends. But others may be more challenging. Obviously, we should seek out fellowship and community with other believers. But if we only hang out with other Christians, then we will likely miss opportunities to share our faith with the people who need it most.

This is why asking God for his wisdom about our relationships is so important.

Today ask God to direct you to the people you need to invest in.

Power Lift

Lord, give me your wisdom so I can know which relationships you want me to invest in today.

A gentle tongue is a tree of life, but perverseness
in it breaks the spirit. (Prov. 15:4 ESV)

Several years ago, our daughter Catie came bursting into our bedroom
to tattle on her little sister, "Mommy and Daddy! Anna said a really,
really bad word!"

Accustomed to their sisterly drama, Amy and I calmly asked what
the really, *really* bad word was.

"It's so bad, I can't say it," she explained soberly. Leaning in some,
Amy asked, "Catie, can you tell me what letter the word started with?"
Our distressed little tattler leaned in and whispered, "Anna said the
one starting with *s*."

Since younger sister Anna was only six at the time, this definitely got
out attention. Trying not to show panic, we wondered aloud where she
heard such bad language. Then Amy said to Catie, "I promise you that
you won't get in trouble, but can you please tell me exactly what she said."

At first Catie resisted. After continuous prodding, she whispered
ever so softly. "You know—she said 'shut up.'"

To this day, we can't tell if that makes us pretty good parents or
way too strict. Either way, we laugh every time we retell it. And it also
reminds me of the importance of watching what we say, no matter what
age we might be.

Our words have incredible impact, and as the Bible points out, can be
life-giving or life-taking. We can bless others by what we say around them,
or we can hurt their hearts and destroy them. When we focus on being
more like Christ, our words will bring Good News to those around us.

• • • • • • • • • • • • **Power Lift** • • • • • • • • • • • •

Jesus, give me the power to hold my tongue when I'm tempted to say things that
will tear others down. Following your example, I want to bless others when I speak.

Bear with each other and forgive one another if any of you has a grievance against someone. Forgive as the Lord forgave you. (Col. 3:13)

One time when Amy was running late, our whole family loaded into our minivan behind schedule. Extremely frustrated, I punched the gas pedal and raced the Suburban like it was a Mustang GT. When Amy told me to slow down, rebelliously, I sped up. After missing a turn, I wheeled our vehicle around like something from the *Dukes of Hazzard* and did a one-eighty in the middle of a four-lane street.

Kids flew in all directions and screamed in fear. Fortunately, no other cars were near enough to get hit, and none of us were hurt. While I straightened our vehicle, the whole car was silent. No one spoke. No one moved. No one breathed.

Finally, our oldest daughter, age twelve at the time said, "Daddy, you need to pull this car over, and Mom needs to give you a hard spanking!"

She was right. I had just acted like a total you-know-what. The only thing I could do, was fall on my sword and ask for forgiveness. "I messed up really bad. I'm so sorry. What I did was wrong. Will you please forgive me?" I said sincerely.

Of course they all forgave me and still retell the "Daddy needs a spanking" story. They know I'm not perfect, nor do I pretend to be. But they also know that I love God and want to please him. When I don't, I do what we all should do and ask for his help and forgiveness.

Is there someone you need to ask to forgive you? Today be mindful of the consequences your decisions have on the people around you.

· · · · · · · · · · · **Power Lift** · · · · · · · · · · ·

Dear God, I'm far from perfect and often fail to obey you. Forgive me when I mess up, and give me the strength to ask those I've sinned against to forgive me as well.

Be made new in the attitude of your minds. (Eph. 4:23)

Sometimes we forget how much control we have over our daily attitudes.

We've all had those days when nothing seems to be going right, and then a friend, family member, or coworker stops and asks us how we are doing. They aren't satisfied with our polite reply, "Oh, I'm fine. How about you?" But they sense there's more and keep talking, listening, and caring until we begin to sense our attitudes shifting.

We realize we have so much for which to be thankful. We're reminded of God's goodness and sovereignty. We regain our eternal perspective and recognize our little inconveniences are no big deal. Maybe we can even laugh about what seemed like a monumental struggle earlier in the day.

The Bible tells us we have the ability to renew our minds by taking our thoughts captive to Christ. If we filter our negative thoughts when they occur, refusing to give them room to grow and fester into our attitudes, then we hold onto our peace and joy. No longer does our mood depend on our circumstances. Regardless of what happens from hour to hour, if we focus on Christ, then our thoughts, words, expressions, and actions will reflect a positive, loving spirit.

Power Lift

When negative thoughts come to mind today, Jesus, help me submit them to your authority. Let my attitude reflect the grace, gratitude, and gentleness that I see in you.

> If any of you lacks wisdom, you should ask God, who gives generously
> to all without finding fault, and it will be given to you. (James 1:5)

Each year, as our church grows, it gets more difficult to make the best decisions. Should we remodel a campus we already have? Purchase more property and build larger facilities? Add an additional service to one of our new locations? Usually, there's no right or wrong decision—it's a matter of impact.

Good decisions are often relatively easy to make. But your best decisions are usually much more difficult. They may cause you to struggle between what feels safe and comfortable versus what seems risky and uncertain. They may challenge you, because you face several good options but struggle to know which one is best. Or they may carry a steeper price than other, easier options. Your best decisions may even defy logic or go against the recommendations of those around you.

Ultimately, however, there's no need to panic. If you're walking closely with God, then he will guard your steps and guide you. Even if you stumble into a ditch, take a detour, or get stuck, he can redeem your bad decisions into a positive outcome. Our God is that good.

No matter what decision we're facing, we will always be required to trust God.

. . . . **Power Lift** . . . .

Lord, sometimes it's difficult to discern which choices will yield the greatest impact for your kingdom. Today give me wisdom to hear your voice and follow your lead.

> Do nothing out of selfish ambition or vain conceit. Rather in
> humility value others above yourselves. (Phil. 2:3)

Several years ago, I agreed to go with my friend John to look at a house he and his wife might buy. After touring the inside, we headed to the back yard and were looking up at the roof when we heard a low, ferocious growl behind us.

We spun around just in time to see one of the original hounds of hell bearing down on us. It looked like the offspring of Marmaduke and Cujo with a little Rottweiler thrown in. I'd like to say I stood my ground and used my God-given talent as a dog whisperer to tame the savage heart of the evil beast.

But that's not what happened.

You know how athletes push off to get a strong start? That's what I did. Only what I pushed off of was my friend John.

Now, to hear him tell it, I shoved him to the ground and ran like a five-year-old. Reflecting on it now, I can see how he might have interpreted it that way. Certainly I did put both my hands on him, and I did push him toward the dog—accidentally, of course—with my full strength. But for whatever it's worth, I wasn't pushing John *toward* the dog; I was pushing myself *away* from it.

If I'm honest, I'm selfish. I'm committed to protecting myself. I wasn't worried about John, just myself.

If you want to connect with others and build strong relationships, you must put others first. Just maybe not in the face of a big mean dog.

Power Lift

It's hard to put others first, Lord, so give me your strength to consider their welfare above my own.

"Whoever wants to be my disciple must deny themselves
and take up their cross and follow me." (Matt. 16:24)

We don't have to teach people to be selfish. We are selfish by nature.
When push comes to shove (as my friend John can attest), we're looking out for number one—me, myself, and mine. Not only do we have
our sinfulness working against us, but much of what we see in culture
affirms our self-centered tendencies. Some argue that a massive shift
in culture in 1973 changed everything. I was only six at the time, but I
certainly took note, mostly because of the catchy jingle.

In a move that would rock the fast-food world, Burger King boldly
declared that you had choices, options, decisions to make. If you wanted a
burger, you could "have it your way!" Hold the pickle, hold the lettuce—
whatever you wanted, you could have it that way.

As far as competing with McDonald's, BK nailed it. But if you
want to be closer to God and connect with others, then it's not going
to work. According to Jesus, life is not all about us. Even when everything in culture tries to tell us that it is.

We are not called to celebrate, promote, defend, or advance ourselves—
but to deny ourselves. To pick up our cross, to suffer through not having
everything our way, to die to our selfish tendencies.

God wants us to have it *his* way.

And we're not talking burgers.

Power Lift

It's tough to put others first, Lord, when everything around me encourages me to
have it my way. Today give me the strength to take up my cross and follow you.

> "My food," said Jesus, "is to do the will of him who
> sent me and to finish his work." (John 4:34)

Jesus had just finished ministering when his disciples realized their Master had not eaten in a while. Never one to miss a teaching opportunity, Christ said, "I have food to eat that you know nothing about" (John 4:32). Now, if your mind is a bit odd like mine, you might imagine the disciples thinking, *You've got food we know nothing about? Maybe some of those new fig-and-olive power bars under your robe? Do you have pockets in there? Sneaking lamb kabobs from the temple concessions?*

Maybe we're not so weird after all, because the disciples also took the Lord's response literally. "Could someone have brought him food?" they asked (John 4:33). But Jesus was talking about something much more substantive than lunch. Basically, he told them, "My food is to serve God. My food is to please him. My food is to complete the assignment that God sent me to do. My food is to do the will of my Father and to finish his work."

God wants us to contribute rather than to consume. When all of culture says, "fill yourself," God tells us to fill others. He didn't create us to be takers. Our Father created us to be givers. Rather than focusing on our self-centered desires, God calls us to focus on the needs of others. Instead of cutting to the front of the line, God calls us to wait at the end.

He created you to serve.

Power Lift

I hunger for your Word, Lord, and I want to serve those around me like the example of your Son. Today let my food be the satisfaction that comes from serving you and putting others above myself.

"Whoever serves me must follow me; and where I am, my servant also
will be. My Father will honor the one who serves me." (John 12:26)

If you want to have deeper relationships, stronger connections, and more
effective teams, then good communication is essential. It's important
to know where you stand with each other and who is responsible for
what. Without trust and the freedom to speak openly, it's impossible
to grow together.

While on earth, Jesus clearly had this kind of closeness with his
Father in heaven. Christ frequently went away to pray and be alone with
God. He knew that the more time he spent pursuing God, the more
effectively he could minister to those around him.

The same holds true for us today. The more time we spend with
God, the better we get to know him. And the better we get to know our
Father, the more we grow to trust him. The deeper our trust grows, the
more we become transformed into being like Jesus.

When we follow Christ's example, we can be sure we're pleasing
our heavenly Father. He wants us to live purposefully and passionately,
enjoying the abundant life Jesus came to bring us. God knows that we
find our lives when we lose them in service to others. Today look for
opportunities to serve those you encounter.

· · · · · · · · · · · **Power Lift** · · · · · · · · · ·

I want to follow you, Jesus, and become a leader who puts others first. And when
I serve like you, I know God our Father is pleased.

Love one another . . . Outdo one another in showing honor. (Rom. 12:10 ESV)

As a young pastor, I learned so much about ministry from an older lady named Lana. She knocked on our church door one day, and I felt moved to take personal responsibility for helping her. I recruited some other church members, and we spent several days addressing each of her critical needs. We helped her get cleaned up, got her into some clean, comfortable clothes, and got her some medical attention for her skin infections.

As we had the honor of serving Lana, she became more and more open to talking about spiritual issues. She had sold her body for money, and she carried more guilt than I was comfortable imagining. But the grace of Jesus swept her away. Lana cried out to him for mercy, asking him to make her his disciple.

By God's grace, Lana remained sober, found work, and got her own place. Amy and I threw her a housewarming party, and I've never known anyone to be as proud of their home. When we didn't hear from her in several days, we went to check on her and confirmed our worst fears. Suffering from significant health issues, Lana had passed away.

I was sad that day, but not so much for Lana. She had met Jesus. Her suffering was over. Now she was with him. I was sad for the rest of us. Lana gave us a reason to get out of our comfortable lives. She taught us how to love someone most other people wouldn't even touch. She gave us the gift of giving our lives to serve her.

Lana helped grow my faith. Because of Lana, I realized that serving isn't something we do. A servant is who we're called to be.

Power Lift

Take me out of my comfort zone today, Lord, so I might receive the blessing of serving those in need around me.

"A new command I give you: Love one another. As I have loved you, so you must love one another. By this everyone will know that you are my disciples, if you love one another." (John 13:34–35)

When I was in college, it was pretty easy to identify other students based on what they were wearing. Those in fraternities and sororities almost always wore something sporting their Greek letters. The jocks usually had on team shirts or some other apparel related to their sport. The preppies had polo ponies and alligators on everything. Dance majors wore tights. And business majors often kept their dress shirts tucked in and buttoned down.

It wasn't so different once I got out of college either. It's so tempting to see a uniform, a business logo, or team mascot and assume we can know a lot about someone. Christians are no different and love to wear a cross, tattoo a Bible verse, or display a faith-based twist to a familiar saying. But Jesus told us the best way we can make sure others know who we are is by the way we love each other.

When we love others with the selfless, sacrificial love of Christ, then others notice. We stand out. We don't need to dress differently, cover our cars with bumper stickers, or wear a certain symbol or emblem.

We just need to love.

Power Lift

Jesus, I want others to know I belong to you by the way I love the people around me. Give me a tender heart so I can see beyond their surface impressions.

"For God so loved the world, that he gave his only Son, that whoever believes in him should not perish but have eternal life." (John 3:16 ESV)

It happened again the other day. I met someone new to our community. Like always, I asked them how they're adjusting and how they like their new home. When I brought up church, I found out that this person was already a Christian—and a very frustrated one.

Within seconds, they had already told me about seven different churches they had tried since moving here. Then they listed off the various reasons that none of those churches could "meet their needs" and "minister to their family." Then they delivered the line that's a critical deathblow to my pastor's heart: "We're still church shopping."

Too often, we view ourselves as spiritual consumers with the church as the product. Before long, this polluted mindset creeps into our theology. Well, since I'm going to church and doing good things, then God should answer my prayer, get me the job I want, help my sports team win the championship, and ensure that my twelve-year-old becomes class secretary. And if any of this doesn't happen the way I want it to, then God has failed me. Because remember: everything is all about me. Right?

We seem to forget that we are not made to be spiritual consumers. As Jesus gave his life for us, we are to give our lives by serving and loving others. And the church is not some place we go. The church is who we are. So be the church today as you show the love of our Savior.

Power Lift

I pray you will use your church, Lord, to attract and serve those who do not know you. Protect us from becoming consumers focused only on ourselves. Give us your heart for those who are lost.

> "And if anyone forces you to go one mile, go with
> him two miles." (Matt. 5:41 ESV)

I've had the privilege of hearing the stories of several people who grew closer to Christ when they decided to serve. One is a thirteen-year-old boy named Gavin. After a friend invited Gavin to church, Gavin met the grace of Jesus, surrendered his life to Christ, and was baptized. And even though Gavin wasn't an adult, he started serving.

Now every week he worships in one service on the weekend, then serves at the other six. You read that right. A thirteen-year-old boy serves at six services every weekend. Rain or shine, you'll see this fired-up kid welcoming people to church week after week. Serving impacted Gavin's life so much that he asked for permission to get other students involved serving. Now this middle-school student has personally recruited and oversees *fifty other students* who serve on our host team. Talk about a gift of leadership! Gavin doesn't just occasionally and sporadically serve. He is a servant. That's who he is.

No matter what your gift, God has given it to you not just to make your life better but to use it to serve him and others in the church. If you're just "going" to church and not serving in church, I can promise you that God wants to do more in you and through you.

Power Lift

Dear God, work in my heart so that I can be your humble servant, giving my gifts to all those around me.

> My dear brothers and sisters, take note of this: Everyone should be quick
> to listen, slow to speak and slow to become angry. (James 1:19)

The choice to connect with someone can produce benefits beyond our wildest dreams. He's gone on to heaven now, but Lyle Schaller was around seventy-five years of age when we met. He was a legendary church consultant, and our church was only a couple years old at the time.

Because our space was so small, we had to hold three services just to accommodate everyone who wanted to attend. When I spoke with Lyle, I was considering adding a fourth service, but after hearing my explanation, he said, "That's the problem with you young guys: you all think so small."

Ouch. Not what I expected to hear. "You shouldn't be thinking three or four services. You should be thinking about doing *seven* services at your first location and then seven at your second, third, fourth, and so on."

My jaw hit the ground. Was this old dude insane? SEVEN?! I considered politely thanking him for his time and making my escape.

But I had to hear more. The more he talked, I realized that my new friend Lyle wasn't crazy. He could simply envision a future no one else could see. And he was right. Today our church conducts over a hundred and fifty services each week at more than two dozen locations in eight different states.

God brought Lyle into my life at the perfect time to have maximum impact for others. God brings certain people into your life for the same reason.

Power Lift

Dear Lord, help me pay attention and listen to those people you've brought into my life for your purposes. What seems impossible for me is easy for you.

> Listen to advice and accept discipline, and at the end you
> will be counted among the wise. (Prov. 19:20)

Years ago I made friends with a guy at my gym named Bart who has helped me change my body physically in more ways than I can count. I had worked out for most of my life, exercising faithfully for more than twenty years. But I also ate whatever I wanted. And by whatever, I mean anything with sugar or salt (and especially sugar *and* salt): donuts, cinnamon rolls, cake, ice cream, and chips and whatever was within reach that I could dip them in.

But I was one friend away from changing my "physical" future. I noticed that Bart didn't work out much harder than I did, but he looked very different from me. He was ripped! I always attributed that to genetics, but Bart helped me see that diet is actually more important than exercise. Little by little, he helped me make small changes. First I added protein. Then I cut carbs. Then I added vitamins. Then I cut down on desserts. And together we tweaked my workouts. Over time, I became stronger and leaner, and I felt better. But more important, I was healthy, probably healthier than I'd ever been.

One friend.

Too many changes to count.

Do you have a few friends that make you better, people who see your potential? Think about it. Do your buddies at the gym make you better? Or do the friends in your support group help you grow? Do the people you work with make you sharper? Do the moms you run with make you stronger?

If not, decide to connect with someone new—someone who makes you better.

Power Lift

Lead me to the right person, Lord, who can help motivate, inspire, and propel me forward. Help me to be that person in someone else's life.

"And lead us not into temptation, but deliver us from the evil one." (Matt. 6:13)

Sometimes it's hard to resist the attention we get when we do the right thing. We help someone, give more than expected, stretch beyond our comfort zone. And when others notice, it has to feel good. Even though we don't want to become prideful and self-righteous, the temptation is there. And the more others notice, the more likely we are to think we're doing a great job.

Ironically, the best way to avoid this trap is to allow others to see our weaknesses and shortcomings. When we are transparent in appropriate ways, those around us get to see that God is the one accomplishing his purposes through us. It's not that we're perfect or extraordinary or superstars. It's simply that we serve a holy, amazing, stellar God.

This kind of honest vulnerability often illustrates a godly life more than any attention-getting good deed. We can shine the light of Christ in our dark world without making it a fireworks show. The glow of one lone flame is more than enough to illuminate the darkest night.

When we share our struggles and weaknesses with others, we also remain humble and dependent on God. We resist taking credit for anything but our availability for God to use us. Such admissions keep us grounded and make us more approachable and identifiable for non-believers, and more encouraging and real for other Christians.

Today let others know what God is doing through you.

Power Lift

Dear God, you empower me to do things I could never achieve in my own power. Today I want everyone to know you are the source of my strength, hope, and inspiration.

Oh give thanks to the LORD, for he is good; for his steadfast
love endures forever! (1 Chron. 16:34 ESV)

My grandma was an amazing lady. As someone who grew up in the
Great Depression, she deeply valued hard work, discipline, and financial responsibility. She was one who never spent much on herself, but
was often generous with others.

Since my sister Lisa and I share the same birthday (three years apart
to the exact day), we always looked forward to receiving Grandma's card
in the mail, always stuffed with a check for some extra spending cash.
Year after year, I'd wait for Lisa to open her card first. "Twenty bucks!"
she'd shout, already thinking about how she would spend it.

Then I'd open my card, read what was written, then unfold the
check. Each time it was just like Lisa's, exactly twenty dollars. But instead
of celebrating the same amount, I'd fake Lisa out and shout, "Wow! I
got $100!" Of course, I was just joking, but she would get so upset. The
funny thing is that she'd fall for the same trick year after year.

Then one year, Grandma must have caught wind of it. Because that
year I opened my twenty-dollar check and pretended like it was $100!
But when Lisa opened her check, it wasn't for $20. It was actually $100!

There is never a winner when we compare. As Theodore Roosevelt
said, "Comparison is the thief of joy." Remember, the most joyful person
isn't the one who has the most but the one who is thankful for the most.

Power Lift

Dear God, you provide so much and I'm more than grateful. Help me not to compare but to see the abundance of blessings in my life each day.

I give thanks to my God always for you because of the grace of
God that was given you in Christ Jesus. (1 Cor. 1:4 ESV)

When my daughter Mandy was just a little girl, we bought a box fan at a neighbor's garage sale to cool her room. The fan was perfect except for a small hole in the corner of the protective plastic grate. My wife and I felt confident that Mandy wouldn't find it, especially if we placed that side of the fan against the wall.

Then one evening after work, I lifted Mandy out of her crib to play with her. She had just started walking, and I basked in every minute of watching her tottering around. But that evening, my heart stopped.

Mandy bounced across the room, making a beeline straight toward the fan. To this day, I'm not sure how the fan got turned around with the exposed grating facing out. But Mandy seemed to eye the small hole with her fingers pointing directly toward the spinning and exposed blades.

Fueled by a rush of adrenaline, I dove across the room and managed to nudge Mandy aside before she could put her tiny fingers in the fan. When she hit the ground, dazed and confused, she started wailing in disappointment. Why hadn't I let her do what she wanted to do? It was obvious: I saw a danger she couldn't comprehend.

I wonder how many times we beg our heavenly Father to do something for us, but he doesn't. When we don't understand, it's so easy to be disappointed, downtrodden, or discouraged. If God doesn't let you have something you wanted to have, take a moment to thank him. Remember, his ways are higher than ours.

Your Father is always good.

Power Lift

Lord, thank you for protecting me from the dangers of getting what I want sometimes. Today I praise you for always having my best interests at heart.

And he said to them, "Follow me, and I will make you fishers of men."
Immediately they left their nets and followed him. (Matt. 4:19–20 ESV)

Have you ever ordered something online and then when it arrived been disappointed to discover it's not what you thought it was? Marketers call this the classic "bait and switch" technique of selling a product. You advertise one thing, but the product is something else. Infomercials and mail-order products used to be notorious for this. Not that I've ever ordered anything like a "Viking Warrior Workout Bench VII." Fortunately the old bait and switch is not as prevalent as it once was because customer reviews and viral warnings about scams let others know to avoid these products.

I'm so grateful God never uses this approach in his relationship with us. His gifts are the exact opposite. Once we accept the gift of salvation through Christ and welcome God's Spirit into our hearts, then we get more than we ever imagined. Our Father delights in giving us an abundant life that's so much more than we dreamed. We have purpose and joy, peace and security.

You can rest in the assurance that God is who he says he is. Your salvation has been secured by Jesus' death and resurrection. You can live in confidence of his love and share it with others. Give thanks today for what an amazing God you serve!

Power Lift

Thank you, Father, for loving me so much and blessing me with your abundant life. Today I will live in the fullness of all your blessings so that I may be a blessing to others.

Because he himself suffered when he was tempted, he is
able to help those who are being tempted. (Heb. 2:18)

When I was a young pastor, I was doing one of my first baptisms. Since I idolized my pastor, Nick, I studied how he did them. I quickly noticed how Pastor Nick would often say "the old self was dead." He was quoting Paul and describing how our sin nature no longer had power over us. We were dead to sin and alive to Christ.

So when I baptized Susan, a lady in our church in her late fifties (I was in my early twenties at the time), I thought I would do the same thing. Armed with my partial script from Pastor Nick, I stood by her in waist deep water and put my hand on her shoulder. "We celebrate the amazing news about Susan today!" I said in my best preacher's voice. "In a moment, I'll put her underwater and the old woman will die!"

It sounded a lot better in my mind than it came out. Everyone gasped. I didn't know if I should apologize, correct it, or pretend it never happened. I decided to try to explain what I meant. All I know is, within a few seconds, everyone was laughing hard at what I had said, including Susan.

Even though I didn't get it quite right on that day, we can celebrate the good news. Sin used to be our master. We were under its power. But because of the death and resurrection of Christ, sin no longer holds us. We are dead to it.

If you're facing a temptation that seems greater than your power to resist, thank God that Christ in you is greater than any struggle you will face.

Power Lift

I'm so grateful today, Lord, that when I'm weak, your strength empowers me to resist temptation.

God did not call us to be impure, but to live a holy life. (1 Thess. 4:7)

When Amy and I were first married, I was so frugal that I would often buy grocery items that had been marked down because they were close to their sell-by date. Amy never complained and somehow always managed to produce something delicious out of over-ripe apples or that package of chicken wings.

But then one day, I brought home some yogurt that was already beyond its best-by date. Of course, once we opened it, we could tell right away. It had spoiled and was no longer good for us to eat. Even I agreed the only reasonable thing to do was to throw it away.

I suspect some of our lifestyle habits work the same way. They were good when we started them, but eventually they're no longer in our best interests. As a result, we go through the motions to do something that's really not helping us grow closer to God.

From my experience, a big part of living a life set apart for God is learning to adapt to change. God asks us to obey him regardless of our circumstances, and he also promises to provide his wisdom and strength to us when we ask him. I'm convinced we often don't have what we need, not because God isn't willing to provide it but because we're still clinging to outdated habits.

Today let go of those expired items to make room for the fresh blessings God wants to give you.

Power Lift

Give me wisdom and discernment, Lord, so that I can eliminate habits, routines, and relationships that are no longer needed. Thank you for providing what I need according to your perfect will and time.

*Give thanks in all circumstances; for this is God's will
for you in Christ Jesus. (1 Thess. 5:18)*

One time a young boy named Billy stepped into his back yard, clothed in his favorite baseball team's uniform. With dreams of playing in the big leagues one day, he fantasized about future greatness.

Billy grabbed his favorite bat, choked up on it slightly, taking a couple of practice swings before picking up a ball. Preparing to toss the ball up in the air and hit it across the back yard, Billy shouted enthusiastically, "I'm the greatest hitter who has ever lived!" With that he tossed the ball slightly, swung with all his might, and missed.

Undeterred, Billy followed the exact same ritual. Grip perfect. Stance just right. Tongue slightly to the left. Again he exclaimed confidently, "I'm the greatest hitter in the whole wide world!" Another swing and a miss.

The third time was exactly like the first two. The declaration. The swing. The miss. Without missing a beat, the young boy declared, "Wow! Who would have ever thought? I'm going to be the greatest *pitcher* in the whole world!"

When life doesn't go your way, God often has something totally different for you. Be careful not to despise what you don't have or what you can't do. Embrace all that God has given you. You are exactly the way he wants you to be. God knew what he was doing when he made you. And you have everything you need to be everything God wants you to be.

Power Lift

When things don't go my way, Lord, help me to trust you for something better—your good and perfect will for my life.

But Christ is faithful as the Son over God's house. And we are his house, if indeed we hold firmly to our confidence and the hope in which we glory. (Heb. 3:6)

Our family was recently looking through old photos—the kind we took with a camera, not a phone, and had developed at a drugstore. We laughed at some obvious fashion mistakes we had all made but also marveled at how faithful God has been to us. When our kids, who are now mostly grown, looked at the first house Amy and I ever lived in, they couldn't believe just how good God has been to us. One of my daughters laughed and said, "It's a good thing we don't all live there now."

Looking at these pictures of where we used to live got us talking about "dream homes" and where we would live if we could choose anywhere in the world. Amy wanted someplace close enough and big enough for visits from the kids and future grandkids, while I was thinking about something more remote, like maybe a cabin in the mountains or a little place on a beach.

How about you—what's your dream home? No matter what kind of house you might live in, the good news is that nothing here on earth can compare with our heavenly home. This verse tells us that Jesus rules over God's house and that we maintain it through our courage, faith, and hope. Why? Because we *are* God's house. He dwells in us and transforms our lives.

Give thanks today for where you live right now but also for the place being prepared for you after this life is over.

Power Lift

Lord, I'm so grateful that one day I will dwell with you in heaven after my life here has ended.

And the world is passing away along with its desires, but whoever
does the will of God abides forever. (1 John 2:17 ESV)

At a pastor's conference one time, I shared a hotel room with another pastor friend named Paul. Pastor Paul was a very godly man with an amazing sense of humor. By the end of the first day, I had been on the receiving end of at least three practical jokes from my new roommate.

Not to be outdone, I decided to wait and get him when he least expected it. I planned to wake up in the middle of the night and body-slam him. I pictured leaping sideways into the air pro-wrestler style and landing an elbow to Paul's side while he slept soundly.

While my plan was decent, my depth perception was not. I leaped into the air but landed short of my target. Instead of hitting Paul, my elbow dug deep into the mattress and shot my clenched fist directly into my chin.

Yes, I actually punched myself in the middle of the night.

The joke was on me.

Paul woke up to the commotion and saw me half-conscious on the floor by his bed. Once I explained what had happened, he laughed for what seemed like a half hour and now tells that story every chance he gets.

I fell short of my target. Unfortunately, no matter how good we are, we fall ridiculously short of God's target. God's law demands perfection. Jesus did for us what we couldn't do for ourselves. He gives us his grace freely.

Thank God today for salvation through Jesus.

Power Lift

Dear God, you know all the mistakes I make and all the times I fall short of your standards. Thank you for sending your Son to die on a cross and forgive me of my sins.

"The LORD himself goes before you and will be with you; he will never leave you nor forsake you. Do not be afraid; do not be discouraged." (Deut. 31:8)

In the Bible we often see the Israelites sending scouts ahead as they wandered in the wilderness looking for the Promised Land. These spies reported on potential dangers and enemies, many of which they had encountered and defeated on their journeys. They also blazed trails so that when they returned with the entire group they would know how to proceed within the untamed area. They made sure it was safe for everyone to proceed before they all went charging in.

They learned something that we as believers still know today: God is the ultimate scout, going ahead of us and preparing the path we are to follow. He equips us for the route we should take, warning us of danger and protecting us from assaults by our Enemy. Even when we can't see what's ahead, we can step out in faith, confident in God's guidance. The uncertainty of the future doesn't have to cause us fear or worry.

Today you don't have to worry about what lies ahead—God has already scouted it out. He will lead you. Just follow the trail of faith.

Power Lift

Lord, I give you thanks for all the ways that you go before me and prepare the way. Today I want to follow you, stepping out in faith even when I don't know what's around the corner.

Therefore, with minds that are alert and fully sober, set your hope on the grace to be brought to you when Jesus Christ is revealed at his coming. (1 Peter 1:13)

Learning to play tennis is easy; playing it well requires a lot of hard work. One of the best tennis coaches I ever had taught me to visualize my serve before the ball left my hand and I raised my racquet. He helped me imagine each part of the process in slow motion so that I could learn greater control and improve my speed and strength. From him I learned that the mental aspect of the game is every bit as important as the physical part.

Years later as I was trying to teach one of my kids how to serve, I realized that we can also benefit from visualizing our obedience to God. When we see ourselves facing temptation and obeying God, we increase the likelihood of successfully resisting sin when our Enemy attacks. It's no guarantee, but such "obedience training" can definitely help us.

So often the devil tempts us in weak moments, when we're physically tired, mentally fatigued, or emotionally troubled. If we've mentally rehearsed a God-honoring response to tempting situations beforehand, we can remain strong. We will be prepared when the Enemy tries to exploit our weakness. We will focus on pleasing God instead of the immediate gratification that our sin offers.

Today imagine yourself facing temptation and obeying God rather than giving in. Prepare mentally today for what you will face tomorrow.

Power Lift

Thank you for my imagination, Lord, and for the way it can help me remain obedient and faithful to your calling on my life. Strengthen my resolve today as I face temptation.

Your word is a lamp to guide my feet and a light for my path. (Ps. 119:105 NLT)

Sometimes when I'm making decisions about the future, I wish that God would give me more information to help make the decision easier. He already knows the future. Why won't he share more of it with me?

During those times, I try to remind myself of today's verse from the Psalms.

When we seek him in his Word, God will often speak to us, prompting us on what steps we should take next. But if he is offering a lamp to our feet and light to our path, that may only help us for a few steps. And no more.

Most of the time we want more details about the future. However, it would probably be more than we bargained for. I'm guessing that God knows we wouldn't deal well with some of the details if we could see exactly what was coming. If he had shown me much of what I've had to endure leading the church, I would not have said yes to starting it more than two decades ago.

God's grace is always sufficient for today—or for the moment.

If you ever find yourself wanting more details, remember that God will show you all you need to make decisions that honor him. He may illuminate our path for two or three steps, but he likely will not show us steps four, five, or six. We have to take the first few before he'll show us what to do next.

Power Lift

As I make decisions in my life, Lord, I will trust you to illuminate the next step I should take. Forgive me when I want to see more than you are ready to reveal. I will wait on you to guide me.

In peace I will lie down and sleep, for you alone,
Lord, make me dwell in safety. (Ps. 4:8)

When my kids were little, I loved holding them as they fell asleep in my arms. We would be at some event, a school program or concert, and they would inevitably beg to be held. Next thing I knew, they'd nestle into my shoulder, close their eyes, and cling to my neck as they drifted off. I like to think they fell asleep so easily in those moments because they felt safe. They knew that I would hold them, protect them, and keep them safe from anything or anyone who might try to harm them.

We can rest in the security of our Father's arms the same way. There's nothing we have to fear because he's never going to leave us. He will hold us close and protect us.

God always has your back. When you feel overwhelmed and anxious, remember that you can experience his peace simply by praying and sensing his Spirit within you. As you lie awake at night, your mind spinning through all the demands and struggles of your day, you can let go. No matter how big, scary, or intimidating the circumstance, he's got you.

Let yourself relax today and give God thanks for being such a loving Father, one who holds you close and reassures you of his presence no matter what you're facing.

Power Lift

Dear God, I'm so grateful for your peace when life's worries begin to overwhelm me. Thank you for holding me close as your beloved child.

Through Jesus . . . let us continually offer to God a sacrifice of praise—
the fruit of lips that openly profess his name. (Heb. 13:15)

It's hard to believe the year is almost over. The final leaves are falling
and all the crops have been harvested. Fields are lying fallow and the
days are growing shorter. Instead of dew on the grass when we wake,
there's frost. Sweaters and hoodies have replaced T-shirts and shorts.
The seasons have passed the baton from summer to fall, and before long
winter will take its cold icy turn.

The holidays will also be here before you know it. But before you
start planning family dinners and office parties, checking flight schedules and weather forecasts, take a few minutes today and offer God your
deepest thanks. Reflect on these past months and all the ways he has
blessed you and comforted you, protected you and strengthened you.
Maybe you encountered some obstacles, and a few may be lingering
still, but God has been so faithful to you this year.

Think about the people in your life that mean so much: family,
close friends, people you see every day at work, prayer buddies from
church, people in your small group and neighborhood. Before you get
caught up in the holiday madness of planning, shopping (maybe you've
already started), decorating, cooking, traveling, and fellowshipping—
stop and catch your spiritual breath.

Ask God to refresh your spirit. Let him know how much you love
him. Share with him the people, places, and moments that have meant
the most this year.

• • • • • • • • • • • **Power Lift** • • • • • • • • • • • •

Thanksgiving should be every day, Lord, but I want to acknowledge you, praise
you, and thank you for the many, many blessings in my life today. Keep my heart
truly grateful now and in the weeks to come.

> Then Peter said, "Silver or gold I do not have, but what I do have I give you. In the name of Jesus Christ of Nazareth, walk." (Acts 3:6)

I've heard people say that God often guides by what he provides. Not only is this true, but the rhyme makes it fun to say out loud. But even though God often does open doors of provision to show us the way to go, this isn't the only way God guides.

I'd argue that God occasionally will also guide by what he withholds. Perhaps there are seasons when God won't allow us to have what we think we need so we can see his provision or direction in an unexpected way, just as when the crippled man at the gate asked Peter for some money and Peter responded with something else. And at Peter's word, the man was miraculously healed. If Peter had had what the man wanted, he might not have given the man what he needed.

You might experience something similar in your life. Although you may be convinced with all your heart that you need something from God now, he may withhold it from you. His plan isn't to torture you, discourage you, or insult you. He may simply be loving you in a way you didn't expect. Instead of giving you what you want, God may show you what you really need. And when you experience his perfect provision, you may thank him later.

Power Lift

I trust you today, God, to know what's best for me. I surrender my will to yours. I trust that you love me and want me to grow.

You know that the Lord will reward each one for
whatever good they do. (Eph. 6:8)

A few years ago, one of our kids' pets went missing. Because I wasn't a cat fan to begin with, I wasn't nearly as upset as the rest of the family. But I hated seeing my kids so upset and agreed to help them search the neighborhood. Then one of my daughters got the idea to make signs to post and offer a reward. We hung them on every light post and stop sign for miles around our house.

The sad news is that we never found Cutie Pie, and another cat eventually took her place in my children's affections. But I'll never forget how amazed the kids were that the reward didn't work; no one came forward to claim the $100 reward by returning their beloved pet. That whole experience taught my kids that so much of life revolves around making an extra effort in order to claim the benefit.

Fortunately for us, God has already given us his assurance of the greatest reward we could ever imagine: being with him for eternity in heaven. Once we've invited Jesus into our hearts, we are washed clean and our sins are forgiven. There's nothing we can do to earn God's favor, no works that we could accomplish to make ourselves worthy of him. As believers in Christ, we are joint heirs with him, adopted into God's family as sons and daughters.

Our inheritance is in place and our reward is secured.

Power Lift

I'm so grateful for your grace and mercy, Father. Thank you for the eternal reward you have given me through my faith in Christ.

Then Jesus said to them, "Be careful and guard against all kinds of greed. Life is not measured by how much one owns." (Luke 12:15 NCV)

The first home that Amy and I purchased was built in 1910. It only had one closet, about three feet wide, in the whole house. In the early 1900s, many men had only one pair of work jeans, a couple of casual shirts, a suit, dress shoes, and casual shoes. And that was about it. This small closet was room enough not only for his storage but also for his wife's.

Fast forward to today, and most homes have multiple closets, pantries, cupboards, cabinets, and bookshelves throughout. Not only do we have many options for storing our stuff, but the options are usually quite large. Many homes now have "walk-in closets." I even toured a house that had a walk-*around* closet. I'm not certain, but I'm guessing ten or so laps around this closet might have equaled a mile.

Yet many people still don't have room for all their stuff. Their bedroom closet overflows, so they put stuff in the hall closet, the attic, and even the garage. It's not uncommon to see a garage so full of stuff that cars won't fit. I even know people whose houses are so full that they rent storage space to store—you guessed it—more stuff.

We must work hard to remember the words of Jesus. Our life doesn't consist in the abundance of stuff. I'm almost certain that if most of us had less stuff, we'd have more intimacy, more time, more peace, and more joy.

Today eliminate some of the stuff that doesn't matter so you can pursue the things that really do.

Power Lift

I'm blessed with an overabundance of material possessions, Lord. Help me to let go of what I don't need in order to make room for what I need the most.

> "But seek first his kingdom and his righteousness, and all
> these things will be given to you as well." (Matt. 6:33)

It's always interesting to me how different people do things in different orders. Like when I'm finished showering, I like to dry off first, then get out. But some people get out of the shower first and dry off while dripping on the floor (at least that's what I've been told). When I get dressed, I put on deodorant first, then my shirt. But some put on their shirt, then somehow roll on their antiperspirant afterward. When I put on my shoes, I'm a sock-sock, shoe-shoe guy. But some people go sock-shoe, then sock-shoe.

When it comes to your daily routine, order matters. What do you do first each day? Do you check social media? Read your news apps? Listen to music while drinking coffee? Jesus told us to "seek first his kingdom." Not only did he teach us to seek God first, but he modeled it. Jesus would often rise early in the morning and leave the crowd in order to spend intimate time with his Father.

Whatever you do, seek God first. Open your heart to him. Lift your praises toward heaven. Absorb the truth of his Word. Let him purify your heart, cleanse your motives, and direct your actions. When you seek him first, he will add everything that matters into your life.

Power Lift

I want to spend time with you, God, before I face other priorities in my day. Thank you for giving me the power, strength, and peace to prepare me for what's ahead.

But godliness with contentment is great gain. For we brought nothing
into the world, and we can take nothing out of it. But if we have
food and clothing, we will be content with that. (1Tim. 6:6–8)

One of my friends serves in an international ministry that provides clean water, food, and medicine to people in underdeveloped areas around the globe. These places are sometimes called "third-world" countries, implying how far behind our "first-world" locales they are in terms of infrastructure and human services—things we usually take for granted. Like having a roof that doesn't leak, water that doesn't cause diseases, and more food in our fridge than many people see in a year.

When my friend returns to the US after serving in places like Haiti, Kenya, or Kosovo, he often experiences culture shock. He told me he's always stunned at how many people here get upset by the smallest things: sitting in traffic, waiting at the dentist's office, drinking a half-caff latte without soy milk. These are all what many people call first-world problems, issues that are trivial and somewhat inconsequential when compared to the life-or-death struggles so many families face daily in other parts of the world.

We entered this life without any possessions, and we will exit it the same way. God wants us to be good stewards of all we're given, not good organizers of larger storage units. So often we take for granted the big things in our lives and complain about the little discomforts and inconveniences. Today notice how many blessings you take for granted—fresh food, warm clothes, clean water, and people who love you.

Power Lift

All good gifts come from you, Lord. I'm so overwhelmed by the many ways you bless me. Help me notice all my blessings and take nothing for granted, giving to those in need around me.

> The Lord has heard my supplication, the Lord
> receives my prayer. (Ps. 6:9 NASB)

A couple of years ago, I started journaling in a five-year journal that Amy gave me. Honestly, this process of journaling was a spiritual game-changer for me. From a purely practical perspective, it works because I'm allotted only five lines on one page per day. This takes the pressure off so I don't feel like I have to write a chapter every day. The shorter format ensures that I'm consistent.

One of the best parts for me is seeing the same day from the previous year and what I wrote back then. When I write about what happened today, I also get to see what happened the same day last year, and the year before, and the year before that.

It's fascinating to see what was weighing on my heart in years past. A problem to solve. An issue to address. A person to coach. A challenge with a child. A hurdle to overcome. When I see my thoughts on a problem I was facing back then, I can honestly say that God has resolved almost every issue that seemed big at the time.

This perspective totally changes whatever I'm facing right now. I remind myself that God was faithful in the past to work things out. God will be faithful in the present. And one year from now I will look back on this challenge and thank God for whatever he did. In the moment, I don't know what he will do or how he will do it, but I know he will prove himself faithful.

· · · · · · · · · · **Power Lift** · · · · · · · · · ·

Lord, sometimes I get so caught up in the daily grind of life's demands that I lose my perspective on the many ways you answer my prayers and bless me. Thank you for being so faithful and consistent and for loving me so well.

> There is a time for everything, and a season for every
> activity under the heavens. (Eccl. 3:1)

Planning holidays sometimes feels like air traffic control at Chicago's O'Hare Airport. Now that two of my children are married, even planning family dinners has gotten more complicated. They obviously want to spend time with their spouse's family as well as ours. As the rest of my children become adults and move away for school and work, we also need to factor in their schedules and geographical distances. It's not as simple as when they were little and we could invite Grandma and Grandpa over, maybe include some aunts, uncles, and cousins, and be done.

When you toss in some ugly weather, last-minute flu bugs, and unexpected airport delays, it gets even crazier. We do our best to manage all the variables and get everyone together for an enjoyable, memorable family celebration. But life remains constantly unpredictable. Despite our best efforts to plan and adjust, we're forced to rely on God. He's the only one who's truly in control and knows what's going to happen.

So often we assume we can manage our time, our schedules, and our expectations each day, each month, each season. But only God knows the best time for everything and everyone. We can plan all we want as long as we remember that God's timing trumps everything.

Today let God guide your plans according to his timing and not your own.

Power Lift

Dear God, I yield my schedule to you today. You give me life and breath. I know that your timing is better than anything I can plan.

Give thanks in all circumstances; for this is God's will
for you in Christ Jesus. (1 Thess. 5:18)

Like many families who enjoy a big meal at Thanksgiving, we started a tradition when the kids were little to go around the table and have each person tell what they are especially thankful for. Over the years it has been both fun and encouraging to see the list grow from items like toys, cats, and pumpkin pie to jobs, relationships, and family. Now that our children are growing up and starting families of their own, I hope this tradition continues. I can't wait to hear what my grandkids will thank God for!

At this time of year, we're supposed to be mindful of all our blessings and be especially thankful. While I love this traditional time to pause and thank God, to make sure we're not taking all that we've been given for granted, I also encourage you to make it an ongoing practice. Thanksgiving is truly a holiday that should be celebrated throughout the year.

Today let God see your spirit of gratitude as you recognize all that he's given you during this past year. Let your praise for him be an ongoing part of your relationship with him every day.

Power Lift

When I stop and count my blessings, Lord, I'm amazed at all you give me. My heart overflows with gratitude for my family, friends, home, and all the little daily things I sometimes take for granted. Thank you, God!

"The Lord is my strength and my defense; he has become my salvation. He is my God, and I will praise him, my father's God, and I will exalt him." (Ex. 15:2)

When my buddy started cycling passionately, I thought it looked like fun and great exercise. So I borrowed a nice street bike, grabbed a helmet, the right shoes, a water bottle, and most of the outfit. (I couldn't make myself wear the biker shorts on my first ride.)

Knowing my friend would ride up to a hundred miles at a time, I didn't want to overdo it on my first trip out. So I charted a nice, easy fifty-mile ride. Twenty-five miles from my house and twenty-five miles back. Easy enough, right?

I had almost made the halfway point when I seriously thought I might die. Instead of dying, though, I just parked my bike on the side of the road and puked out approximately the last seven meals I'd eaten. Then I called a friend on my cell phone to pick me up and drive me home. And that was the end of my cycling career.

Many of us start out with enthusiasm, only to flounder within a short period of time. That's why the gym is packed early in the year. But it's easy to find a parking spot in November. As the end of the year approaches, take a quick glimpse in the rearview mirror of your year. When you launched into this year, hopefully you set some goals, some markers to achieve. If you dropped something important to you along the way, there is still time to pick it back up.

Power Lift

I've let certain areas of my life slip, God, and I want to do better. Give me the strength and stamina to persevere and to accomplish the little habits that produce big results.

Just as you received Christ Jesus as Lord, continue to live your lives in him, rooted and built up in him, strengthened in the faith as you were taught, and overflowing with thankfulness. (Col. 2:6–7)

As a pastor, I've learned that the holidays are not always joyful times of celebration for everyone. Many people become depressed around this time of year as they watch others enjoying special times with family and friends. They feel lonelier than ever and more acutely aware of how isolated they are from others around them. Many feel burdened by ongoing struggles with their health, finances, or relationships. Others grieve the loss of loved ones who are noticeably absent at this special time when people usually come together.

While I try to be as compassionate and understanding as possible, I also try to remind them there's still much for which to be thankful. That's how the Thanksgiving holiday started. The early pilgrims in our country struggled way beyond what they imagined in this new, untamed land. Without the assistance of Native Americans willing to share food and teach them how to survive, the first colonists likely would have died.

Out of their hardship, those early settlers recognized how much God had blessed them and provided for them. After all, most of them had traveled to the New World to experience the kind of religious freedom they were denied back home. What better way to exercise their new freedom than to worship and praise God for sustaining them?

No matter what you may be going through, look for the ways God continues to demonstrate his love, care, and faithfulness to you.

Power Lift

Lord, for all the hard times you've brought me through this year, I thank you. You are always with me and always protect and provide for me.

> "For the LORD sees not as man sees: man looks on the outward
> appearance, but the LORD looks on the heart." (1 Sam. 16:7 ESV)

When I asked one of my kids to do a chore, it was obvious this chore wasn't their top priority or passion at the moment. My slightly grumpy child obliged, obeying out of necessity, but only putting in partial effort. That's when I slipped into fatherly lecture mode, teaching about the importance of putting your heart into what you do.

I've learned that whenever your heart isn't right with God, whatever you do will be a struggle. Perhaps that's why Jesus told us that before we give a gift at the altar, we should make sure we are right with other people (see Matt. 5:23–24). Jesus also quoted Isaiah and said that some people would honor him with their lips but their hearts were far from him (see Matt. 15:8).

Any time we obey God but demand that he give us our desired results, we are not obeying with the right heart. We don't obey God so he will bless us. We obey him because we love him. I'm convinced that there are times God doesn't change our situations because he is trying to change our hearts.

Take a moment to examine your heart. Are you struggling with being thankful and praising God for what he's given you? Where is your true devotion? Are you seeking God with true purity of heart?

If not, it's time to change.

Because more than anything else, God wants your heart.

● ● ● ● ● ● ● ● ● ● ● **Power Lift** ● ● ● ● ● ● ● ● ● ●

Jesus, I surrender my attitude and motives and want to make sure my heart is right with you. Forgive me for my sins and restore my focus on loving you.

Now we see things imperfectly, like puzzling reflections in a mirror,
but then we will see everything with perfect clarity. All that I know now
is partial and incomplete, but then I will know everything completely,
just as God now knows me completely. (1 Cor. 13:12 NLT)

If you've ever played with Photoshop or used some of those apps that make your pictures look funny, then you know appearances are not always accurate. You may look around at church and think everyone else has it together, or that you're the only one who feels unworthy and inadequate.

If you're like me, sometimes you look in the mirror and really struggle with the person looking back. Usually this happens when you've blown it, or hurt someone you love, or compared yourself to someone else and come up short. You think, "How could God ever love me when I'm such a big mess?"

But he does.

Too often, we work hard to hide the burden we're carrying and end up feeling even more alone. But God doesn't want us feeling this way, doubting his love for us and falling prey to our Enemy. We don't have to live perfectly or have our act together all the time. That's the very reason God sent Jesus to us—not to bring religion to the world, but to set us free from the law, and to give us something better: a relationship with him.

Sometimes the hardest part of starting over is seeing yourself the way God sees you—as his beloved child.

• • • • • • • • • • **Power Lift** • • • • • • • • • •

Father, today I want to let go of the old ways I tend to see myself. Help me to accept the truth about how much you love me.

These trials will show that your faith is genuine. It is being tested as fire tests and purifies gold—though your faith is far more precious than mere gold. (1 Peter 1:7 NLT)

How do you respond when you're facing a trial? While some people resist having their faith tested, they often overlook how trials make us stronger. A faith that has been tested is a faith that can be trusted.

We see this truth lived out when King Nebuchadnezzar, the most powerful man in his era and King of Babylon, conquered the tribe of Judah. This evil king captured Judah's best and brightest young men. The king commissioned a gold statue that was ninety feet tall and nine feet wide and invited every government leader, advisor, judge, and magistrate to come to the dedication.

When everyone heard the sound of music, they were commanded to bow down and worship the golden statue. Anyone who didn't would be thrown into a blazing furnace. So when the music started, everyone bowed low, except for three faith-filled teenagers who continued standing tall. So the king had the furnace heated up to seven times its normal temperature and threw them in.

These brave young men didn't bend. They didn't bow. And because of God, they didn't burn. By the grace of God, the boys didn't die, and they didn't even smell like smoke. God reveals his power in many places, but you'll know his presence best in the fire.

Just as these believers were not in the fire alone, neither are you. If you are facing a challenge today, remember that God is with you and he is building your faith. A faith that is tested is a faith that can be trusted.

Power Lift

I choose to thank you today, Lord, for the trials in my life. I don't like them and how they make me feel, but I trust that you are using them to make me stronger.

Grace and peace be yours in abundance through the
knowledge of God and of Jesus our Lord. (2 Peter 1:2)

One of my favorite parts of Thanksgiving is eating the leftovers. You can't beat turkey sandwiches piled high with stuffing and cranberry sauce. Maybe I love these leftovers so much because with six kids in our house (especially during their teenaged years), we didn't have many leftovers. I'm starting to realize a perk of being an empty nester is enjoying leftovers more often, as well as just having my favorite cereal last more than a day.

Most retailers in our culture today encourage us to buy their products in bulk. The whole premise of stores like Costco and Sam's Club is that we'll save money if we buy an acre-sized box of macaroni and cheese or a thousand pounds of ground beef. While it's good to save money and plan ahead, it's easy to fall back into that "more-is-better" mindset. (You know, the one that got me in trouble with Sprees at the movies that time.)

Fortunately, spiritual abundance is not about collecting more stuff. We don't have to stockpile Bibles, purchase discounted choir robes in shocking pink, or hide boxes of Christmas candles for our church's candlelight service. The quantity of our material possessions doesn't determine true abundance—it's the quality of our souls. When we dwell on the character of God and the example of Christ, we grow and develop an abundance of peace, grace, and joy.

Power Lift

Dear God, I'm grateful for the abundance of blessings you give me materially. But I'm even more thankful for our relationship and for the gifts of your Son, your Word, and your Spirit.

> Blessed is the one who always trembles before God, but
> whoever hardens their heart falls into trouble. (Prov. 28:14)

Most people want to see God as a loving Father, but not as many want to see him as a righteous judge. They want his love, but not his wrath. They crave his mercy but will pass on judgment. They desire blessings but despise discipline.

But Proverbs tells us we are blessed when we tremble before the Lord. Though God loves us and we can rest assured of his care for us, he is still holy. When we know him as he truly is, we will embrace his love and also respect his righteousness. The Bible calls this the "fear of the Lord."

This type of fear doesn't mean that we hide from God; it means that we respect, revere, and worship him. This is a foreign concept to many in the world today. Perhaps it's because as a culture we've become too familiar and comfortable with the idea of God. But this overfamiliarity creates great misunderstanding about his character.

God is not the "big guy in the sky." He's not "the man upstairs." And Jesus is not your "homeboy." God is so holy that mortals cannot look upon him in his purest essence and live. Jesus is our rock, redeemer, judge, the Lion of Judah, and the Lamb of God. He's the soon-returning, all-conquering, supremely reigning King of Kings and Lord of Lords.

Don't let your heart grow hard. Reflect on who God is—and be in awe of his splendor, majesty, and holiness.

Power Lift

Dear God, you are most holy and worthy to be praised. Thank you for desiring to relate to me as your child. Thank you for sending your Son to die for my sins.

And God will generously provide all you need. Then you will always have everything you need and plenty left over to share with others. (2 Cor. 9:8 NLT)

If you've ever lived through a home improvement project, then you know that it always takes twice as long (and twice as much money) as you projected. If you're doing it yourself, then it's also going to require at least three extra trips to Home Depot, one stop at Lowe's, and a few borrowed tools from neighbors. If you're doing a major renovation and hire a contractor to do the work, then God bless you!

Seriously, these experiences are incredibly stressful, because no matter how much and how well you plan, something unexpected usually comes up. The pipes are rusted and need to be replaced. The roof has a hole in it and must be patched. The electrical panel wasn't done to code and needs a new breaker box installed. And that sets off a whole new round of trips to the hardware store or conversations about increasing your renovation budget.

Can you imagine what it would be like to remodel your house and have everything you needed at your fingertips whenever you needed it? Crazy, right? It's almost impossible to imagine because it could never happen. But God promises us that when we're doing his good work, we will have everything we need.

This is the essence of grace—the free gift of God that we can't buy, earn, or build for ourselves. He loves us so much that he sacrificed his most precious Son. We have grace in abundance, including plenty to share with others.

• • • • • • • • • • **Power Lift** • • • • • • • • • •

God, I'm so thankful for the gift of grace. Thank you for giving me all I need to do your good work—today and always.

> Those who sow with tears will reap with songs of joy. Those who go out weeping, carrying seed to sow, will return with songs of joy. (Ps. 126:5–6)

While we're not sure who wrote the psalm from which today's passage is taken, clearly it was written after the people of Israel had returned from Babylonian captivity. They had been enslaved by the proudest, most violent and pagan culture at the time and had finally been set free. There must have been so many tears during their captivity—and so many after their liberation as they rejoiced and praised God for delivering them.

It's hard to imagine our tears as an offering to God, but the psalmist clearly thought they could be. We're told to sow them as seeds in order to produce a harvest of joy. Our tears can produce growth and maturity leading to a stronger, deeper faith in God. We can grow into someone who sings with joy despite whatever hardships we may endure.

Your tears bring growth. If you're hurting, wounded, or see an injustice, don't hold back. Let your heart open before God as you shed tears. If you have sinned against God, cry out in repentance. Worship with your tears and make them a sacred offering.

Tears open us to healing our hurts as well as cleansing our hearts after we sin. The good news is that when we sow in tears, we reap with joy. Notice the text doesn't say happiness; it says *joy*.

Happiness is based on happenings.

Joy is based on God's goodness.

. . . . **Power Lift** . . . .

Lord, I lift my tears to you today. Heal my heart and forgive me of my sins. I seek you as my light so that my seeds of sadness will blossom into shouts of joy.

Do not forget to do good and to share with others, for with
such sacrifices God is pleased. (Heb. 13:16)

For the longest time after Amy and I got married, we didn't give each
other gifts. Not for birthdays or anniversaries—not even for Christmas.
Once we started our family, we found the cheapest ways possible to buy
clothes, toys, and strollers for the kids. We shopped in thrift stores and
at yard sales and made a game of it. How little could we spend and still
have everything we needed?

This wasn't that hard for me. As I've explained, my nature is to
save and to be frugal. When I first entered into adulthood, I was really
careful with every penny and reluctant to spend it or give it away. After
becoming a Christian, however, I sensed God working in my heart to
transform me into a generous person.

It really is more blessed to give than to receive.

No matter what your personality or natural inclination might be,
when you practice generosity, you remember to give God your thanks and
praise. If you're not clinging to possessions, wealth, and financial power
as the source of your security or identity, then you realize you don't need
to hold on to them. God is the source of all you have, which frees you
up to be a conduit of blessing for those around you. You can use what
you've been given to serve others and to advance your Father's kingdom.

Today surprise someone with your generosity, whether that be with
your time, attention, money—or all three.

Power Lift

You are always so generous to me, Lord. All that I have comes from you. Give
me eyes to see those in need around me and show me how I can bless them
with your abundance.

Every good and perfect gift is from above, coming down from the Father of the heavenly lights, who does not change like shifting shadows. (James 1:17)

Both my parents were tremendous givers, but my dad remains one of the most generous people I've ever known. When I was a kid, he gave me a rookie Nolan Ryan baseball card from 1968. We lived in Houston then, and Ryan, one of the greatest pitchers of all time, played for the Astros. Today, in mint condition, that little card is worth about $1,500, but to me, both as a kid and now, it's priceless.

I'll never forget the joy my dad had presenting that card to me. And I was blown away and couldn't believe it. I wanted to give something equally special and cool and meaningful to him, but it was tough as a kid. However, thirty-something years later, I happened to be in a sports store and saw an autographed picture of Nolan Ryan pitching. It was way out of my budget, but I had to get it and couldn't wait to give it to him.

When he opened it, he just smiled and shook his head. Then he said, "Whoa, son, that's a grand slam, home run, out of the park!" He's always talked in baseball slang and baseball metaphors. If he wants to ask me how my preaching went last week, he'll say, "How was it on the mound? Keep it down the middle, low and inside." That's how much he loves baseball. But it doesn't come close to how much he loves me.

Who's the most generous giver you've met? What did you learn about giving from them?

• • • • • • • • • • • **Power Lift** • • • • • • • • • •

Lord, you take delight in surprising your children with good gifts. Let that be my motive for all the gifts I give this holiday season—to show others your unexpected, crazy-generous love.

"Every man shall give as he is able, according to the blessing of the Lord your God which He has given you." (Deut. 16:17 NKJV)

The first time I tithed, I was a junior in college. I'd worked all summer teaching tennis lessons and made what I considered a lot of money back then. Then I heard a message on giving, and I thought, *Okay, I'm doing this, and I'm doing it with the right attitude. This is going to be an act of worship.* And I wrote out what seemed like the biggest check in the world.

I remember putting it in the offering plate with this thrilling sense that I was putting my money where my mouth was. I was trusting God with everything—my heart, my mind, my time, and my money. And as you've learned by now, for someone as frugal as I was, that was no small thing.

The same day, my grandmother called me and said, "Craig, God has put something on my heart. I'm so excited that you're now a follower of Jesus, and I want to buy you a car." I was speechless. This was my grandmother who was raised during the Depression. We never saw her spend any money, and I had even wondered if she lived on air.

And she bought me a car. Not just any car, a biblical car. You know, a Honda Accord—because all the disciples gathered in one Accord. My grandmother's surprise gift made a huge impact on me. She modeled incredible stewardship but also knew how to listen to God and give generously.

Today talk to God about what he wants you to give—to him and to others.

· · · · · · · · · · · **Power Lift** · · · · · · · · · ·

Father, I'm so grateful for the many ways you provide for me. Today use me to provide your blessing for someone in need.

> "Bring the whole tithe into the storehouse, that there may be food
> in my house. Test me in this," says the LORD Almighty, "and see if I
> will not throw open the floodgates of heaven and pour out so much
> blessing that there will not be room enough to store it." (Mal. 3:10)

After my grandmother surprised me with my little Honda Accord, she created a ripple effect she could never have imagined. At the time I had several thousand dollars saved for a car, and because I was committed to paying in cash, I was saving up for the rest. After being given a car, I decided to use the money to purchase a tiny older home as my first rental house.

As a result of God's faithfulness after I started tithing, it wasn't long before I bought another small house. By the time I graduated from college, I had four small rental units. When we started the church, there was almost no money to pay me a salary, so we lived mostly off the income from those rental properties. I can literally trace every financial blessing we have today back to my very first tithe. When we give God our first and our best, we can trust him to bless the rest.

Now, I'm not saying that if you tithe, you're going to get a new car and rent houses. What I am saying is that God proves himself faithful. Today's verse is the only place in all of Scripture where God encourages us to test him. No matter how much we give, we will never out-give our Father.

Power Lift

Lord, help me to be as generous as you are with your children. Give me wisdom about how to be the best manager of the resources you've given me.

"Give to everyone who asks you, and if anyone takes what
belongs to you, do not demand it back." (Luke 6:30)

I am thrilled beyond measure that our church continues to give away
my favorite app, the YouVersion Bible App, free to people all over the
world. People often say, "I can't believe a church created the app." But
I'm overjoyed that our church was able to create this. Right now we've
got about forty full-time staff members who create, build, maintain,
and expand this unbelievable, amazing app.

Despite what others have recommended, I've never considered charging for this app. "But people don't value something they get for free!
You should charge at least 99 cents for it," these people argue with me.

But because we can give the Bible away, we will. The Bible is living and active, and we are honored to give it to everyone who wants
one. And personally, I *love* to give this app away, and you know why?
Because years ago, someone from the Gideon organization smiled more
broadly than you can imagine and handed me a free Bible. And my life
was transformed by the living Word of God, so now I am overjoyed to
return the favor and provide digital Bibles.

We recently celebrated giving away over two hundred and seventy-
five million free downloads. People all over the world can have God's
Word wherever they go, on their phones or tablets, and read it at their
convenience. My goal is to lead the way with irrational generosity. We
truly believe it's more blessed to give than to receive.

Power Lift

God, thank you for the gift of your Word and the many ways you reveal yourself
through its pages.

"Therefore the Lord himself will give you a sign: The virgin will conceive and give birth to a son, and will call him Immanuel." (Isa. 7:14)

Have you ever had a hard decision to make and asked God to give you a sign? For most people, we rarely get the bold skywriting from God that we would like to have regarding our next steps. Instead we often have indicators that are more subtle—a verse from God's Word, wise advice from a trusted friend, or circumstantial evidence.

The people of Israel had been promised a Messiah, a savior for God's people, for so long. Year after year they waited, until finally they were losing faith. But throughout the more than four hundred years they waited on the arrival of Jesus, God never forgot his people or his promise to them. Speaking these words from today's verse through the prophet Isaiah, God clearly outlined the birth of his Son to a virgin. It's no coincidence that this name, Immanuel, means "God with us."

Christmas often gets so defined by its commercial, decorative aspects that we overlook it as a celebration of God keeping his promise. But like a loving parent dropping hints to a child eager to know what's inside a present, God provides reminders of his generosity. He gave us the best, most perfect gift he was able to give. He allowed his Son Jesus to be born as a baby in a manger in a little, backwoods town called Bethlehem.

Beneath all the bright lights and shiny tinsel, look for reminders that God is with you today—and every day.

Power Lift

Open my eyes, Lord, and open my heart so I can see the many ways you reveal yourself to me during this wonderful holiday season.

"In everything I did, I showed you that by this kind of hard work we must help the weak, remembering the words the Lord Jesus himself said: 'It is more blessed to give than to receive.'" (Acts 20:35)

Early in our marriage, we had a problem with our car and took it to the mechanic. After examining it, the man explained to me how much it would cost to do the repair. Many people would have said it wasn't terribly expensive. But at that point in our young financial lives, any amount was too much.

But I was in for an even bigger surprise than the cost of the repair. The mechanic explained that his daughter had recommitted her life to Christ at our church. As an act of gratitude, he wanted to do this repair for us for no charge at all! I think I danced right there in front of him. It was a massive blessing to receive.

Years later, I found myself at an auto repair shop again. This time I saw a young mom with small children get the news of what it would cost to repair her minivan. She burst into tears and slipped to the side to call her husband, obviously panicking.

So I discreetly approached the guy at the counter and said I'd like to cover the cost anonymously. After paying, I slipped quietly back to my seat. When the mom reappeared, the guy explained, "Good news! Your repair is free." She looked confused. He said, "Uh, it's buy-one-get-one-free day. The last guy bought one, so yours is free."

She cried even harder than before, overwhelmed with joy.

It is always more blessed to give than to receive. Look for ways to bless others today with your generosity.

Power Lift

Lord, I want to bless others with the abundance of gifts with which I have been blessed. Today guide me to an opportunity where I can surprise another with your generosity.

Give generously to them and do so without a grudging heart;
then because of this the LORD your God will bless you in all your
work and in everything you put your hand to. (Deut. 15:10)

When I look back, I can't remember a single time when I got all choked up reflecting on a purchase I'd made. I can't remember ever crying at the checkout when I was about to bag my groceries and walk out of a store. Not even when I was buying donuts!

I also can't remember anyone else telling me their tremendously moving "getting" story. No one ever said, "I cried for two days after getting a flat-screen TV," or "I worshiped God with all my heart when I got my first pair of Jordans," or "I was speechless when I purchased my fifth Coach purse."

Although I don't know anyone who was moved beyond measure by getting, I know plenty who were moved deeply by giving. I've heard countless stories that go something like this:

"We prayed and prayed and prayed. God led us to sacrifice to give to our building fund at church. We've never felt closer to God than when we gave."

"We just met the girl we have been sponsoring for the past eight years. This may be the most important thing we've ever done."

"We were planning on selling it, but God led us to give it instead. Wow! We need to give more often."

When you give and impact someone's life, it's a feeling you will never forget. And no "getting" story ever compares to the joy of giving.

Power Lift

God, it's amazing that when we're obedient and give generously, you bless us and draw us closer to you. Help me to give beyond my comfort zone to someone in need today.

> "She will give birth to a son, and you are to give him the name Jesus,
> because he will save his people from their sins." (Matt. 1:21)

Just as he provided the long-awaited Messiah, God also provided his name. He told Mary and Joseph to name the baby "Jesus" and went on to explain why he had chosen this name. As a derivative of the name "Joshua," the name given to Mary's baby wasn't uncommon at that time, and it means "God rescues" or "God delivers."

But I wonder if Mary and Joseph understood the full extent of what Jesus' name means. Having the full story in God's Word, we can see the big picture and how this name revealed his entire mission here on earth. Jesus came to save us and pay a debt we could not pay ourselves. Because the Jewish people were looking for an earthly king, many of them struggled to accept Jesus, the carpenter from Nazareth. With his ragtag group of former fishermen and tax collectors, he didn't live up to their royal expectations. Even Jesus' birth in a lowly cattle stall in Bethlehem didn't make sense. Why would the King of the Jews be born in a smelly animal barn instead of a palace? It didn't seem possible.

Today remember that we can't always see all that God is up to from our vantage point. We have to trust him as he completes the epic design of his perfect will.

· · · · · · · · · · · **Power Lift** · · · · · · · · · · ·

Like the shepherds on the hillside hearing the news of the newborn king, Lord, help me to trust you even when things don't seem to make sense.

> But generous people plan to do what is generous, and
> they stand firm in their generosity. (Isa. 32:8 NLT)

If you're like me, when you want something, you do your best to figure out how to get it. Whether it's the best deal on a new tech gadget, the perfect jacket, or a cool new pair of shoes, it has never been easier to surf online and shop for the best deal—and hopefully with free delivery.

If we find what we want but it's slightly beyond our budget, many will still make plans to get it. Some might open a new credit account. Another person might skip lunches for a week or work extra hours on the job. Bottom line, many of us will make plans and work hard to get what we want.

What if instead of just planning to get, we also planned to give? Today's verse teaches us that generous people plan their generosity. Instead of just scheming to get what we want, what if we schemed to give what others need? What if you used your clever resourcefulness to meet the needs of others instead of your own?

Imagine sitting down with your spouse or small group and asking, "How can we give more? Who can we help? What do we have that would be a blessing to others?" Think about how our attitudes would change, how we'd become others-focused instead of self-centered, how we would grow to become more like Christ.

Instead of just thinking about what you want, focus on what you can give. How can God use you to bless someone else today? Generous people stand firm in their generosity.

Power Lift

Give me wisdom, God, to plan my generosity so I can show others what a great God you are.

> But the angel said to her, "Do not be afraid, Mary; you have found favor with God. You will conceive and give birth to a son, and you are to call him Jesus." (Luke 1:30–31)

Can you imagine going about your daily routine when suddenly an angel shows up? And how thoughtful of the angel to tell you not to be afraid because you've found favor with God. Sort of like being called to the principal's office not for misbehaving but for good conduct. But then the angel drops the bomb—"Oh, and by the way, you're going to get pregnant and have a baby boy, and you should name him Jesus."

Somehow, though, Mary kept her cool even when she didn't understand how she would conceive without being with a man. She was a virgin and had clearly honored God and found favor with him by having a heart devoted to him. But I doubt she had any idea just how big a role God had in mind for her. This was it—the moment the Jewish people, and people across history, had been waiting for—the birth of the Messiah.

Even without knowing all the details of what would follow, Mary still said yes. Instead of making excuses and asking dozens of questions, like you or I might have done, Mary embraced the role God had for her. She was willing. She surrendered her will to her Master's.

As you go through your daily routine today, look for how God wants to use you in his story.

. . . . **Power Lift** . . . .

Thank you, God, for including me in your plans to bless others and to share the gospel. I am willing, Lord, and want you to use me.

Then the people rejoiced because they had offered so willingly, for they made their offering to the LORD with a whole heart. (1 Chron. 29:9 NASB)

Recently I met a couple at church who told me how God had changed their heart about giving. They had always been faithful to tithe 10 percent of what God blessed them with, but gave only occasionally above their tithe. As they grew in their relationship with Christ, they realized that God was calling them to a more intentionally generous life.

Though they didn't have much extra to give, they agreed they could easily spare twenty dollars each month to give to someone in need. The first month was an easy decision. When an F-4 tornado took out several neighborhoods in their community, this couple immediately agreed to give their first twenty dollars to help those impacted.

The next month, they were in line at a grocery store. The lady in front of them was obviously embarrassed when her government assistance and small wad of cash didn't cover the $48.03 total of basic necessities that she was attempting to purchase. Seizing this opportunity to be a blessing, the couple humbly offered to help. The next month they gave to help someone go on a missions trip.

Month after month, the blessing stories mounted. Now two years later, this couple has grown their monthly offering to two hundred dollars a month. Not only do they not miss the money, but they would never miss the opportunity to be a blessing.

When you open your heart to God, he will help you to grow in generosity.

Power Lift

Lord, use the generosity of others to inspire in me a desire to give more. Show me where I can meet the needs of those around me.

An angel of the Lord appeared to them, and the glory of the Lord shone around them, and they were terrified. But the angel said to them, "Do not be afraid. I bring you good news that will cause great joy for all the people." (Luke 2:9–10)

Once again, we find an angel telling someone—or in this case, a group—not to be afraid. Like her message to Mary, the angel told the shepherds good news from God himself. But it still must have been quite a scary sight, right? You're out there on the cold Judean hillside, minding your business and keeping watch over your sheep, making sure they aren't snatched by predators.

Then suddenly the sky lights up like it does on our Fourth of July! An explosion of light streams God's glory through the appearance of angels, and one of them starts talking directly to you, telling you that this event your people have been waiting on for generations—for over four hundred years—has finally happened. Apparently no one else has heard about it yet, but God has chosen you.

The Christmas story is familiar to us and makes it hard for us to appreciate just how shocking and unsettling it must have been for so many of its key players—Mary, Joseph, the shepherds, and the wise men, just to name a few. But in their case, their initial fear, shock, and uncertainty shifted into obedience, worship, and awe.

The story of Jesus' birth may be familiar, but it's still the most amazing story you'll ever hear.

Power Lift

Thank you for this special time of year, Father, when we can celebrate the gift of your Son being born in a manger.

He who has a generous eye will be blessed. (Prov. 22:9 NKJV)

Some people have an eye for fashion. They can spot a brand a mile away. They know who has it going on and who is striving but hasn't arrived. Some have an eye for cars. They know which year is the best, which model holds its value, which brand is most economical. Others have an eye for talent. They see potential in people that many overlook. Given time, they can help someone who is average at their work become great.

What if you asked God to give you an eye for generosity? Instead of just looking for things that interest you, you could look for a way to bless and serve others. If you ask God to help you see needs you can meet, God will open your eyes to a world of possibilities.

He may lead you to give a few extra minutes to listen to someone who is hurting. God may show you an opportunity to help someone who has car trouble. You might overhear someone who is struggling to make rent, and you offer to throw in some extra to help them get by.

Instead of just developing our "eyes" for what interests us, God can give us an eye to bless others. And when you do give, you will be blown away at how God gives back to you. Because when you develop an eye for generosity, not only will you bless others, but you too will be blessed.

Power Lift

Give me an eye for generosity, Lord, so that I can spot the needs of others and bless them with your abundant provision.

> But they who wait for the LORD shall renew their strength; they
> shall mount up with wings like eagles; they shall run and not
> be weary; they shall walk and not faint. (Isa. 40:31 ESV)

One of my favorite childhood Christmas memories was the daily Advent Christmas calendar. If you never had one, each day there was a small flap on the calendar that we could open to see a cool picture or image on the other side. The image might be a candle, a star, a manger, or a gift. Along with each image, we had a small devotional to read that pointed us to the birth of Christ.

Each day, my sister, Lisa, and I would anticipate opening the flap to see what that day represented. And each day we felt a small sense of delight and satisfaction. Once we experienced the small blessing of the day, we couldn't wait to see what was behind the flap the next day.

As Christmas Day approaches, what if you looked for small glimpses of Christ in every day? If you look for him, I promise you will find him. You might see him in your daily reading plan. You might see an act of kindness that reminds you of his grace. You could see someone serving another person, reminding you that Jesus came not to be served, but to serve this world with his love.

Anticipate seeing Christ today. Ask God for eyes to see where he is working, ears to hear his voice, and a heart moved by the things that move his. Each day is a gift from above. And each day is an opportunity to know our Savior better.

Look for Jesus today. When you seek him, you will find him.

Power Lift

Jesus, reveal yourself to me today as I go about my familiar routines. Help me notice where you are present and at work in others' lives.

"I am the way and the truth and the life. No one comes
to the Father except through me." (John 14:6)

I will never forget the day I found out the truth about Santa Claus. Even though I had been a staunch defender of the big, generous, bearded man in red, I finally discovered the truth. The stack of would-be Santa presents was carefully hidden in the back of the garage—but unfortunately, not carefully enough.

Devastated, dazed, and distressed, I demanded my mom tell me the truth. And so she did. My footing felt unstable. The world seemed to spin faster. And I suddenly felt sick to my stomach. Really sick.

If Santa wasn't real, what else wasn't real? Suddenly the Tooth Fairy was in question. And of course there was the Easter Bunny. And then there was God. Suddenly my childhood faith seemed more unsure.

What is true?

Thankfully over time, I've learned that truth is not just an idea. Truth is a person. Jesus is the truth. It amazes me to know that James, the brother of Jesus, believed that Jesus was truth. What would your brother have to do to convince you he is the Son of God?

And Peter, who repeatedly denied Christ, believed that Jesus was truth. So much so that he died for his belief in Christ. Ten of the twelve disciples died for truth. (Judas hanged himself, and John died in exile after surviving being dipped in boiling oil.)

If you occasionally experience doubts, as many of us do, remember the truth. Jesus is truth. And the truth will set you free.

Power Lift

Jesus, I'm so grateful you were willing to come to earth as a baby and live as a man. But I'm also thankful you are God's Son and the absolute truth.

> For to us a child is born, to us a son is given, and the government
> will be on his shoulders. And he will be called Wonderful Counselor,
> Mighty God, Everlasting Father, Prince of Peace. (Isa. 9:6)

When we were expecting each of our children, Amy and I would pick out a name, usually one for a girl and one for a boy, and then wait until after the birth for the final decision. We waited because there was always the chance that our baby didn't look like the name we were considering. Sounds funny, but there's something about someone so little having to be called by a name that sounds so grown-up. We just wanted to be sure that our little person and his or her name actually fit.

Christ also experienced being born into some big names. The angel had already told Mary to name her baby Jesus, but because the Jewish people had been waiting so long for their Messiah, other names were already established for the one who would save God's people. Some names emphasized God's ability to provide or his perfect holiness, while others indicated his power, peace, or righteousness.

The prophet Isaiah foretold the birth of Christ and revealed names that God's Son would be called, all reflecting different aspects of his character. Interestingly enough, though, they all indicate the perfect holiness of God: *Wonderful* Counselor, *Mighty* God, *Everlasting* Father, Prince of *Peace*.

Jesus continues to reveal himself in these roles to us today, demonstrating his power, love, and peace in countless ways.

Power Lift

I'm amazed at the many ways you reveal yourself to your people, Lord. Thank you for the ways I experience you each day in my life.

For God so loved the world that he gave his one and only Son, that whoever believes in him shall not perish but have eternal life. (John 3:16)

Most years at Christmas, Amy and I practice what we call the "no-gift-giving rule" with each other. Because we have everything we want and need, we just say we're not going to exchange gifts. But inevitably, I break the rule each year and go and buy her something just to show her how much I love her. After it happened enough times, she learned to expect it, despite the fact that we had just talked about following the rule. But I *have* to do it.

Why? Because I'm crazy about her. I can't stop myself from giving her gifts. And she always says, "Hey, you broke the rule!" And I always say back, "I know, but love gives. So take this gift and love it, because I love you so much."

Keep in mind, I haven't always been this way. Sadly, for years, I was often more concerned with myself than with others. Rather than giving, I focused on keeping. Rather than Christ and others dominating my heart, I was focused on myself and what was best for me.

But when I met and married Amy, my heart changed. Now I can't keep myself from giving her good gifts. When you love someone, you give to them. Love gives. The Christmas season reminds us that God gives. Just as God gave us his only Son, we give our lives to him and give to those around us.

Power Lift

Dear God, thank you for giving so generously, including the most precious gift of all, your only Son.

For God gave us a spirit not of fear but of power and
love and self-control. (2 Tim. 1:7 ESV)

When I think about the way the angel told Mary, as well as the shepherds, not to be afraid, I realize how easily I sometimes let fear overtake my imagination. As a self-proclaimed tough guy and faithful follower of Jesus, I'm not proud of my irrational fears, but they're there sometimes nonetheless. One of my biggest fears is that something bad will happen to my family, especially to my wife, Amy.

She is crazy-gifted in so many different ways, and her faith always inspires me to grow closer to God. But if there's one little thing that bugs me, it's that Amy has what I call the "spiritual gift" of being late. She doesn't do it on purpose, and it's never intentional so that others have to wait on her, but it's consistent.

So many times I've been waiting on her, thinking, *Wow, she's ten minutes late. Maybe something came up.* Then when I look at my watch three minutes later, *Oh, my goodness, she's thirteen minutes late; what if she was in a car accident?* By the time she's twenty minutes late, she must be at the hospital and I'm already a widower!

From there my irrational fear spins out of control. About then Amy usually pulls in the driveway and rushes up to me, apologizing for being so late and explaining why. I'm so relieved to see her, I usually hug her and move on.

Like Mary and the shepherds, we don't have to be afraid. God can handle anything, even the worst our imagination might serve up. God keeps us secure in his love.

Power Lift

Lord, I will trust you today even when I'm afraid of the future.

> Magi from the east came to Jerusalem and asked, "Where is
> the one who has been born king of the Jews? We saw his star
> when it rose and have come to worship him." (Matt. 2:1–2)

When I think about the wise men, I'm amazed at how willing they were to interrupt their lives and go on a quest to seek baby Jesus. Surely, they were important leaders in their tribes and nations with seemingly more important things to do than traipse all over the world following a star and looking for a baby. However, that's exactly what they did. And some scholars think the wise men may have been traveling for months, maybe even years, to find the newborn King.

I wonder how often we miss out on God's invitations to experience Jesus because we're not willing to interrupt our daily lives and normal schedules. So often we're too busy, especially during the holiday season, to realize the opportunities that cross our paths each day. Instead we think, "Nah, I don't have time to invite the neighbors to our church's Christmas services. They might want to go and then I'd have to go with them and be late for the office party. Which reminds me, I need to pick up a gift for my boss."

But do you really want to miss out on being part of what God is doing in others' lives?

God's interruptions are often invitations to something more significant. Today don't miss out on the blessing of participating in God's plan because you're too busy. Allow God's Spirit to interrupt your plans and reveal the joy of giving.

Power Lift

This time of year gets so hectic, Lord, and I lose sight of the reason you humbled yourself and came to earth. Help me let go of my agenda so I can bless others with your love.

Each of you should give what you have decided in your heart to give, not reluctantly or under compulsion, for God loves a cheerful giver. (2 Cor. 9:7)

Shopping for Christmas gifts has changed considerably over the past few years. Like most people, I used to fight the crowds at the mall. Now, online shopping has made the experience much easier. Not only is it easier to find exactly what you want, but it's also easier to get a bit more out of control with your purchases.

As you are busy shopping, think for a moment about what types of gifts you most want to give. Rather than just giving sweaters, gift cards, and video games, think about how you can give more of yourself. Perhaps you can commit to having dinner each week with those you love. Maybe you will make a private decision to spend less time on social media and engage more with your kids. Maybe the best gift you could give is the gift of encouragement. Your words have power. Your affirmation can change lives.

Get creative in what you give. Spending money is usually relatively easy. Making something takes time. Being creative shows thought. Personalizing something communicates love.

Think about the gift God gave. God didn't shout his love from heaven. He sent his Son to show it on earth. Instead of just giving like most give, perhaps you can give more of yourself. And discover just how blessed you are when you do.

. . . . **Power Lift** . . . .

Thank you, Lord, for reminding me that it's more blessed to give than to receive. As I finish my shopping, guide me to the presents that will let my loved ones know how much I appreciate them.

"Glory to God in the highest heaven, and on earth peace
to those on whom his favor rests." (Luke 2:14)

I'm not the greatest singer, but at this time of year, you'd think I was Perry Como or Josh Groban. I love the music of Christmas and the special memories associated with certain songs and carols. I mean, can anyone really hear that jazzy music from *A Charlie Brown Christmas* and not start tapping your foot and dancing like Snoopy? Or hear carolers in your neighborhood singing "Joy to the World" and not want to sing along?

It used to bug me that certain stores, malls, and radio stations start playing Christmas music before Halloween. But then one day, I realized those songs and their lyrics are no less beautiful and meaningful just because I heard them in November instead of December. The story of Jesus' birth is timeless, and we should celebrate it every day.

And as we see in the nativity story from Luke, the angels certainly knew how to celebrate this momentous occasion. Their chorus filled the night skies over Bethlehem as they proclaimed the most joyful news anyone on earth has ever heard. While musical instruments and praise songs were around long before the birth of Christ, surely the angels' song created a lasting precedent for the carols and hymns we love to sing at Christmas time.

Today keep a song in your heart as you celebrate the birth of your Savior, Jesus Christ!

Power Lift

Thank you, God, for the gift of music and the many beautiful songs that enhance this wonderful day. Today my heart is filled with a song of praise for the gift of your Son.

Adam, the first man, was made from the dust of the earth, while
Christ, the second man, came from heaven. (1 Cor. 15:47 NLT)

We thought our friends' young son may have accidentally added a new holiday to the Christmas season. Eagerly anticipating Christmas Eve and then Christmas Day, this little boy was counting down the days. As the big day got closer and closer, one morning this little guy rushed into his parents' bedroom and said, "Mommy! Daddy! Get up—today is Christmas Adam!"

Still groggy with sleep, his parents asked what he was talking about. "Well, I figured it out," he said. "If tomorrow is Christmas Eve, then today must be Christmas Adam! Because Adam came before Eve." He went on to suggest that opening at least one present might be a good way to celebrate Christmas Adam, but his parents weren't buying it. Nonetheless, from then on, December 23 became known to us as Christmas Adam.

When I heard this cute story, I smiled and appreciated the little boy's ingenuity. But it also made me pause to reflect on what is mentioned repeatedly throughout the Bible. God created Adam as the first man, then Eve, and gave them the Garden of Eden. He also gave them free will and asked them to obey him and not eat from a certain tree. They blew it and ignited a legacy of sinfulness in human beings to this day.

However, Scripture indicates that Jesus came as a second Adam, a kind of "do-over" who didn't sin but instead sacrificed himself so that our sins could be forgiven. Christ did what Adam failed to do—obeyed God and yielded to his Father's will. So who knows? Maybe celebrating Christmas Adam is a good idea after all!

Power Lift

Lord, I'm so grateful that you were man as well as God. You paid the price for my sins, and now I am being transformed and can spend eternity with you in heaven.

> So they hurried off and found Mary and Joseph, and the
> baby, who was lying in the manger. (Luke 2:16)

If there is any window of time during the year when all seems right to me, it's Christmas Eve. Maybe it's because the hustle and bustle of shopping is finally done. Perhaps it's because all the Christmas cooking is complete. Maybe it's because there's always something special about Christmas Eve church services. Singing the same classic Christmas tunes brings joy to the world. Maybe it's because for the next twenty-four hours, few people are working. Most get to enjoy their families. Whatever it is, that short burst of time is one of my favorite moments each year.

On the day before the day we celebrate the birth of Christ, take a moment to consider all Christ has done for you. Count your blessings. And when you think you are finished, count some more. Don't just stop with your health, your friends, your family, where you live, what you have. Also think about your spiritual blessings. Take note of the joy of salvation, knowing that you are saved by grace. Note the times God has spoken to you. Remember the sins he has forgiven.

As you continue taking count of his goodness, remember the blessings of the Holy Spirit. The spirit comforts, convicts, corrects, and guides. No matter what you do, God is always with you. He never leaves you. He will never forsake you. Even when you are not faithful, God is. He can't be anything else.

Remember, all the good things you have exist because of all that Christ endured for you. Now enjoy the moment. Embrace it. God is with you.

Power Lift

Dear God, I want to pause for a moment and give you glory, honor, and praise. You have blessed me in so many ways this year. Thank you, Lord.

And Mary said, "My soul magnifies the Lord." (Luke 1:46 ESV)

Someone said something years ago that stuck with me. They explained that Christmas is a magnifier. If things are good in your life, Christmas tends to magnify that goodness. That which is good seems better. A good family seems great. A good party seems fantastic. A good memory becomes an even better one. Christmas magnifies the good.

But unfortunately, it also can magnify what's difficult. If you are struggling, Christmas season can almost make the struggle seem more intense. Financial stress is tough any time of the year. In December, it can feel unbearable. A challenged relationship with extended family is never fun. It seems to be accentuated during the holidays. If you normally battle with loneliness, Christmastime may be the loneliest time of all.

Rather than just focusing on yourself this Christmas Day, what you got and what you gave, how much you ate, who you saw, how the kids looked, I'd encourage you to focus on Christ. Today we celebrate the greatest gift in history, our Savior's birth.

As you focus on Jesus, worship God for his goodness, his love, his sacrifice. We are told to magnify him, to glorify him together. What does that mean? Among other things, magnify simply means to make bigger. What if you made God a bigger part of your life? Not just on Christmas Day, but every day. What if you allowed his goodness, his will, his plans to consume your thinking? What if you made his presence the biggest priority in your life?

If you are going to magnify anything this Christmas, magnify the Lord.

Power Lift

I want to focus on you, Lord—not just the presents, parties, and decorations. Today let my soul magnify your presence as I reflect on the miracle of the virgin birth, the gift of your Son, Jesus.

For since the world began, no ear has heard and no eye has seen a
God like you, who works for those who wait for him! (Isa. 64:4 NLT)

I love going to movies, and my family always goes to the same theater, for a couple of reasons. One is because the matinee is cheap. And the other is because the chairs rock, and if no one's in front of you, you can prop your feet up, and just kick back and enjoy the show. It doesn't get much better for under five bucks, right?

But then recently for my birthday, my assistants gave me a gift card for a different movie theater. Because they knew about my favorite place, I asked why they'd chosen another one. "Trust us," they said. "The chairs in this theater are unbelievable." I thanked them and thought, *Wow, for twelve bucks, they better be!*

When we finally went there, the chairs were leather and clean and big. They have a little cup holder—I'm not making this up—that is *refrigerated*. I also discovered a button on the side that turned my dream chair into a recliner. I looked over at Amy and said, "Wow, I had no idea! If only this armrest wasn't between us, we could snuggle and this would be perfection."

My wife smiled at me, pushed a button somewhere, and the armrest between us disappeared. I thought I'd died and gone to heaven! Later I wondered how often I underestimate what God has for me. I'm satisfied with an old rocker, but he has this huge recliner waiting for me!

As you reflect on the gifts you received this holiday season, consider what God wants to give you that you may be missing by holding on to what you have.

Thank you, Lord, for being the source of all good gifts. Expand my vision today, God, so I can receive what you have for me.

> You will be enriched in every way so that you can be
> generous on every occasion, and through us your generosity
> will result in thanksgiving to God. (2 Cor. 9:11)

Perhaps the most meaningful conversations I have are with pastors when I'm at events for church leaders. These rich moments all result from a faith-filled decision of generosity our leaders made just over a decade ago.

At the time, our church finances were tight—very tight. We were at the peak of our financial debt and often barely making payroll. About that time, church leaders started asking if they could purchase some of our materials to use at their churches. They asked to buy transcripts, videos, youth messages, and kids' material. While there's nothing wrong with selling quality products at a reasonable price, we believed God was calling us to a different path.

Even though we weren't sure if we could afford to do it forever, we decided to try to give away as many resources as possible for free. Oddly, as we did, God seemed to bless us and trust us with more. As of today, we are a debt-free church with 27 locations in 8 different states. As of this moment, we have been blessed to give more than 10 million free resources to over 360,000 pastors.

So when other pastors get teary-eyed and tell me that the free resources helped save their church, impacted their lives, or improved their leadership, I pause to remember God's gift to me through Jesus. God blesses us all—so we can bless others. And when you do, people will thank God because of you.

What can you do today that will move people to worship God because of your generosity?

Power Lift

Show me where to give, Lord, that will bless those in need and inspire others to give.

The plans of the heart belong to man, but the answer of
the tongue is from the LORD. (Prov. 16:1 ESV)

After Christmas, there's usually quite a bit of cleaning up to do—all that wrapping paper, some of the leftover treats, tinsel tracked all over the house. Over the years, I've learned that my wife likes being a good steward of whatever activities take place in our house. Who knew that some types of wrapping paper can be recycled but not others? Or that the dishes should be loaded into the dishwasher a certain way? They don't teach us in Man School that you should leave parallel lines in the carpet while vacuuming.

I've learned to surrender those areas to Amy. The only things I try to control are, well, everything else. We joke about it, but it can be a real problem. I like to control when we leave, when we arrive, how everyone is dressed, how they act, what they say, and the list could go on and on. Controlling is a problem for me—not just during the chaotic holidays but all year long.

How about you? Are there areas of your life that you try to control that aren't yours to control? Are you trying to manipulate outcomes rather than trusting in God? Are you frustrated when you don't get to have things your way?

I'm trying to live the important principle that you can have faith, or you can have control, but you can't have both. If you're trying to control something that isn't yours to control, try trusting it to God. Surrender it to him. He's way more experienced at being God than you are. And you can always trust him.

· · · · · · · · · · · **Power Lift** · · · · · · · · · ·

As this year comes to a close, Lord, I give you thanks and praise for all you've done for me. Today I surrender control for the year ahead and give it to you.

> Being confident of this, that he who began a good work in you will carry it on to completion until the day of Christ Jesus. (Phil. 1:6)

When I was hired into ministry, I felt overwhelmed with insecurity. I knew that I didn't know enough, wasn't good enough, and certainly wasn't holy enough. Hoping it didn't show, I did my best to blend in with the church staff, but underneath it all, I was paralyzed with fear and insecurities.

One day a lady named Mary said, "Good morning, Pastor Craig." No one had ever called me "Pastor" before. I froze in my tracks. Later that day I was chatting with my boss, Pastor Nick. I told him how unworthy I felt when she called me by such an important and reverent title. Nick smiled a knowing smile and said, "Yep, I used to feel the exact same way. But don't worry," he continued, "you'll grow into that title."

I'll never forget those words. "You'll grow into it." He was right. Over time, with God's grace and some experience, I'm now confident in the title. And it's not because I have it all down. It's because I know that God has called me and is with me.

As you reflect on this past year, you may not yet be all you want to be. You may not know all you'd hoped to know. You may still have issues that you deal with daily. But don't worry. God calls you an "overcomer." God says you are "blessed." He says you are the "righteousness of God in Christ."

God is still working in you. He's conforming you to the image of his Son. You'll grow into it.

Power Lift

I've made mistakes this past year, Lord, and haven't always been as faithful to you as I want. Thank you for never giving up on me. I'm excited about the year ahead with you!

"I will give them a heart to know Me, for I am the Lᴏʀᴅ; and
they will be My people, and I will be their God, for they will
return to Me with their whole heart." (Jer. 24:7 NASB)

One of the police officers from our church went on a sting operation.
Several fully armed guys in riot gear stormed a drug house and successfully made the arrests. They caught three known dealers and confiscated
a sizeable amount of illegal substances.

My officer buddy kept certain details about the case confiden-
tial, but he was excited to show me a photo they had taken of one guy's
nightstand. On the nightstand was a bottle of liquor, cigarettes, drug par-
aphernalia, a condom, and a Bible and a Life.Church weekend bulletin.

At first, I felt a bit discouraged. Obviously the church hadn't made
much difference in that guy's life. But my buddy saw it from a whole different point of view. With enthusiasm he said, "Isn't it awesome this guy
had come to church and had his Bible out? It's amazing that someone so
lost would have felt welcome. He was obviously searching for something.
If only he had had more time, maybe our church could have reached him.
I love that a guy like this would be coming to our church."

His insight helped so much. Because that guy who was arrested was
the type of person Jesus would have befriended. Even though he was
far from perfect, or perhaps especially because he was far from perfect.
This guy was "in-process." And Jesus loves those in-process.

Our Savior accepts us as we are, but he never leaves us there.

• • • • • • • • • • • **Power Lift** • • • • • • • • • • •

As I start setting goals for next year, Lord, I want to make you the priority in all
of them. Give me wisdom about what things I should change and what things I
should keep the same in the months ahead.

May the God of hope fill you with all joy and peace as you trust in him, so that
you may overflow with hope by the power of the Holy Spirit. (Rom. 15:13)

How would you describe this past year? Was it harder than you expected,
filled with ongoing struggles and discouraging news? Or were you surprised by blessings beyond what you had imagined, seeing God's hand at
work in miraculous ways? For most of us, it was probably some of both.

The good news is that regardless of how we feel about the past
twelve months, we can trust that God is still in control. Even if you
can't see how he could possibly use some of the painful moments from
your past, he loves to do the impossible.

As you look ahead and set goals or resolutions for the new year,
put God first. Trust him with every area of your life. Ask him to draw
you closer to Christ and to open your heart. Start small and know that
he is with you every step of the way. No matter what lies ahead, you
can have peace. God didn't bring you this far to give up on you now!

Tomorrow is a new day and a new year.

Give God the glory for all he's done—and for all he's about to do!

. . . . **Power Lift** . . . .

Dear God, wow—I can't believe this year went by so quickly! Help me to learn
from this past year and to look ahead toward what you are doing in my life moving forward. I trust you with my life and believe your best is yet to come!